# Contents

*(preceding pages) The intricate design and meticulous care needed in the restoration of classical Chinese architecture is apparent in this example to be seen in the Summer Palace, Beijing— something that is sadly lacking in many recent restorations of historical buildings in China*

Pu.Qun, Canton, Delin.

Dadley, London, Sculp.

Published May 4, 1799, by W. Miller, Old Bond Street, London.

*Plant seller, Canton 1799*

# Introduction: Tours and Expeditions

There was a time when one could visit China only on a group tour organized by China International Travel Service (CITS), the state tourism agency. Nowadays, while most tourists to China still travel on a package basis, the options have multiplied. Not only are there many kinds of itineraries offered by travel agents and airlines worldwide, but one may also travel independently. Either way, careful research and planning beforehand is essential. This guide has been designed to help you plan your itinerary before you go, and to give you up-to-date information on the most attractive destinations once you get there. It is not comprehensive, but it includes the places most worthwhile to visit as well as a selection of exotic and adventurous expeditions that can be enjoyed either as part of a tour or be undertaken independently. The layout of the book has been designed to reflect the way in which many people arrange their travel programmes for China: an itinerary which includes a selection of cities or an extended journey to one or more special regions. City destinations in this book have been divided into four categories: Cultural Capitals, Cities Traditional and Modern, Cities in a Landscape and Secondary Destinations. While there should not be any rules for choosing destinations, picking one from each category will provide the opportunity to see the range and contrasts of Chinese urban life and to gain an insight into the development of China's cultural heritage. The 'Expeditions' chapters cover the other possibilities that can be combined with a 'standard' tour—from the popular Yangzi River cruise to off-the-beaten-track exploration of China's border regions.

## Tours

The organized China tour, with its ready solution to the problems of time, language and money, is a blessing for first-time China travellers. A well-organized tour with a local escort is highly recommended even to those who would arrange their own itinerary elsewhere in the world. People who have lived and worked in China also like the problem-free nature of a tour, since they are all too well aware of what can go wrong in some of China's more far-flung regions.

As the Chinese open more and more destinations to international tour operators, independent travellers are finding their options both extended and restricted. There are more places to visit, but there are also more people travelling. The economic reforms since 1978 have meant that ordinary Chinese people now have more money to go sightseeing. This has strained to the limits China's inadequate transport systems, and the independent traveller often has to fight and cajole his or her way onto a plane, boat or train. During the boom years of China travel in the mid-1980s, hotels in the major cities were invariably full to bursting during the popular tourist seasons of spring and autumn. Independent travellers who had not booked in advance found themselves having to sleep on floors or to journey out to dormitory hostels far from the centre of town. Although the supply of hotel rooms in the main cities has increased dramatically in recent years, you may still need to expend time and effort on locating one that suits your pocket and requirements. On the other hand, hotel tariffs in China are now very competitive; many of them, especially those in cities which have been oversupplied as a result of a construction boom, offer special deals such as discounted weekend rates or winter packages, so it pays to shop around. Travellers now find that it is possible just to turn up at the front desk of a hotel and to negotiate for a room price considerably lower than the advertised rate (unless it is a state-operated hotel where the pricing policy tends to be inflexible).

Booking tickets for long-distance transport remains difficult for the independent traveller. It is rarely possible simply to go to a railway station, buy a ticket and then board the train of your choice. Unless you have connections in China (which could mean anything from an official contact to a friend in a foreign embassy), getting things done while 'on the road' is so time-consuming that basic organization can spoil the holiday. Your status and connections in China may be the only deciding factor in the allocation of flights, seats and rooms, for 'first come, first served' is definitely not a Chinese motto.

If, for reasons of time and convenience, you choose a tour, remember that you can select either a special-interest tour (anything from bicycling to botany) or a series of general tours with a good mixture of contrasting destinations. If you have a scientific or educational interest, it may be worth your while to contact the relevant professional or specialist organization in China (whether it is bird-watching or acupuncture) for help with organizing visits to places of specialist interest or setting up exchange programmes.

Those on a general tour who wish to see an institution or site because of professional interest need not hesitate to ask their tour operator if a visit can be fitted into the schedule within any given city or region. Tour operators, if notified in advance, can pass on the request to CITS, which can then apply for admission and make the appointment. Advertised schedules are not always set in stone anyway: CITS ha⸱ᶜ exasperating habit of changing an itinerary at the last minute, when ther⸱ the tour operator's representative can do except argue.

# Regional Map of China

KAZAKHSTAN

Almaty

KYRGYZSTAN

Urûmqi

Kashi

Turpan

TAJIKISTAN

▲ Muztagata

XINJIANG

Hotan

Dunhuang

Jiayuguan

G

QINGHAI

Xining

TIBET
(XIZANG)

New Delhi

NEPAL

Xixabangma   Shigaze

▲ ▲ Mt. Everest   Lhasa

Kathmandu

SICHU

Gongga ▲
Shan   ▲
Emei

BHUTAN

INDIA

INDIA

BANGLADESH
Dhaka

Dali   Kunmin

YUNNAN

Calcutta

BURMA
(MYANMAR)

Mandalay

BAY OF BENGAL

LAOS

Rangoon

THAILAND

ok Company Limited

If you do decide to make your own way somewhere while on tour, it is easy to arrange transport (by hiring a taxi from your hotel for a half or a whole day at a fixed rate, for example), to use your own maps and the advice of a sympathetic guide. Although CITS guides are like good shepherds who want to keep their flock together for their own peace of mind, there is usually no problem if you decide to forego a pre-arranged excursion and go off on your own.

# Expeditions

This section has been devised for those choosing a regional tour in China, as well as for those wanting to make their own travel arrangements. Indeed, the word 'expedition' should not discourage the comfort-loving traveller who may think that choosing an adventurous itinerary in China necessitates hardship. Every year, new areas of China that were either closed to foreigners or solely the domain of Chinese-speaking backpackers have been opened up by enterprising travel agents. These agents, in co-operation with the Chinese government, have helped to develop facilities where previously there were none, and they have also urged that more historical and archaeological sites be included on tourist itineraries—sites which once were known only to scholars.

An organized itinerary for adventure travel does not mean that the adventure is lost. Often it can mean that the tourist has more access to little-known places, which would be difficult to visit independently. Perhaps this is best illustrated by the tours to the Yangzi River. The independent traveller has the fun of booking a berth on a regular passenger steamer and travelling downstream in the company of a boat full of Chinese people on their daily business or on holiday themselves. The tourist who chooses to go on a luxury cruise loses this day-to-day contact with ordinary people, but does get the chance to make side-trips and stop at small towns which the scheduled steamer just glides past. As a generalization, one could say that the organized expedition is for those with less time but few financial restrictions, while the independent journey is for those with plenty of time but less cash.

If you decide to forego the organized tour in favour of a do-it-yourself journey, then take Baden-Powell's maxim to heart: *Be prepared!* A China tour that is not well thought out can entail a series of very expensive, bureaucratic nightmares. Gather as much relevant information as you can before setting out. CITS has representative offices in Hong Kong and some major Western cities, including New York, London and Paris; the advice and knowledge of their staff can come in useful. The parallel travel organization for foreign nationals of Chinese descent, China Travel Service (CTS), has opened branches in some of the cities where there are large Chinese communities, such as Sydney, Los Angeles, San Francisco, Vancouver, Bangkok, Tokyo, Singapore and Jakarta. In the past the separation between CITS and CTS was rigidly adhered to, but nowadays the line has become somewhat blurred, and you may find a CTS office abroad a good source of information even if you are not an overseas Chinese. The officials of your national China friendship society (in Britain it is called the 'Society of Anglo-Chinese Understanding'; in America the 'US-China Peoples Friendship Association') can be helpful because they are often people who have travelled extensively in China and have organized tour itineraries for other people.

Check up on vaccination requirements, especially if you plan to visit some of the poorer border regions, and make sure you have altitude sickness tablets if you are visiting Tibet. Unless you are planning to scale a Himalayan peak, you will not need specialist equipment for mountain walking. The best thing you can take to China is a pair of well-worn, stout walking shoes; most other daily necessities for budget travelling (including sleeping bags and ensolite pads) can be bought in specialist stores in Beijing, Shanghai and Guangzhou.

The list of do's and don'ts for independent travel in China will vary according to your age, health, and willingness to pick up some of the Chinese language. Make sure that you buy a phrase book before you go to China, since most people encounter language difficulties when venturing beyond the larger cities. When sightseeing, you can always join up with a CITS-organized day tour in major cities like Xi'an, where getting to the sights beyond the city is not always easy or cheap. Going by bus is fun but time-consuming. Meeting up with someone and sharing a taxi for the day can often be the best solution. In fact, it is good to share meals too, since Chinese food is always better when there are a few people eating together.

A useful middle course which takes some of the effort out of making your own travel arrangements in China is available. Large branches of China International Travel Service (CITS) usually have an 'FIT' (Foreign independent travel) section (known as *sanke bu* in Chinese), which will make reservations or buy tickets on your behalf for a small charge.

Above all, China travellers who go it alone should be models of patience, tolerance and forbearance in adversity. The Chinese have never admired someone who loses his temper easily. There is a Chinese saying that you should be able to 'hold a boat in your stomach', the English equivalent of which is 'turn the other cheek'! Common problems on China expeditions range from no hot water to occasional power failures. If minor discomforts are going to cause you to lose your cool, then avoid travelling outside of the main cities in China. And bear in mind that travel in China has been known to test the patience of sages.

There are many off-the-beaten-track destinations in China waiting to be explored. Increasingly, there are also programmes that incorporate some adventurous activity

# The Good Life

*Far away in the East, under sunshine such as you never saw (for even such light as you have you stain and infect with sooty smoke), on the shore of a broad river stands the house where I was born. It is one among thousands; but every one stands in its own garden, simply painted in white or gray, modest, cheerful, and clean. For many miles along the valley, one after the other, they lift their blue- or red-tiled roofs out of a sea of green; while here and there glitters out over a clump of trees the gold enamel of some tall pagoda. The river, crossed by frequent bridges and crowded with barges and junks, bears on its clear stream the traffic of thriving village-markets. For prosperous peasants people all the district, owning and tilling the fields their fathers owned and tilled before them. The soil on which they work, they may say, they and their ancestors have made. For see! almost to the summit what once were barren hills are waving green with cotton and rice, sugar, oranges, and tea. Water drawn from the river-bed girdles the slopes with silver; and falling from channel to channel in a thousand bright cascades, splashing in cisterns, chuckling in pipes, soaking and oozing in the soil, distributes freely to all alike fertility, verdure, and life. Hour after hour you may traverse, by tortuous paths, over tiny bridges, the works of the generations who have passed, the labors of their children of to-day; till you reach the point where man succumbs and Nature has her way, covering the highest crags with a mantle of azure and gold and rose, gardenia, clematis, azalea, growing luxuriantly wild. How often here have I sat for hours in a silence so intense that, as one of our poets has said, "you may hear the shadows of the trees rustling on the ground"; a silence broken only now and again from far below by voices of laborers calling across the water-courses, or, at evening or dawn, by the sound of gongs summoning to worship from the temples in the valley. Such silence! Such sounds! Such perfume! Such color! The senses respond to their objects; they grow exquisite to a degree you cannot well conceive in your northern climate; and beauty pressing in from without moulds the spirit and mind insensibly to harmony with herself. If in China we have manners, if we have art, if we have morals, the reason, to those who can see, is not far to seek. Nature has taught us; and so far, we are only more fortunate than you. But, also, we have had the grace to learn her lesson; and that, we think, we may ascribe to our intelligence. For, consider, here in this lovely valley live thousands of souls without any law save that of custom, without any rule save that of their own hearths. Industrious they are, as you hardly know industry in Europe; but it is the industry of free men working for their kith and kin, on the lands they received from their fathers, to transmit, enriched by their labors, to their sons. They have no other ambition; they do not care to amass wealth; and if in each generation some must needs go out into the world, it is with the hope, not commonly frustrated, to return to the place of their birth and spend their declining years among the scenes and faces that were dear to their youth. Among such a people there is no room for fierce, indecent rivalries. None is master, none servant; but equality, concrete and real, regulates and sustains their intercourse. Healthy toil, sufficient leisure, frank hospitality, a content born of habit and undisturbed by chimerical ambitions, a sense of beauty fostered by the loveliest Nature in the world, and finding expression in gracious and dignified manners where it is not embodied in exquisite works of art—such are the characteristics of the people among whom I was born. Does my memory flatter me? Do I idealize the scenes of my youth? It may be so. But this I know: that some such life as I have described, reared on the basis of labor on the soil, of equality and justice, does exist and flourish throughout the length and breadth of China.*

*Anonymous,* Letters from A Chinese Official; Being an Eastern View of Western Civilization, 1903

like mountaineering and trekking. The Expeditions sections of this book will point you to those areas that offer something more challenging than the standard China tour. The list is by no means comprehensive, but it does cover the most exotic—as well as some of the most popular—destinations in the remote regions and in a few of the most scenic provinces.

Finally, Hong Kong, now a Special Administrative Region of China, has been included. Its function as a 'Gateway to China' makes it the most popular and the most logical of stopping-over places in which to begin or end a tour to China itself. No companion to China travel would be complete without some reference to Hong Kong's unique blend of Chinese and Western experience.

# Facts for the Traveller

## Getting to China

By air, the major international gateways to China are Beijing, Shanghai and Guangzhou (Canton). From Hong Kong, there are scheduled direct flights by Chinese airlines to the cities of Beijing, Dalian, Fuzhou, Guangzhou, Hangzhou, Kunming, Ningbo, Shanghai, Shantou, Shenyang, Tianjin, Xiamen and Xi'an. A large number of other destinations can also be reached from Hong Kong by regular chartered flights operated by the Chinese aviation authorities: Beihai, Changchun, Changsha, Chengdu, Chongqing, Guilin, Guiyang, Haikou, Harbin, Hefei, Huang-shan, Jinan, Lanzhou, Luoyang, Meixian, Nanchang, Nanjing, Nanning, Qingdao, Taiyuan, Wuhan, Zhanjiang and Zhengzhou. Dragonair, the Hong Kong-based airline, flies to Beijing, Changsha, Chengdu, Dalian, Guilin, Haikou, Hangzhou, Kunming, Nanjing, Ningbo, Shanghai, Tianjin, Xiamen and Xi'an. These flights are bookable in Hong Kong, as are domestic flights on Chinese airlines. Airport taxes are levied on both international and domestic flights. Domestic flight taxes are cheaper than international ones. Amounts for both vary from airport to airport.

There are other points of entry by rail, by road and by ship. Several express train and bus services run between Hong Kong, Shenzhen and other Guangdong cities, and highway buses also go regularly to Fuzhou and other main cities in Fujian Province. China Travel Service (Hong Kong) is able to supply details and book tickets. For inveterate train lovers the Trans-Siberian Railway leaves twice a week from Moscow. The Karakoram Highway (linking Pakistan and Xinjiang in northwest China)

*Thousand-armed Goddess of Mercy at Puning Temple, Chengde*

and the Kathmandu-Lhasa highway (linking Nepal and Tibet) are now travelled by the patient and hardy. Motorized catamarans and hovercraft can be taken from Hong Kong to ports in south China, there is a nightly steamer to Guangzhou (except for the 31st of each month), a steamer to Shanghai on the 2nd, 7th, 17th and 22nd of each month, a steamer to Ningbo twice a month. A number of cruise lines include a China tour on their itineraries. A passenger liner service operated as a joint-venture plies between Osaka and Kobe in Japan and Shanghai.

## Visas

Tourists travelling as part of a group enter China on a group visa— a single document listing all members of the group. The visa is obtained by the tour operator on behalf of his clients. Individual visas can be obtained through China International Travel Service (CITS), a number of travel agents in Hong Kong, the Visa Office of the Ministry of Foreign Affairs of the People's Republic of China in Hong Kong, or at Chinese embassies or consulates in your respective country. Applying for a visa before you travel is fairly routine; all you need to do is fill in a form, supply a photograph and hand over a fee. However, the processing time could vary from only a few hours to several months, depending on where you are. Hong Kong remains the easiest place to obtain a Chinese visa.

As a tourist visa gives access to all open cities and regions (1,288 as of April, 1997), there is no need for further documentation. The fees for individual visas vary considerably, depending on the source of the visa and the time taken to get it. In Hong Kong, for instance, a visa can be obtained in one day for an extra fee. Those who have a previous China visa in their passport may apply for a double or multi-entry visa for an extra fee. Applications for extensions—usually for a further 30 days—are granted by public security bureaus (*gongan ju*) within China. At present, group members on tours visiting the Special Economic Zones of Shenzhen or Zhuhai only (just over the border from Hong Kong and Macau respectively) do not require visas if the tour is less than 72 hours.

## Customs

Customs officials rarely bother foreigners, so you need not expect long hold-ups in the customs hall. There is a green channel for those who have nothing to declare and a red channel for those bringing in any of the following: over US$5,000 in cash in any currency; video tapes; professional film equipment; expensive electronic goods that they plan to leave in China, such as computers and VCRs and also commercial samples. Each person is allowed to bring in two litres of spirits and 600 cigarettes duty-free.

The export of antiques is controlled. It is forbidden to export any artifacts made earlier than 1795, unless they are common, such as Han-dynasty coins. Most antiques sold in Friendship Stores or curio shops are not very old, and as long as they carry a red wax seal or a paper label indicating that the authorities approve of the exportations, you may take them out of China. You should keep your sales receipts in case the customs officers ask to see them. Generally speaking, you will have no trouble taking out other old artifacts which you may have bought in a market—but if any question arises, the decision is left to the discretion of the customs officer on duty.

# Money

## RENMINBI
Chinese currency is called *renminbi* (meaning 'people's currency') and is abbreviated to RMB. The standard unit is *yuan* (referred to as *kuai* in everyday speech). The yuan or kuai is divided into ten *jiao* (referred to as *mao*) and 100 *fen*. Ten fen make one mao and ten mao make one kuai. Yuan (kuai) and jiao (mao) are available in note forms and fen as small coins. At present RMB is only convertible in China and Hong Kong. Therefore it is important to keep foreign currency exchange receipts, as you will need to present them to the Bank of China official when you change RMB back into foreign currency before leaving China.

## FOREIGN CURRENCY
There is no limit to the amount of foreign currency you can bring into China. All major freely negotiable currencies can be exchanged at branches of the Bank of China, in hotels and stores. The rates of exchange fluctuate with the international money market. Traveller's cheques are changed at a slightly better rate than cash.

## TRAVELLER'S CHEQUES AND CREDIT CARDS
All the major European, American, Hong Kong and Japanese traveller's cheques are accepted. International credit cards are now also quite freely accepted in shops and hotels of major cities.

# A Liberated Woman

One day as Wang Ta-pao's wife returned from a meeting of the Farmers' Committee she said, "I have something I want to tell you."

Wang supposed that it was some committee business or else fresh news of the victories of the Red Army and he replied in good spirits, "Please go ahead and tell me."

"What I have to say is very simple," she began. "During the last ten years you have not treated me badly. And of course, as you yourself know, my behavior toward you has been correct. You have looked after me and I have done a lot of work for you. In the first place, I have managed your home, and in the second place, I have borne you two sons. But now I want to leave you, and I am preparing to go tomorrow with Comrade Chen to register."

Wang Ta-pao listened in stupefaction, his heart beating furiously. The veins stood out on his reddening face.

"You can't do that!" he stammered out miserably.

"Why can't I? Do you think we are still living in the times of the landed gentry? Don't forget that this is the Soviet age. You must be more careful what you say."

She was right. Wang Ta-pao could not oppose her. He hesitated a while and then bethought himself to say, "Why do you want to leave me?"

"For no very important reason," she replied reddening, "Only— well—I feel that living with Comrade Chen would be better than with you. The soviet allows this. You mustn't be cross with me about it. If you feel bad about losing me, remember we can still see each other always at work . . . dear Comrade Wang."

She left him rather cheerfully and busied herself in packing up her things.

Hu Yeh-p'in, 'Living Together', 1930

*Cook's Far Eastern Traveller's Gazette, April–June 1937*

## Tipping

Though officially prohibited, tipping has appeared in major cities. Service staff in restaurants and hotels, particularly joint-venture ones, as well as tour guides and tour bus drivers, will generally welcome tips if not always expect them.

# Health

The Chinese authorities ask those who are unfit because of 'mental illness, contagious or serious chronic disease, disability, pregnancy, senility or physical handicap' not to take a China tour. Experience has shown this to be sound advice. A tour that is exhausting but stimulating for the fit becomes a gruelling experience for those who are not.

If you do become ill in China, you will be taken to the local hospital and given the best treatment available (not always of a standard that Westerners are used to) and you will be put in a private room if possible. Costs—particularly of medicines—are high, so it is important to invest in some form of health insurance before visiting China.

There are no mandatory vaccination requirements. However, you may be advised by your doctor or government health authority (the US State Department, for example) to take certain precautions. In recent years, the US Consulate in Hong Kong has recommended inoculations against hepatitis A and B, Japanese B encephalitis, tetanus, polio, cholera and malaria. This is a long and daunting list, but it should be considered alongside the specifics of your itinerary. For a trip to Beijing, Xi'an, Shanghai, Suzhou and Guilin at any time except the height of summer, the possibility of contracting any of these diseases is minuscule. It is only when travelling to southwest China in the summer or to very out-of-the-way areas that such a regimen should be considered.

The most common ailments contracted by tourists in China are upper respiratory infections and chest colds. Some physicians prescribe a quarter-dose of an antibiotic like tetracycline as a mild preventative. In the north, places like Beijing are extremely dry and cold in the winter, and it is sensible to wrap up warmly and drink lots of fluids. Visitors are often surprised by the tendency of the Chinese to dress much more heavily than seems necessary during the transitional seasons of fall and spring. The Chinese believe that keeping warm is the key to staying healthy at these times.

Drink only boiled water while you are in China; hotel rooms are normally supplied with thermos flasks of boiled water—both hot and cold—which are replenished daily, or they will provide mineral or distilled water in the mini-bar. If eating at street stalls, make sure the food is freshly cooked.

Chinese standards of sanitation lag behind those in the West—as will be quickly evident when you see people spitting in the street—so it makes good sense to wash your hands carefully before eating anything. Peel all fruit and avoid raw leafy vegetables unless you are in an up-market restaurant.

# Climate and Clothing

Within the nearly ten million square kilometres (four million square miles) of China's vast territory it is hardly surprising to find immense variations in climate. Even generalizations about relatively small areas are difficult because of the effects of altitude and other local conditions. Before deciding on the best season to take a tour, it is worth checking carefully the weather conditions of each city on the itinerary. Of course, if you choose the most attractive season to visit a city, you also choose the time when tourist spots and hotels are most crowded.

As a basic guide, winters in the north are harsh: Beijing's average minimum temperature between December and March is only -5°C (23°F), and its maximum is around 0°C (32°F). If you go further north towards Shenyang in the northeastern province of Liaoning, or west into Inner Mongolia, it is much colder. By contrast, summer can be uncomfortably hot and sticky; temperatures in Beijing, for example, may soar to over 38°C (100°F) during July and August, which is also the rainy season. Spring and autumn are undoubtedly the best times for touring in the north, when you can expect less rain, clear skies and comfortable temperatures.

Moving south, the Yangzi valley area (which includes Shanghai) has semi-tropical conditions. Summers are long, hot and sticky, with notoriously unpleasant conditions at Wuhan, Chongqing and Nanjing—cities which the Chinese have, with good reason, called 'the three furnaces'. Winters are short and cold, with temperatures dipping below freezing, while spring and autumn are the most attractive seasons with cool nights and daytime temperatures of around 24°C (the mid-70s°F). Humidity remains high throughout the year—the average rainfall in Shanghai is 114 centimetres (45 inches).

The sub-tropical south (Guangzhou is on the Tropic of Cancer) has a hot and humid six-month period from April to September, with days of heavy rain (Guangzhou's average annual rainfall is 345 centimetres or 136 inches), but the region has a very pleasant dry, sunny autumn, when daytime temperatures hover around 24°C (mid-70s). Spring can be cloudy and wet, while the short winter from January to March produces some surprisingly chilly days.

Apart from mid-summer, when virtually everywhere open to foreign tourists is hot, most tour itineraries lead the tourist through several different weather zones. But people who decide to travel with several complete changes of wardrobe may find themselves with crippling excess baggage charges—the Chinese tend to be strict about their 20-kilogram (44-1b) baggage allowance for air travellers. A more practical

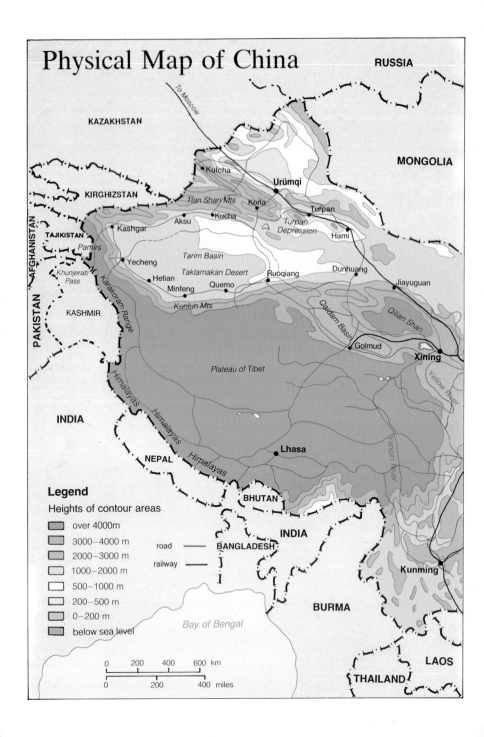

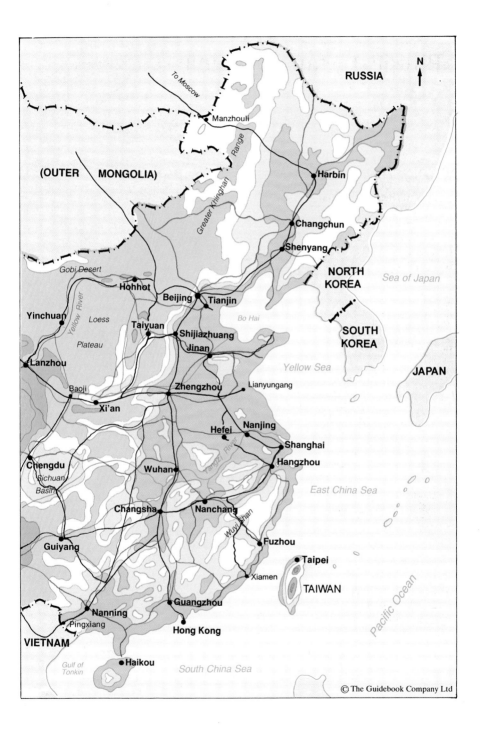

policy would be to plan on wearing layers that can be discarded or added to as the weather dictates.

The Chinese themselves are informal about dress, and will not expect tourists to dress formally. (Business visitors, though, will find suits or dresses the normal wear at meetings in the main cities.) Unless the itinerary includes an official reception, men need nothing smarter than a sports jacket and perhaps a tie, and women can feel properly attired in an everyday dress or a trouser suit. So take casual, practical clothes, and strong, comfortable shoes—you are bound to be doing a lot of walking. Although the Chinese are becoming a little more adventurous with their own clothes, they are still unused to anything too flamboyant, and offended by exposure of too much flesh. But in rapidly changing China even attitudes towards dress are relaxing, and nearly two decades of economic reform—bringing with it an improvement in the standard of living—has made the young people much more fashion conscious and eager to adopt Western styles. Nevertheless, women should leave their skimpy shorts and décolleté dresses at home.

Winter in the far northwest and in Tibet demands very heavy clothing—thermal underwear, thick coats, sweaters, lined boots, gloves, and some form of headgear as protection against the biting wind. Hotel and tour buses are usually well-heated, while museums, offices and even some theatres and restaurants are not.

For summer anywhere in China keep clothes as light as possible —many of the places you visit will not be air-conditioned. You may be sightseeing during the heat of the day, so take plenty of protection against the sun, particularly if you are planning to visit Tibet or Xinjiang, where sunglasses are a must. A light raincoat is a wise addition to your luggage at any time.

You need bring only a few changes of clothing since hotel laundry everywhere is fast, cheap and efficient. Dry cleaning is possible, although it may be wiser to wait until you are home to get your most treasured clothes cleaned.

## What's Available

### FOOD, DRINK AND TOBACCO

China has more than 600 breweries, and 51 of the top 60 have formed joint ventures to produce lager, or light beer. Foreign brewers such as Heineken, Carlsberg, Budweisers and Miller all have factories in the mainland. A surprisingly wide choice of wines and spirits are available, even in medium-sized cities in the hinterland. Whiskies and brandies have become popular with China's nouveau riche, and are marketed aggressively. As for wines, there are some quite drinkable locally-made ones available. Look out for Dragon Seal and Great Wall. Foreign cigarettes are available everywhere, at a much cheaper price than back home. Conclusion: unless your taste for a toddy or smoke is extremely unusual, then use your baggage allowance to pack something else. Coffee is also easy to find. Nescafe has a factory in Guangdong and travellers find that the 3 in 1 or 2 in 1 sachets, made by Maxwell House and Nescafe at about US$2 per box of 10, offer the best convenience when on the move. Thermos flasks of freshly boiled water are always available. For those who like chocolate, there is also good news. Cadbury's, Mars and Nestles have all set up operations in China and their goodies are easy to find in provincial capitals.

## FILM

Fuji and Kodak manufacture basic grade colour films—Fujicolor and Kodakcolor—in China. They import and distribute better emulsions, including Fuji Super HG and Gold, but Reala is difficult to find. As for transparency films, Fujichrome Sensia, Provia and Velvia can be found in Beijing, Shanghai and Guangzhou, as can Kodak's positive films. Always check the "process before" date when you buy, and buy from a specialist shop. One is allowed to import 72 rolls of film and 3,000 feet of movie film. Videocam cassettes are also available in the big cities.

## MEDICINE AND TOILETRIES

Naturally, one should bring any prescribed medicine and a small first aid kit with a few painkillers and elastoplasts, and maybe a broad spectrum antibiotic if one plans to go into the countryside, merely for convenience. Some books advise travellers to bring toiletries. There is absolutely no need to—it is easy to buy Colgate toothpaste, Lifebuoy soap, Rejoice shampoo, Gillette razors and blades, Duracell batteries, toilet paper, tissues, sanitary towels and tampons—even in the smallest of cities in the far west.

## ELECTRICAL APPLIANCES

Voltage may vary slightly from region to region, but it is within the 220-240V range. Some travellers have reported their laptop keyboards and printers being damaged by surges in current. If you are going to small cities and towns, supplies are often cut off for much of the day, so bring batteries for your laptop, razor, Walkman and the like. Electrical points in China are either two-pin, both round and rectangular, and three-pin rectangular in an unusual triangular form, therefore it is vital to bring a universal adaptor such as the "World Wide Adaptor" or "Go Adaptour" both manufactured by "Go, the Travel Products Company".

*(following pages) On the Li River, near Guilin*

## READING MATERIAL

*China Daily*, launched in 1981, has grown to 12 pages on weekdays and provides a good insight into reforms-promoting journalism, with noteworthy spice in the form of its pun headlines courtesy of a team of foreign copy editors. It is distributed free of charge in 3- to 5-star hotels in tourist cities. On Fridays in Beijing look out for the city what's on—*Beijing Weekend*. On Sunday comes *Business Weekly*. In Shanghai, there is the bi-weekly *Shanghai Star*. Hong Kong-printed papers, the *South China Morning Post, Hong Kong Standard, Asian Wall Steet Journal* and *Herald Tribune* are availbale in Beijing, Shanghai and Guangzhou on the same day of issue. *Time* and *Newsweek* are also available from most luxury hotel newsstands.

# Travel Arrangements

The standard of travel arrangements in China has improved enormously over the past ten years. There are comfortable international-standard hotels, new airports and many more areas are open to tourists. Yet it should be remembered that China is a developing country which has only been open to tourists since 1978; tourism has been developed almost from scratch in a very short time. Thus English-speakers are still in short supply and guides and hotel staff may not always be very fluent. Attitudes to service jobs are improving, but many Chinese consider them demeaning and you may encounter surly and slow service.

Whether on a group tour or travelling independently, the key word for travelling in China is flexibility. Be prepared for itinerary changes, particularly flight changes and delays. There are simply not enough planes to go round; sometimes plane seats (and even entire cruise ships!) are commandeered by government officials with no advance warning. Bad weather in one area can wreak havoc with plane schedules across the country.

## GROUP TOURS

Although an increasing number of foreigners travel around China independently, most people, daunted by the language barrier, time restraints and the difficulties of obtaining plane and train tickets, choose to go on a group tour. Group tours offer substantial savings on hotels and other travel arrangements, the advantage of having English-speaking guides at all times, and freedom from worrying about the nitty-gritty of travel—reservations, baggage handling and so on. They are definitely the best way to see a lot of China in a short time.

There are many reputable tour operators in Europe and the United States who specialize in China tours. They usually book hotels and Yangzi cruise ships directly and go through one of the Chinese travel services for guides, sightseeing, some or all meals and transportation. The biggest of these travel services are the state-owned China International Travel Service (CITS) and China Travel Service (CTS), although there is now a plethora of smaller agencies as well. CITS and CTS have offices in all major cities in China, as well as representative offices abroad. They also run their own group tours out of Hong Kong.

The days are gone when Chinese guides insisted on starting sightseeing at 8:00am sharp and included obligatory factory visits with briefings about the miraculous production increases under socialism. Today's itineraries are more relaxed and free of ideology. However, they are still quite strenuous; there is a lot of walking (sometimes it seems as though every sight in China is at the top of myriad flights of steps!) and a full programme of sightseeing is planned for every day, often finished off with a Chinese opera or dance show in the evening. These days shopping is also included in itineraries, as guides urge you to 'keep China green' (with banknotes, that is). As long as you inform your guide first, it is perfectly acceptable to break away from the group for a day or an afternoon. Your guide or the hotel can arrange for a taxi to take you on an expedition somewhere, or you may choose to just take a rest!

Tour groups will usually have an escort provided by the foreign tour operator who accompanies them throughout the trip, plus a Chinese guide in each city. On some of the longer itineraries, particularly if they involve overnight train trips, CITS and CTS also provide a 'national guide' who accompanies the group throughout their journey in China.

## INDIVIDUAL TRAVEL

Some tour operators and travel agencies will handle FIT (foreign independent travel) arrangements in China, arranging hotels, transport and also private guides, with car and driver in each city if requested. This is expensive, but works quite smoothly.

If you decide to travel without arrangements set up in advance, be prepared to spend frustrating hours chasing after plane and train tickets, especially at peak times: Chinese New Year, May to June and September to October. All transportation in China is invariably crowded and tickets are at a premium. Beware of touts selling train tickets—sometimes they are fake. While some CITS and CTS offices in China are helpful to independent travellers, others are too busy coping with tour groups and have no time for individuals. Some of the cheaper hotels are open to Chinese and 'overseas compatriots' only and refuse to take other foreigners. With these provisos in mind, you will find most Chinese to be friendly and helpful, although with limited English.

# Transportation

Joining a tour saves you the trouble of making your own arrangements for transport. The local Chinese travel service is responsible for selecting the date, time and type of transport, making reservations, seeing to the neccessary security clearances, and ensuring that luggage gets from the hotel on to the appropriate train or plane. It is only left for the tourists to pay their own excess baggage charges. Most foreign tourists travel the long distances between China's major cities by air, and the shorter inter-city distances by train.

## AIR TRAVEL

The Civil Aviation Administration of China (CAAC) once had the monopoly on domestic flights; now a number of semi-independent domestic airlines are appearing, such as China Eastern (based in Shanghai) and China Southwest (based in Chengdu). Routes and services have greatly expanded over the past few years. But there is still an element of adventure in flying within China. Flights may be cancelled if bad weather is forecast, reserved seats may mysteriously be filled by others, and sometimes aircraft simply do not turn up. An interesting array of aeroplanes are used on internal flights.

You will experience few of the extras associated with commercial airlines in the West. In-flight service has a distinctive Chinese quality to it. Demurely dressed air hostesses serve light refreshments together with gifts of key-rings, fans, handkerchiefs, or perhaps a butterfly papercut. During longer flights planes may make a special stopover to allow crew and passengers to have a more substantial meal at an airport restaurant. Airports tend to be spartan places with a minimum of services. Cities which serve as international points of entry have upgraded their terminal buildings in recent years, and Xi'an recently opened its new airport at Xianyang, but these are still strictly functional places compared to their Western counterparts, and have few of the usual trappings such as glossy arcades of duty-free shops.

## TRAINS

Most foreign tourists enjoy the long-distance train trips, however reluctant they may be at first to embark on their journey. 'Soft Class'—the class most foreigners choose— combines comfort with efficiency. Clean, white embroidered seat covers, an endless supply of hot water and green tea, effective heating in winter, and dining cars which can produce adequate and sometimes excellent Chinese meals (beer and bottled fizzy drinks are available)—all add up to ideal conditions for sitting back and watching China's diverse countryside speed by. Overnight passengers are comfortably housed in velvet-curtained, four-bunked compartments, with a potted plant in each. Each car has washing and toilet facilities. Another plus for Chinese trains is their good record for punctuality—to be on time in China it is still safest to travel by train.

*A sketch of the first railway train at Shanghai, June 1876, artist unknown*

## Tour Buses

There is a range of buses for sightseeing. Foreign groups are usually put in luxury 40-seater Hino buses imported from Japan. These are equipped with air-conditioning, heating that works, and an effective public address system. Smaller groups may be allocated 16-seater buses, vehicles described colloquially in China as *mianbao che*—'bread vans'. Occasionally, tourists may find themselves touring in older, unsprung Chinese-made buses.

## Taxis

In all tourist cities, taxis cruise the streets looking for fares. Larger, more expensive taxis tend to queue up outside hotels. If you want a cheaper one, just wait on the roadside and flag down a car yourself. Most drivers use their meters. In some small and cities, one may have to strike a deal with the driver. Before is best, to avoid getting ripped off. A problem exists at railway stations, where drivers lurk in the hope of making a fast buck. Once again, a short walk should allow you to hail a cab whose driver is willing to use his meter. In the smallest of towns, various motorized transport is available, and it is always necessary to haggle about the price. If you cannot speak, write figures down.

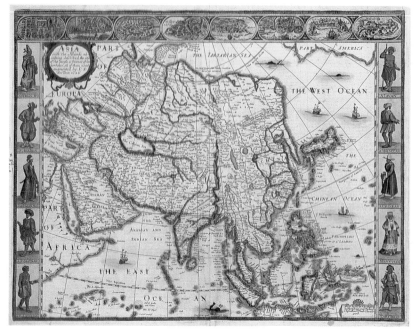

*A map of Asia drawn by John Speed, 1676*

## PUBLIC TRANSPORT

Only the most enterprising short-stay visitors would attempt to find their way around on public transport. No doubt there are many efficient bus and trolleybus services in China's cities, but it is difficult to come to grips with the system right away, especially if you do not speak Chinese. Route maps are in Chinese and, since the fare is based on distance travelled, you should also be able to say in Chinese where you are going. You may also have to muster considerable strength to push yourself both on and off the bus.

# Communications

China is developing its international communications systems, so it is possible to make long-distance telephone calls or send telexes and faxes from most major cities. All of the up-market hotels have business centres where guests as well as walk-in customers can send telexes and faxes. Airmail letters and cards do reach their destinations, although they may take some time. If you are thinking about sending any large purchases home, bear in mind that while shipping costs are average, crating charges are high, and the crate may not arrive for many months. Small boxes sent by seamail are often the best solution.

## Costs

A Westerner visiting China is travelling halfway across the world. The chief component of the travel budget is therefore the return airfare from his or her home country. Because of the relative cheapness of fares between London and Hong Kong compared with costs of direct flights between, say, a European city and Beijing, many tours begin or end in the Special Administrative Region. A large proportion of tours from North America also opt for the routing via Hong Kong, since trans-Pacific flights to Hong Kong are both frequent and increasingly competitively priced. (For individual travellers as well, Hong Kong—with its abundance of China-oriented travel agencies and quasi-official Chinese organizations authorized to issue visas—is an extremely convenient starting point.) The savings on airfares may be offset, however, by the expense of staying in Hong Kong for a few days.

*Steam locomotives are still to be seen today, particularly in the coal-rich north, although they are slowly being replaced as the country modernizes its vast railway network*

When travelling in China, as anywhere else, the benefits of group tours apply. You pay much less for the same standard of accommodation and other services than if you were doing it on your own. Tour prices vary widely, depending on the destinations and length of stay. Very roughly, for a 'classic' 14-day tour covering Beijing, Xi'an, Shanghai, Suzhou, Guilin, Guangzhou and exiting from Hong Kong, count on a ground price averaging US$200–250 (£120–150) a day, exclusive of airfares to Beijing and from Hong Kong. This gives you first-class accommodation, meals, all internal transfers and excursions to the most notable sights in each city. Prices vary according to the time of year. They are highest in May, June, September and October, and lowest from December through March. Obviously, the longer your stay, the lower becomes the average price per day. On the other hand, the more remote destinations can appear to be disproportionately more expensive. Sipping coffee, the visitor to Lhasa is unlikely to spare a thought for the enormous expense of supplying it to a few hotels in Tibet, just so that tourists may order their favourite brew at breakfast. Costs are high as much because of the special effort involved in providing tourist facilities in those places as because of their distance from, say, Beijing or Shanghai.

Unless you are backpacking and going 'hard class', do not expect China to be a bargain for individual travellers—the present official policy is to charge rates for tourist services similar to those prevailing elsewhere in the world. Those who knew China 'in the old days', when nothing seemed to cost more than a few *jiao*, may feel rather resentful of this. It is as well to recognize, though, that food items, transport, housing and other necessities of daily life are heavily subsidized by the Chinese government, and there is no reason to allow foreigners to benefit from the artificially low prices. This will change. Already, as the Chinese economy is slowly freed from total central control, domestic prices are moving closer to market rates.

The two-tier pricing policy which was the bane of China travel in the 70s and 80s is thankfully on its last legs. Foreign Exchange Certificates were abolished in 1994; China Railways made foreigners' tickets the same as for Chinese in October 1995; in March 1997, the State Pricing Commission issued a circular to all parks, museums, temples and other historical sites to anounce that dual-pricing should be stopped by December 31, 1997 at the latest; and the Civil Aviation Administration of China (CAAC) announced in July 1997 that foreigners and 'compatriots' from Macau and Taiwan would all  enjoy the same ticket tariffs. After such sweeping reforms, foreigners will, from early 1998, be free from government-sanctioned 'overcharging'.

# China Travel Today
—*Madeleine Lynn*

The first handful of Western tourists allowed into China in 1978 were grateful simply for the privilege of entering the country at all. Thus they were willing to put up with dismal Soviet-style hotels, bad service and itineraries that were arbitrarily changed from day to day. As many of them agreed, visiting China was an educational experience that they wouldn't have missed, but hardly a vacation. Today not only has China tourism changed beyond recognition, but in many ways so has China itself.

With the disintegration of communism worldwide, China is one of the few countries left to proudly call itself socialist. But to cope with the changing times China has its own unique ideology: 'socialism with Chinese characteristics'. This useful phrase means that any changes, no matter how drastic, can still come under the label of socialism, Chinese-style. In reality the country is evolving from a totally planned economy where all land and property were owned by the state, to a partial free market system. More and more state enterprises are being privatized, and those which remain in state hands are expected to turn a profit—an unsettlingly revolutionary idea for many of them. The slogan of the Mao era 'Serve the people' has been replaced by 'To get rich is glorious', uttered by the late paramount leader Deng Xiaoping himself.

Many have taken him at his word and a new class of entrepreneurs has grown up. Thus for locals and tourists alike, Chinese cities are more colourful and interesting now. The streets are alive with small private restaurants, markets and shops, most of which stay open till late, seven days a week. At night, street stalls selling noodles and other snacks do a brisk business under precariously swinging electric bulbs or by the light of paraffin lamps; by day, tourists are besieged by hawkers selling souvenirs, often handmade. Not only the streets, but the people too have a new look. Gone is the sombre uniform of green Mao suit and short pudding-basin haircut for men and women alike. Department stores are full of local and foreign cosmetics, and permed hair is fashionable for both sexes.

With the opening up of the country, tourism facilities, communications and transport have improved beyond measure. Major cities now offer a wide choice of international- standard hotels, many of them as extravagantly luxurious as the best five-star properties anywhere in the world. If you crave Western food, they offer everything from haute cuisine to hamburgers. McDonald's and other fast food-chains have come to some of the larger cities and are very popular among local Chinese. Some things have not changed much, however. Once outside your hotel or the better restaurants, be prepared for filthy public toilets of the squat type, and generally low standards of hygiene. Improvements are being made all the time in the most popular tourist sites (pay toilets with attendants have been introduced in many places for instance), but there is still a long way to go.

In the early 1980's, travellers to China were quite cut off from the outside world. Today they can return to their hotels to watch CNN, and call or fax home. Meanwhile urban Chinese in Beijing and Shanghai can hook up to the Internet to send e-mail and surf the Web—providing they sign a declaration to guarantee that the technology will not be used to subvert the government. Home telephones are more commonplace, mobiles are not a rare sight in cities, while pagers are widely used.

New roads have cut travel times to such famous sites as the Great Wall outside Beijing and the terracotta army excavation near Xi'an. Comfortable, air-conditioned tour buses have also made the journeys pleasanter. Airports are being upgraded, new ones built and the old Soviet planes are being replaced with the latest American and European aircraft. However, the expansion still cannot keep pace with the ever-increasing demand, particularly since the new affluence and freedom to travel has brought a surge of domestic tourism. Thus travellers can still be plagued by delays and difficulties in getting tickets.

One way to avoid this is to travel off season, during the winter months. The cold weather is compensated for by the delight of having sites like the Great Wall almost to yourself, empty of throngs of other tourists. Lhasa, though cold, boasts brilliant sunshine and deep blue skies and the unforgettable sight of hundreds of people from all over Tibet on winter pilgrimage. Southern China is quite mild throughout the year, while Kunming in the southwest is known as the 'city of eternal Spring' because of its pleasant weather year-round. Indeed, China is so vast that it would take many visits to fully explore its wide variety of landscape and ethnic groups, not to mention the innumerable historical sites. As transport and accommodation improves and as more areas are opened up for tourists, it is becoming easier (though still an adventure!) to visit remote regions as well as the more familiar destinations. Often when people think of China's scenery, they visualize the strangely-shaped mountains of Guilin or the humpbacked bridges and canals of the area around Shanghai, which inspired the popular blue-and-white willow pattern on Chinese porcelain for export. Yet there is so much more to be explored for the intrepid traveller, from the deserts of Gansu and Xinjiang to the wooded mountains of Sichuan. The Three Gorges of the Yangzi River, long famous for their beauty and their historical and cultural associations, can now be travelled in style on a variety of comfortable, international-standard cruise ships. Local Chinese are flocking to the Yangzi, as they know that with the building of the gargantuan Three Gorges Dam, slated to be the largest hydro-electric project in the world, this magnificent scenery will soon be changed forever.

These days natural scenery vies with man-made entertainments. The large numbers of Asian tourists plus the phenomenal growth of domestic tourism has led to the creation of numerous golf courses (over 40 in Guangdong Province alone and several around the Beijing area), theme parks and funfairs. At one time all of China rose and went to bed with the sun. Now the cities offer not only traditional entertainment such as Chinese opera and acrobats, but also nightclubs, discos and bars, particularly in the many joint-venture hotels. Like other countries in Asia, a craze for *karaoke* (literally 'empty orchestra' in Japanese) has taken the country by storm. A video and backup soundtrack play while you provide the vocals to your favourite song. Taiwanese and Hong Kong pop tunes are especially popular, another sign of the changing times. Al-

*The new, younger breed of shopper outside Tangcheng Department store on Dong Dajie, Xi'an*

though most Westerners (and many young Chinese) find the screeching falsettoes of Chinese opera to be a hard taste to acquire, everyone will enjoy the spectacular costumes and the more 'acrobatic' or 'martial' operas. Look out for any opera that features the Monkey King; it will definitely have its share of fighting and also humour. In Beijing there are often shows made up of short extracts from a variety of the more action-filled and accessible dramas.

Although over 90 per cent of the population are from the majority Han Chinese group, China has 56 ethnic groups altogether. Even in Xi'an, the heartland of China, there is a sizeable community of about 60,000 Hui people, Muslims who came to Xi'an along the Silk Road many centuries ago. As you wander through the market bazaar in Kashgar, a trading post on the Silk Road to Afghanistan, it is easy to forget you are in China and imagine yourself in a Turkish bazaar. Yunnan and Guizhou Provinces in the southwest have magnificent rugged scenery and a host of different minority groups, many of whom still wear traditional costumes and make exquisite embroidery and hand-dyed textiles. Guizhou, a province still largely undiscovered by tourists, celebrates nearly 1,000 minority festivals a year. The sight of Miao girls in their festival finery, with their elaborate, top-heavy, silver head-dresses is a feast for photographers. Then there is the chance to stay in a yurt (felt tent) on the grasslands of Inner Mongolia, touristy but fun... the list goes on and on.

Most tourists naturally focus on China's historical sites, relics of a civilization that boasts of having written records that go back as far as 2,000 years. During the Cultural Revolution (1966-76) there was a backlash against everything old and therefore 'feudal' and 'backward'. Temples were destroyed or turned into warehouses, books were burned—incalculable damage was done. Yet today, the Chinese value their heritage again. China's museums, though full of treasures, used to be dusty, uncared for places with few, if any English captions. Today, many of them have been totally revamped and rival museums anywhere in the world for their layout and presentation. What's more, many artifacts that were previously not on show because of lack of space are now on display in new museums, such as the beautiful Shaanxi Provincial Museum in Xi'an and the Shanghai Museum which house world class collections. Those revisiting China will be surprised to find how many new things there are to see. The Chinese continue to excavate in Xi'an and at other tomb sites around the country and to open areas and mount new exhibits, such as hitherto closed halls and pavilions in Beijing's Forbidden City and Summer Palace.

The Communists imagined that with the advent of socialism, religion, that 'opium of the people,' would gradually disappear. During the Cultural Revolution the process was forcibly hurried along. Temples were closed and monks sent to the countryside to work the fields. After the fall of the Gang of Four in 1976 many temples were re-opened, largely for the benefit of foreign tourists. Usually manned by a mere handful of elderly monks, they were ghostly museums rather than places of worship. Today, however, much to the consternation of the Communist Party, Buddhist and Daoist (Taoist) temples, Islamic mosques, and Protestant and Catholic churches are all flourishing. The temples are full of worshippers and local sightseers, old and young, and many have been lavishly restored with the help of donations from at home and abroad. New ones are also being built; is this what they mean by socialism with Chinese characteristics? In the past Chinese were reluctant to debate questions like these because of possible repercussions. While political discussions with foreigners are no longer taboo, today most people are simply not very interested. To quote Deng again: 'Who cares if a cat is black or white, as long as it catches mice?' After the suffering and loss of life caused by the endless ideological campaigns since 1949, and the unrest of 1989, the majority of people just want to get on with their private lives and stay away from political issues. The perennial questions you will be asked are ones which may seem rather bad mannered to a Westerner, but which are the Chinese equivalent of inquiring about the weather: what is your salary, the price of all your possessions from your watch to your home, your age and depending on how old you are, the ages of your parents, and the number and ages of your children and grandchildren. All Han Chinese are now supposed to have only one child, so many are envious of Westerners' freedom in this regard.

When dealing with problems, always remember that the concept of 'saving face' is very important. An angry head-on confrontation with someone will only embarrass them and make them 'lose face' (particularly if you loudly prove that they are in the wrong). Someone who has been made to 'lose face' usually reacts by being as unhelpful as possible. Negotiating anything in China, from an important business deal to changing a plane ticket, is nearly always best accomplished by using a combination of patience, politeness and good humour. These days unfortunately, a tip or bribe may be required as well, depending on the circumstances. Consult with those familiar with the situation before trying this. What may seem like simple problems often take a long time to untangle. Save your temper for important battles and lose it only as a last resort! If you are travelling with a group, it is often best to channel all complaints through the tour escort.

Traditional Chinese good manners demand that the speaker should constantly belittle himself and praise the other person. Thus Chinese will often tell you that they speak bad English, that the food they are about to serve you is terrible, and that their country is poor and backward. An American was aghast when the doctor about to operate on her for acute appendicitis started apologising for his 'lack of experience' and 'poor skills'. She was finally persuaded to remain on the operating table by a Chinese who whispered that this was merely the very senior and highly-qualified doctor's way of being polite. These humble phrases are forms only; you are not expected to take them too seriously nor to answer by agreeing with them! Bear in mind that most Chinese are intensely patriotic; they may criticise China themselves but understandably do not take kindly to criticism from casual visitors. As a guest it is polite to give the nation's 'face' some respect.

These days, although large areas (mainly the poorer regions and military sites) are still closed to foreigners, tourists have much more freedom of movement than before. Some of the most rewarding moments of a visit to China are to be found by taking time out from regular sightseeing to wander around the streets. Especially recommended is an early-morning visit to one of the many city parks and squares. Those situated by a river or lake are particularly popular (and photogenic), such as along Guilin's Li River or around beautiful West Lake in Hangzhou. Around 6.30 am is generally the busiest, although retirees with time on their hands enjoy the parks at all hours of the day. Groups of people perform the stately and graceful *tai-chi* exercises, while sometimes you will be lucky enough to see practisers of sword-play. One of the latest exercise fads for older people is Western dancing. You may find groups of pensioners waltzing to old familiar tunes, or doing disco-style aerobics to pop songs. It is all for the sake of their health, they solemnly explain. Old men come to meet their friends and air their caged birds. Hanging the cages in the trees, they settle down to games of cards and chess while the birds sing overhead. Other retirees come to parks throughout the day to sing Chinese opera, to the accompaniment of the two-stringed *er hu* or Chinese violin.

Most tourists spend the bulk of their time in China's cities; and in a country where a medium-sized town may have a population of one million inhabitants, it is easy to forget that urbanites are actually a very small minority here. Over 80 per cent of Chinese live in the countryside, where life for most people is still one of backbreaking manual labour. But even here, life has improved for many, particularly for those living in fertile areas close to large cities. Charge of the land (although not ownership) has been given back to the peasants under the 'individual responsibility system.' After selling a fixed quota of their produce to the state at state prices, they are free to sell the rest as they please. Instead of spending all their time farming many have started cottage industries such as furniture making, or whatever is most profitable. In the prosperous farmlands around Shanghai and Guangzhou, farmers are building modern, two-storey houses, but in many areas village life remains essentially the same as it has been for centuries. A walk off the beaten tourist path into one of China's villages could well be the highlight of your trip. Peasants and water buffalo plough the rice fields, women with babies strapped to their backs beat clothes by the river, while small boys chase flocks of white ducks. Many of the farming implements and houses are exactly the same in style as the models found in Tang tombs dating back over 1,000 years. Villagers are friendly and hospitable and may invite you into their houses for a cup of tea or hot water. In areas where few or no foreigners have been before, be prepared to be surrounded by a sea of curious, but not hostile, faces. Especially in the countryside, a poloroid picture of a prized child or grandchild is the perfect gift. But expect to be mobbed by the whole village!

To visit China is to visit a whole world in itself. It is a land of tremendous geographical and ethnic diversity, where historical sites spanning 2,000 years and breakneck modernisation projects exist side by side. Each person will come back with a different set of favourite memories and images. Will it be the children's faces, the Great Wall, or maybe cormorant fishing on the Li River? Discover China for yourself. As the Chinese say, 'One look is worth a thousand books'.

# Shopping in China

The first thing to say about shopping anywhere in China is that it does not have to be at all expensive. There are many modest items that can give great pleasure, such as cotton T-shirts, vests and *neiku*, which are 'inner trousers' worn in winter for extra warmth. They come in a bright array of colours, shocking pink and electric blue being popular, and make excellent, inexpensive jogging suits and sports clothes. For those interested in folk crafts, the deep indigo-dyed cloth of Guizhou—with its patterns of dragonflies, peonies and frogs—and ceramic rice bowls, medicine jars and casserole dishes made for the country homes of Guangdong Province are inexpensive buys. In Xi'an, brightly coloured children's waistcoats, embroidered and appliquéd with the traditional 'five poisonous creatures', as well as hats and shoes, are widely sold around the sites visited by tourists.

The choice of textiles and clothing in China is astonishing. However, the best often goes to export markets and is more easily sought out in the large emporiums run by the Chinese in Hong Kong. As for silks, cottons, cashmere and other woollen garments, the selections stocked in China's Friendship Stores are often the most appealing to the overseas shopper. But that should not stop the adventurous buyer

*A Canton grocer's shop, William Prinsep*

from shopping in local Chinese department stores. Boutiques selling good-quality casual clothes and leather jackets have proliferated in the larger cities in recent years.

If you see something you like, do not hesitate. There are hundreds behind you all looking for something special.

Silks are one of China's special attractions. Even the most stuffy men have been known to buy silk shirts. Tailoring is easily available if you are in one place for more than a week, but tailors in Hong Kong are even faster—and usually better at interpreting a foreign style. Heavy brocade silks, displayed in swathes of glittering gold, crimson and emerald, are popular with overseas Chinese visitors. A favourite with many shoppers is Shantung silk, woven with bold checks and stripes, which is of a suitable weight for jackets and trousers. Silk scarves are now better designed than in the early 1980s, and cities have excellent selections in their department stores.

For those who enjoy tea and trying out new varieties, a visit to the southern provinces of China affords a chance to taste some of the finest teas available. Excellent Oolong tea is produced in Fujian; Hangzhou is renowned for its Longjing green tea, as is Yunnan for its Pu Er. You can buy teas from all over China in the major cities. The best accompaniment to a fine caddy of tea is a Yixing teapot. Yixing, in Jiangsu Province, has a centuries-old tradition of making unglazed teaware. The unglazed teapots are remarkable for their stylish simplicity of form. Look out for the pumpkin-shaped versions which have a dragon's head on the lid. When the teapot is tilted for pouring, the dragon will stick out its tongue.

China's precious stones can be enjoyed in the form of jewellery or in carved ornaments made from larger pieces of stone. There are excellent precious-stone-carving factories in many Chinese cities where lapidaries with water drills can spend years carving just one work in jade, coral or rose quartz. Some of the carvings are of strange landscapes, others of Taoist immortals, with the texture or markings of the stone cleverly worked into special features. Chinese jewellery can be either extremely unattractive or stunning to the Western eye. Chinese river pearls are very pretty and cost less than cultured pearls. Many shops offer ropes of coral beads, amethysts, pearls and other precious stones.

Embroidery remains one of the most popular purchases for overseas visitors. It is not hard to see why. Few Western countries maintain a tradition of hand-embroidered goods because of the high labour costs, so Chinese embroidery is increasingly sought-after. The shopper can spend a fortune on the double-sided embroidery which is a feature of Suzhou. The embroiderer works both sides to equal perfection and can often cleverly create a front-and-back effect. More everyday items which can also make excellent gifts are hand-embroidered tablecloths, napkins, guest towels, handkerchiefs and aprons.

Many travellers to China like to return home with a painting or a piece of porcelain. A word of warning, however—there are few bargains to be found in the antique shops of China. (You are more likely to find what you are looking for on Hong Kong's Hollywood Road. Occasionally fine pieces of very early Chinese pottery appear in the curio shops in Hong Kong, where a great number of smuggled antiques from illegal mainland digs end up, and it is also possible to find old Chinese paintings.) Beijing's antiques district—Liulichang— has never had much of great antiquity or rarity, though good antiques are sometimes offered by private dealers. Liulichang is nevertheless worth visiting for its good choice of copies from paintings, traditional art supplies, rubbings of stone carvings and second-hand books.

If you are not daunted by the cost of shipping, Chinese carpets and lacquer screens and furniture are of very fine quality. Smaller items which will take up hardly any room in your luggage include cloisonné ashtrays and dishes, sandalwood fans and a seal carved with your name in Chinese.

Minority handicrafts are becoming widely available in big city stores as well as in the shops of the minority regions. You need not go to Yunnan's Stone Forest to buy a Sani cross-stitch satchel, since they can now be found in arts and crafts shops in Beijing, nor to Lhasa for prayer wheels, daggers and turquoise-and-silver jewellery, which are sold in Chengdu. However, it is still true that the best of the minority handicrafts are available in their places of origin. Particular favourites are Tibetan rugs, Mongolian saddle rugs (for their hard wooden saddles), jewellery and clothes from Yunnan, and boots, embroidered caps and daggers from Xinjiang.

It is not only the minorities who have their specialities. The provinces and individual cities are often famous for one particular craft or art. In Fujian, it is lacquerware; Shantou has a tradition of painted porcelain and fine linen sheets with lace-crocheted edging; Shanghai has a wonderful choice of carved wooden chopsticks inlaid with silver filigree; and Sichuan is famous for its bamboo and rattan goods. The list is endless. Ultimately, however, shopping in China is all about finding your own particular treasure.

# Eating in China

A long history, vast territory and extensive contact with foreign cultures have all contributed to the evolution of Chinese cooking into one of the world's great culinary traditions. But with regional cuisines of such startling diversity as that of Sichuan, Canton and Shandong, can we really speak of a single 'Chinese cuisine'?

Perhaps the best place to start answering this question is the kitchen. Nearly all Chinese dishes, as opposed to snacks or staple foods, are cooked in a *wok*, a thin-

Many culinary delights await the visitor to China, and not just in expensive hotel restaurants. Numerous street-side establishments serve delicious snacks such as baozi—dumplings stuffed with minced pork or vegetables (above)—noodles or shaobing—palm-sized breads baked inside a 'tandoori-style' oven (below)

walled, round-bottomed cast-iron pan. Woks can be used for stir frying, deep frying, stewing, steaming and smoking. To conserve both freshness and fuel, most of the ingredients used in Chinese cooking are cut into tiny slices, strips or cubes and cooked as briefly as possible. These principles are almost universal in China proper. Thus what more readily distinguishes regional dishes in China is flavour rather than technique.

There are four major cuisines in China, corresponding to geographical regions, though many everyday dishes are common to them all, so that the boundaries between the cuisines are often difficult to distinguish, and there can be much nitpicking. The regions are:

- Shandong, the traditional model for Beijing cuisine, is known for its seafood, particularly dried products such as shrimp, scallops and sea cucumber, prepared with salty sauces. (The most famous dish associated with the capital, Peking duck, originated in Mongolia.)
- Sichuan, hearty cooking flavoured with an exotic palette of spices: red and black pepper, sesame paste, flower pepper and fermented bean paste, though not all great Sichuan dishes are spicy-hot.
- Canton (in Guangdong Province), with its remarkable range of ingredients (such as dog, snake and salamander) cooked with a light touch, and featuring roast meats, oyster sauce, black beans and shrimp paste.
- Yangzhou (or Huaiyang), little known outside of China, is the general rubric for the cuisine of the lower Yangzi delta, including Shanghai, Suzhou and Hangzhou. Yangzhou dishes make much use of dark vinegar, sugar and rice wine.

The northern regions of China are generally arid, with long, bitterly cold winters. Food in the north used to be severely limited in the winter season. Thus the northern schools of cooking have more limited menus than their southern counterparts. The cuisine of Guangdong Province is widely regarded by the Chinese themselves as the best in China, because of its variety of ingredients and imaginative techniques of cooking. This is not surprising, since the province has a benevolent climate which ensures a long growing season, and an extensive coastline with a tradition of deep-sea fishing. Cantonese cuisine is also, of course, most well known in the West, thanks to the large number of restaurants opened around the world by emigrants from Hong Kong.

Throughout China, rice and wheat (in the form of noodles and steamed and baked bread) constitute the bulk of the diet. In fact, Chinese people in general think of cooked dishes as an accompaniment to their staple starches, and not the other way round as in the West. A banquet in China—a rare event in most Chinese lives, but frequent occurences for foreign tourists—can be defined as a meal at which more meat, seafood and vegetables are consumed than rice and wheat.

As a general rule, rice is served more regularly at meals in the south than in the north of China. The staples for northerners are wheat noodles and steamed breads. In the northeastern provinces (formerly Manchuria), there is a tradition of eating steamed sorghum bread known as *wotou'r*. The breads of China are nothing like the breads of Europe or America, but they should be tried because usually they are delicious. The traditional northern steamed bread bun is called a *mantou* and is often served at breakfast together with rice porridge (*zhou* or *xifan*) and soybean milk (*doujiang*). As a treat, try a steamed bun filled with sweet red bean paste (*hongdoubao*). In Shanghai, bread buns are popular even though the region is in the rice-growing belt. A Shanghainese meal is often served with a *huajuan*, a twisted steamed bread, which is wonderful for mopping up any sauce remaining on the dish. True to their culinary sophistication, the Cantonese prefer a more varied breakfast. *Dim sum* (*dianxin* in Mandarin) consists of an astonishing variety of steamed, fried and baked breakfast snacks. These can be stuffed with sweet or savoury fillings such as lotus seed paste, barbecued pork and shrimps. The traditional Chinese breakfast is perhaps the first meal on which you should try your new-found sense of culinary adventure—that is, if you can just once renounce the coffee, toast and eggs served at most first-class hotels.

The three cardinal virtues by which Chinese food is judged are colour, fragrance and taste (*se xiang wei*). Critics have noted that these categories are purely superficial, and exclude concern with the nutritional value of a dish. This is a philistine view, as the Chinese diet with its emphasis on vegetables, vegetable oils and vegetable protein is an extremely healthy one. The close link between diet and a person's physical well-being is taken for granted by the Chinese. In fact, there is a long established tradition which designates food as either 'heating' or 'cooling'—not according to their literal state but as an indication of their effect on the body. Thus snake and dog meat are eaten by the Cantonese in the winter months because they are 'warming'. When treating patients, Chinese doctors will adopt a holistic approach to healing, and not only prescribe medicine but also advise what foods should be eaten or avoided. Many foods which Westerners regard as strange are delicacies to the Chinese due to their 'strengthening' qualities. Sea slugs and shark's fin are often included in a Chinese banquet not only because they are rare and costly but also because they are 'good for you'. Foreigners usually do not know or are simply unexcited by this approach, but recognition of its background will make you more sympathetic to Chinese culinary idiosyncracies.

The years of the Cultural Revolution (1966-76) did much to damage the tradition of Chinese cuisine. The art of cooking was deemed as bourgeois and decadent as other traditional arts; old master chefs were thrown out of their jobs, and good restaurants were closed down to be replaced by workers' canteens staffed by untrained and unmotivated cooks. Since farms and factories were also in turmoil, there was little incentive and poor facilities to produce or process good ingredients, spices and seasonings.

China is still recovering from that decade of culinary puritanism. Nonetheless, the impact of the Cultural Revolution has meant that few restaurants outside five-star hotels in China reach the high standards achieved by chefs in Hong Kong, Taiwan and other overseas Chinese communities such as Singapore, Vancouver and New York. There are of course notable exceptions.

In the past few years, a number of established restaurants dating from pre-communist days have resumed business after refurbishment and are trying to win back their reputation for fine food. They are proving immensely popular, not least because the new-found prosperity of local Chinese now enables them to be selective when dining out. Inevitably, prices have risen sharply in line with inflation. The excellent Sichuan restaurant in Beijing's Xidan district, Sichuan Fandian, in a converted mansion once owned by the early 20th-century warlord Yuan Shikai, was previously famous only for its spicy food. Now it is famous for its pricy menu too. Nonetheless, the food is still good and the surroundings of traditional courtyards and one-storeyed buildings make it enduringly popular with Beijing's foreign and local residents and visitors. More economical meals consisting of standard dishes are available in the large dining room patronized by local people.

Most tourists still eat in hotel dining rooms where the food can be average to good, depending on the area and the season. Yet hotel dining rooms are not the best introduction to the regional variety of Chinese food. One result of the economic reforms launched some twenty years ago has been the re-emergence of small family-run restaurants, which are restoring a sense of competition and hence quality to cooking in China. These restaurants offer the best value for money, even if the surroundings can be rather basic. You may find yourself perched on a stool under a canvas awning as half the town passes by, but you may also be tasting a family recipe developed over centuries! Do not be too hasty in judging restaurants by their outward appearance. On the other hand, these places may not be very clean and it is as well to bear in mind that hygiene is as important as authenticity.

If you want to eat out on your own, your guide or a local contact may be able to recommend a couple of local restaurants. Ask for their names to be written down in Chinese, along with instructions for the taxi driver. You can also ask for a good selection of local dishes to be written down, also in Chinese characters, to give to the waiter when you arrive. Alternatively, you can take an exploratory walk and look for a local restaurant that is busy—always a good sign—indicate that you want to sit down, then order by looking over the shoulders of other diners and choosing something that looks appetising. Most Chinese will not mind if you act with discreet good humour. Indeed, there is often someone who wants to practise his English by helping you. You may even end up with a conversational companion as well as a meal.

# Old Ways Die Hard

Guo Heizi had a problem. He had married after the one-child policy had begun to be enforced more strictly in the area, and his wife had given birth to a useless girl who would no doubt eventually marry into another family and leave him destitute in his old age. Heizi was so angry that finally the woman conceived again, slipping off to her parents' home in another district to avoid local officials during her pregnancy. She gave birth there, so that not even hospital authorities, who might have forced her to have a late abortion, knew about it. She returned in triumph to the Guos with a three-month-old baby boy.

According to local policies, there was now a fine of 400 yuan to be paid to the xiang Planned Birth Office. Although this was low because the region was poor and the population not as dense as in some areas, Guo Heizi's entire savings amounted to only about 200 yuan, which he turned in. Then officials ordered his relatives to carry his furniture and other possessions to the xiang to make up the rest. But how could they take away the belongings of their own flesh and blood? the peasants asked, still outraged. In fact, they were all filled with rejoicing at the birth of the little boy! Finally the officials came themselves and took everything—beds, wardrobe, even Heizi's household wok. All this had happened just the week before our visit, and now Heizi and his wife were away at her family clan, borrowing the basic necessities until they could get the money to replace them. The child, however, was right here, the peasants volunteered proudly, pushing a shy-looking woman forward from the outer circle of watchers. By the hand she held a fat toddler, naked from the waist down, the evidence of his maleness clear.

In the opinion of the peasants, Heizi had come out of the affair quite all right. After all, the second child had not been a girl, and the fine did not really matter, especially to someone who had little cash and few possessions in the first place. It was worth it. Even in wealthier areas, where the fine was said to be as high as 2,000 yuan, people often preferred to pay; one family was said to have nicknamed their extra son Caidian, "Color TV," for he had cost them just as much as one. All the newlyweds the Guos knew were waiting for boys. The situation was very clear: under the responsibility system, the more labor power you had, the wealthier you would be. As it was being applied in their district, you got more land each time a child was born, but lost some when a girl married off and left you. If you had only a single daughter, you would have to work in the fields for your rice until you died, poor and lonely.

Not everyone had been as fortunate as Heizi, the peasants said. In another village, the Yang clan had consulted fortune-tellers for months in order to find a bride who would produce a boy for one of their sons. They finally found one, and the marriage feast was as lavish as any that had been seen in many years. Even the Guos had been invited, from several li away. All the old customs had been followed. The red-clothed bride had been fetched from her home, with the plaintive, festive sound of the suona horn in accompaniment; in a long train, the relatives carried the new bedding on shoulder poles to the bridegroom's home. There kowtows were made to the images of the ancestors, and a huge banquet was served, for which five pigs were killed. Glutinous rice cakes were consumed in abundance, and rice wine flowed. It was as if the Yangs were already celebrating the birth of the new baby boy.

Perhaps the fortune was poorly told, or perhaps the pregnant young wife encountered a spirit, a peach ghost. The birth was a tragedy.

The baby girl was ignored by her father; the clan spoke of revenge. Some threatened to beat the soothsayer, others to send the woman back to her family. Then, quietly, the problem was resolved. The baby disappeared during the night. The Yangs let it be known that she had been taken away by the same ghosts who had entered her mother and robbed her of the boy that was hers by right.

Then the county officials came and made an investigation. To everyone's surprise, the unfortunate father was taken off to spend a year in prison for murder! It was so unfair, the Guos complained. What else could a man in his position have been expected to do?

Liang Heng and Judith Shapiro, After the Nightmare

# Chinese History: A Brief Chronology

## PREHISTORY

The beginnings of Chinese culture have been traced to Neolithic settlements along the middle Yellow and Wei river valleys in northern China around the fifth millennium BC, but the earliest of the dynasties mentioned by traditional Chinese texts is the Xia (c. 2205–1766 BC). The dynasty is said to have been founded by Yu the Great, a king credited with controlling the floods that afflicted the river valleys of China. Since no archaeological evidence has been discovered in support of its existence, the Xia is considered mythical by some scholars.

## THE SHANG (c. 1600–1027 BC)
## AND THE WESTERN ZHOU (1027–771 BC)

The Shang kingdom, which succeeded the Xia, rose in a part of present-day Henan Province, on the edge of the flood plain of the Yellow River. From oracle inscriptions and other relics, archaeologists have pieced together a picture of an aristocratic culture which waged war with the help of horse-drawn chariots and bronze weapons, built cities walled with rammed earth, and made elaborate vessels for use in ancestor worship.

Ancestor worship, which included the offering of sacrifices, was entrusted to the king. His ancestors, it was believed, could intercede with the supreme god of Heaven on behalf of their living descendants. Thus the idea that political power sprang from spiritual power developed very early on, and it became entrenched by the time the Zhou were established. This later evolved into the 'Mandate of Heaven'—the theory that a king's right to rule was dependent on his ability to appease Heaven so that the destructive forces of nature would not be unleashed upon his subjects in the way of floods, drought or other natural disasters. If the king were unjust or immoral, his harmonious relationship with Heaven would be shattered and famine and chaos would follow. Heaven's mandate would be withdrawn and rebellion given legitimacy.

The mandate of heaven was eventually withdrawn from the Shang. Under the new ruling house of Zhou, formerly a vassal of the Shang, a feudal system was developed based on fiefs granted to the kinsmen of the ruler. As its homeland was in the Wei River valley (today's Shaanxi Province) to the west of Shang domain, the new dynasty relocated the capital to a city near modern Xi'an—hence the name 'Western Zhou' for the first two and a half centuries of its reign.

## SPRING AND AUTUMN ANNALS (770–476 BC) AND THE WARRING STATES (475–221 BC)

A long period of prosperity and expansion under the Zhou began unravelling as family ties with the fiefdoms weakened. While nominally acknowledging Zhou sovereignty, feudal states themselves became power centres acquiring their own vassals. In 770 BC invaders from the northern steppes attacked the capital, forcing the Zhou king to abandon it for a new base at Luoyang to the east. The Eastern Zhou period is conventionally subdivided into two phases—the Spring and Autumn Annals, named after a chronological history covering those years, and the Warring States, a time of escalating disorder and power struggles. Finally, out of all the competing states, three gained ascendancy.

It was against a background of profound turmoil, in the late Spring and Autumn period, that a new intellectual elite emerged. Its most notable member, Confucius (551–479 BC) sought to remedy the political and social disintegration around him by advancing the ideal of leadership by moral example: he taught that only when a ruler was possessed of virtue would he be able to call forth the good in all men and exercise authority. Confucius' doctrine did not find much favour with the feudal lords of this time, although it was eventually to be elevated to a state religion.

## THE FIRST EMPIRE, QIN DYNASTY (221–206 BC)

Of the three states jostling for mastery of the Chinese world in the Warring States period, it was the western state of Qin which finally triumphed as the leading military power. Qin had substantially extended its boundaries by absorbing Shu (modern Sichuan Province) in 316 BC, and in the following century it consolidated its territorial gains by further annexations.

The Qin conquest brought the whole of China under a centralized monarchy. Zheng, the young ruler of Qin and architect of that unification, took for himself the title of Qin Shi Huangdi—First Qin Emperor. To administer this vast realm, he created a form of political organization which was to endure for some 2,000 years; perhaps the most remarkable innovation of the Qin was the bureaucratic apparatus that gradually replaced the old feudal structure. The Qin emperor also built a network of roads for the movement of his troops, repaired and reinforced defensive walls along the frontier, unified the writing system, standardized the coinage and codified the law. All this he did in the 11 years of his reign. He wanted to do more, and he wanted to live forever, but immortality eluded him. He died in 210 BC, during one of his tours of the empire (while searching for the elixir of life, it is said), and was buried in a tomb guarded by thousands of lifesize clay warriors interred nearby.

## THE EMPIRE CONSOLIDATED:
## THE HAN DYNASTY (206 BC–AD 220)

Qin Shi Huangdi's successor, a nephew, did not last long. Rebellion broke out and swept to power the humble founder of the next dynasty, Liu Bang. The first Han emperor, though uneducated himself, wisely recognized the value of learned advisers. During Han rule the influence of Confucian philosophy was revived and knowledge of the sage's works became a qualification for passing imperial examinations. The system of recruiting civil servants by examination, started during this period, effectively eradicated the last vestiges of feudalism. In theory and occasionally in practice, these competitive examinations offered a measure of social mobility for commoners unavailable within a feudal system.

As well as many advances in agriculture and technology (the magnetic compass and paper were developed during the Han), there were conquests which at one time extended the imperial sphere of influence beyond its original borders to as far as Korea in the northeast, the seaboard in the south and westwards as far as Central Asia. It was during the reign of one Han emperor, Wudi, that expeditions were made far to the west of China's boundaries. In 139 BC an official, Zhang Qian, was sent on a mission to find allies against the Xiongnu (Hun) horsemen who were a constant threat in the north. His journeys to Central Asia opened up what was to become the Silk Road, along which Buddhism was brought to China in the first century AD.

The Han dynasty covered more than four centuries, with one interruption (AD 9–24), when the Liu dynastic line was broken by a usurper, Wang Meng, a relative of one of the imperial consorts. As the capital of the first continuous period was at Chang'an (modern Xi'an), the 'Former Han' is also designated as 'Western Han'. In the second period, the court being at Luoyang, the years from the restoration of the house of Liu to the end of the dynasty are known as 'Eastern (or Later) Han'.

### ANARCHY AND PARTITION (220–581)

By about the first century AD, the dynasty was in decline as the growth of factions among the imperial family and the intrigues of eunuchs increasingly debilitated the court. When the centre could no longer hold, the empire fell prey to rebels and pretenders to the throne.

Deprived of authority, the last Han emperor ruled only in name. Power was held by a general, Cao Cao, whose son in 221 forced the abdication of the emperor and founded a new dynasty, Wei. Two rival clans set up their own regional regimes—Wu in the east, and Shu Han in the southwest. Known as the Three Kingdoms (220–265), this period was marked by warfare and turmoil.

Wei emerged the strongest of the three, but it was soon toppled by another clan, which established the Western Jin dynasty (265–316). This spell of unification was also brief, however. Subject to invasions by 'barbarians' from beyond its frontiers, the empire fragmented further. In 316 north China was lost to the nomadic Xiongnu, and thereafter, with the flight of the refugee Jin court to the southern city of Nanjing, the Chinese empire was effectively confined to the Yangzi valley. The north was ruled by a series of short-lived non-Chinese dynasties of the Xiongnu, as well as the Mongols and the Toba Tartars. This profusion of reigns came to be known as the 'Sixteen Kingdoms'. From time to time, the rulers in the south made attempts to recover the Chinese heartland, but their forays were resisted.

This state of affairs lasted until 581. By then, the 'barbarians', who had resorted to Chinese methods of government to control their conquered domain, were thoroughly sinicized. With no experience of agrarian societies, they used the existing administrative apparatus and in the process came to adopt the Chinese way of life themselves. The Toba Tartars, having defeated the rival ethnic groups, founded the Wei dynasty, and abandoned their own language, customs and even surnames.

It was a general of mixed Chinese and 'barbarian' descent, Yang Jian, who rose to seize power in 581. He usurped the throne and consolidated his position in the north, before crossing the Yangzi and overthrowing the southern ruler. Once again, China was unified. The new dynasty Yang Jian founded was the Sui.

## THE SUI DYNASTY (581–618)

This period, though short, accomplished much in establishing an apparatus for government that provided the foundation for the Tang, the next imperial house, to flourish. Yang Jian was extremely frugal; not so his successor, who was enthroned as Yang Di in 605. Yang Di's extravagance included the building of the Grand Canal, a waterway which linked up existing but derelict channels and which, when completed, stretched from Beijing in the north to Hangzhou in the south. Important as it was for integrating the north and south, this transportation project exacted great hardship on countless construction workers and left a legacy of bitterness among Yang Di's subjects. He also launched a series of expensive but futile campaigns against the Koreans. Dissatisfaction flared into revolt, and Yang Di was assassinated in 618.

## THE TANG DYNASTY (618–907)

The new dynasty proclaimed on the collapse of the Sui was to usher in what has been called China's Golden Age. The Tang, building on the system of government left by the Sui, created a strong administration with officials recruited by examination to run the ministries, boards and directorates. There was a great expansion of education, and the spread of literacy was facilitated by the invention, some time during the eighth century, of block printing. If there was one cultural achievement to distinguish the Tang above all others, it was literature. The brilliant poetry of Li Bai, Wang Wei, Du Fu and Bai Juyi attests to a glorious flowering of creativity.

In the economic sphere, trade extended as far as India, and the open and outward-looking attitude which characterized the reign of the second Tang emperor, Taizong (627–649), made the capital, Chang'an (present-day Xi'an), a crossroads of foreign merchants, monks and travellers. Embassies arrived from Persia and the Byzantine Empire. Foreigners and foreign faiths were welcomed, so that the metropolis harboured several non-Chinese communities. When the monk Xuanzang returned from India with Buddhist scriptures in 645, he was received personally by the emperor, who had some years before also granted an audience to a Nestorian priest. Except towards the end of the dynasty, Buddhism enjoyed great favour throughout the empire.

After Emperor Taizong, the court was dominated by a remarkable woman whose rise from concubine to empress was achieved by complex intrigues and utter ruthlessness. For a time, as consort to a weak emperor, she ruled behind the scenes, but as Empress Wu Zetian she took over the reins of government entirely, and even changed the name of the dynasty from Tang to Zhou until she was forced to abdicate at the age of 80.

With the restoration of Tang after Wu Zetian's death, China was able to enjoy a long period of stability and prosperity. The reign of Emperor Xuanzong, who has been called Minghuang (the Brilliant Emperor), was the high point of the Tang. It was marked by enlightened government and splendid achievements in the arts. But his long reign (712–756) was to end in disaster, when An Lushan, a general of Turkish descent who was in command of the imperial forces in the northeast, launched a rebellion in 755. In the latter part of his reign, Xuanzong had become out of touch with state affairs, having fallen under the influence of a favourite concubine, Yang Guifei, and members of her family. When An Lushan threatened the capital, Xuanzong fled to Sichuan, and en route Yang Guifei was killed. The dynasty survived another 150 years, but after the rebellion—finally suppressed in 763—the Tang never recovered the political control it had previously exercised. Like An Lushan had been, the commanders of the military regions remained extremely powerful. Separatist tendencies gained strength and once again the empire fragmented into independent states.

## THE FIVE DYNASTIES AND THE TEN KINGDOMS (907–960)

During this period, five brief dynasties held the north of the country. The capital was transferred from Chang'an to Kaifeng. Over the course of half a century, ten other ruling houses controlled various regions of China, two of them 'barbarian'—the Tangut (a people of Tibetan stock) and the Khitan (a tribe from what was later Manchuria). There was an exodus of officials and scholars from the north to the Yangzi valley, where the heritage of Tang culture was preserved. And as borne out by later events, the impulse for unification had not perished either.

# The Northern Song (960–1126) and the Southern Song (1127–1279)

China was brought under one rule again in 960. The third empire, the Song, was centred first on Kaifeng and later on Hangzhou, hence the division of the dynasty into 'Northern' and 'Southern' phases.

Although the various nomadic races in the north continued to pose a threat, the pacific Song emperors were initially content to appease them. Unlike their predecessors, the Song did not seek to expand their territory beyond the traditional boundaries south of the Yellow River basin. From about 1000 to the end of the Northern phase, peace was maintained. The empire was regulated by an effective civil service, and enjoyed a long period of economic expansion, due in part to fiscal reforms instituted by a brilliant minister, Wang Anshi, which benefited the peasants and shifted the burden of taxes on to landowners and rich merchants. Under the patronage of a series of able emperors there was another efflorescence of artistic and intellectual activity. Painting, above all, attained an excellence never equalled since.

The peace ended when, under Emperor Huizong (reigned 1100–25), a new threat appeared on the scene—the warlike Jurchen who, like the Khitan, were from Manchuria. Huizong abdicated the throne in favour of his son and fled south, leaving the way open for the Jurchen to invade, lay siege to Kaifeng and establish the Jin dynasty. At various times the exiled Song court in Hangzhou tried, unsuccessfully, to recover their lost territory in the north, but for the most part the two empires co-existed in uneasy truce. In 1147, the Jin themselves were attacked by a new, savage conquering tribe, the Mongols, and destroyed by them in 1234.

Genghiz became Great Khan in 1206 and intensified a campaign of conquest that eventually left the Mongols in control of a large portion of China. National resistance to Genghiz and later to his grandson, Kublai, kept Hangzhou in the hands of the Song until 1276. Just a few years later, pursued by Mongol forces, the last of the fugitive Song court retreated to Fujian and died off the coast in 1279.

# The Yuan Dynasty (1279–1368)

Hangzhou, which escaped pillage by the Mongols, deeply impressed Marco Polo, the Venetian traveller and trader who claimed to have served at the court of Kublai Khan. But it was at the site of modern Beijing that Kublai Khan established his winter capital, Khanbaliq. Although Kublai adopted 'Yuan' as his dynastic name, he made sure the Mongols would not be assimilated by the majority Chinese. Different ethnic groups within the empire were formally distinguished, while the southern Chinese (who were suspected of nationalistic sentiments) were relegated to the lowest of four classes. Obviously the Chinese were forbidden to hold important posts in the bureaucracy.

Kublai Khan's reign covered the best years of the Yuan dynasty. Contact was made with the Near East and the West, leading to a flow of scientific and cultural information which brought Arab astronomy to China and a Franciscan mission to Khanbaliq. Europe became more aware of Chinese culture from the reports of the Catholic missionaries.

None of the seven emperors after 1294 had the stature of Kublai Khan. With the weakening of the central authority, social unrest and opposition to the alien dynasty increased. The Yuan was overthrown by insurgents led by a former bandit and monk, Zhu Yuanzhang.

## THE MING DYNASTY (1368–1644)

Zhu Yuanzhang was from a poor peasant family in the southern province of Anhui, where he originally intended to set up his capital. However, it was decided that the strategically located Nanjing would be more suitable, for the Yangzi valley had been the cultural and commercial centre of the empire since the Southern Song. From the start, the commoner-emperor, who took the title Hongwu, was determined to concentrate power in the person of the sovereign. His long reign (1368–98) was marked by stability at home and successful conquest abroad.

It was the third Ming emperor, Yongle, who moved the capital to Beijing, probably for defensive purposes. Preoccupation with securing the northern border against the Mongols led to a spate of wall and fortification building during the Ming, the most notable project being the eastern section of the Great Wall.

Interest in exploration and navigation also reached new heights at this time. In 1405 Emperor Yongle sent the admiral Zheng He (1371-1435) on the first of seven voyages which reached the shores of Arabia and as far as Timor in the east Indian Ocean. Unlike later European voyagers, however, the Chinese did not use their sea power to found a maritime trading empire. The West, on the other hand, was embarking on a period of territorial and commercial expansion. By 1514, the first Portuguese ships had arrived in Guangzhou (Canton), at a time when Chinese policy was unfavourable to foreigners. Although there were specific laws prohibiting Chinese from private trade with foreigners, the Europeans were undeterred. The Portuguese were followed by the Dutch and, in 1637, by the English.

The dynamic rule of Yongle was not repeated by any of his successors. From the beginning of the 16th century, Ming imperial power was on the wane. In a corrupt court, power was increasingly appropriated by eunuchs. The interests of the empire were neglected, even though vast amounts of money were spent on defending the northern frontier. Meanwhile, the Manchus, a northeastern tribe, were consolidating their power. In 1629 the Manchus reached the Great Wall, but were temporarily halted by the barrier. Soon after, the empire was riven by internal insurrections. When Beijing fell to the rebels in 1644, the last Ming emperor, Chongzhen, took his own life on Coal Hill, behind the Imperial Palace. One of his generals, hoping to enlist the Manchus' help in quelling the rebellion, opened a gate of the Great Wall at Shanhaiguan, and let them in. Thus it was that the Manchus, almost by accident, found themselves marching on Beijing, an ill-defended and demoralized capital recently vacated by the emperor. They were able to install themselves as China's new rulers without meeting opposition.

## THE QING DYNASTY (1644–1911)

The Manchu conquerors—founders of the Qing dynasty, as they called themselves—first pacified the rebellious south and eventually consolidated their empire under three capable rulers: Kangxi (reigned 1662–1722), Yongzheng (1723–35) and Qianlong (1736–95). Kangxi and his successors, unlike the Mongols, adopted Chinese culture themselves. The Jesuits who were in Beijing in the 18th century represented the empire as prosperous, splendid, powerful and extensive.

This was all to end in the 19th century. The following hundred years were to witness the gradual decay of an imperial structure that had run its course because of its resistance to change. The first signs of dynastic degeneration gave the Europeans their opportunity to open an isolationist China to the Western world. After a war (1839–42) fought over the ban of opium imports into China, the British forced the Qing government to ratify a treaty allowing foreign traders access to five ports in China. Five years later, the Taiping Rebellion weakened Qing rule irreparably.

Repeated defeats suffered by the Qing armies on a number of other fronts subjected the empire to near-partition by Russia, Germany, Britain, Japan and France. The disintegration reached crisis proportions and inspired a reform movement which advocated the adoption of Western technology and learning for China's rehabilitation. But since the rigidly conservative Dowager Empress Cixi, the most powerful figure at court, was inexorably opposed to modernization, any attempt at reform was doomed to failure. She died in 1908.

In so staunchly resisting change, the late Qing made change inevitable. The dynasty did not long survive Cixi, who died in 1908. When the Chinese people decided that national salvation could be achieved only with the overthrow of the Qing dynasty, they cast in their lot with a revolutionary movement led by a Western-trained doctor, Sun Yat-sen.

## REPUBLIC OF CHINA (1911–1949)

An uprising on October 10th, 1911 in Wuhan sparked unrest throughout central and south China, and within weeks Doctor Sun Yat-sen was declared President of the Republic of China in Nanjing (*see* page 98). Puyi, the boy-emperor, formally abdicated in February 1912, ending more than 2,000 years of imperial dynasties in China. His Nationalist Party advocated nationalism, and people's rights and welfare. But with no military backing, Sun resigned in 1912 and was replaced by Yuan Shikai who proclaimed himself Emperor Hong Xian. In March 1916 he stepped down and China was torn apart by warlordism.

In July 1921, 13 Marxists, one of them Mao Zedong, met in Shanghai to establish the Chinese Communist Party (*see* page 130). From 1923 to 1927 the Nationalists and Communists formed an alliance against warlords in north China, but in 1925 Sun died. The unity became uneasy with Chiang Kai-shek as its leader, and it fell apart in 1927 (*see* page 141).

After a series of failed armed uprisings against Chiang, Mao led his followers to Mt. Jinggang where he established the first communist guerrilla base. The main 'Red Army' then consolidated forces around Ruijin, Jiangxi, which was declared the Soviet Republic of China. This communist stronghold was encircled by Nationalist forces. In October 1934, more than 80,000 Red Army soldiers began a secret exodus west to break out of the siege and find a new base area. The campaign, which lasted one year, ended 11,000 kilometres (6,837 miles) away in Wuqi, northern Shaanxi province, and became known as the Long March (*see* pages 205–206). Less than 4,000 survived, and en route Mao established himself as leader of the Red Army and the Communist Party.

Yan'an became the new red capital while the Nationalists prepared to make further assaults, humiliated by their inability to wipe out Mao's army on its Long March. At the same time the Japanese were taking Chinese territory without opposition from Chiang who considered the 'Japanese a disease of the skin, the Communists a disease of the heart'. But in the interests of national unity, his own generals forced him to join the Communists and fight the Japanese (*see* page 83). From 1937 to 1945 the Sino-Japanese War raged, and once the aggressors were defeated, civil war, the War of Liberation (1945–1949), raged. Chiang's routed forces were forced to flee to Taiwan in 1949 with the mainland under communist control.

## PEOPLE'S REPUBLIC

Mao Zedong proclaimed the founding of the People's Republic of China in Beijing on October 1st, 1949. Land reform was implemented. Government policies were dictated primarily by ideology and often featured extremist campaigns and tumultuous political upheavals, most notably the Anti-Rightist Campaign against the bourgeoisie; a disastrous economic plan dubbed Great Leap Forward (1958); and the Cultural Revolution (1966–76), which aimed to 'prevent a restoration of capitalism'. Mao died in 1976. In 1978 Deng Xiaoping became leader and orchestrated China's normalization program of reform and opening to the outside world after its long isolation.

# Early Archaeological Treasures

Most visitors to China enjoy tours of archaeological sites and museums, but they are often frustrated by the lack of display signs in major foreign languages. The obvious solution is to make sure that you have your guide or interpreter close at hand. However, if you are part of a large group tour, it is sometimes difficult both to hear what is being said and to see what is actually on display. This introduction to early Chinese treasures is designed to help you find your own way around an exhibition or museum, to go at your own pace and to identify what is on display.

China's first known works of art were pottery vessels and carved jade discs, pendants and sceptres, dating from the Neolithic Period (c. 7000–1500 BC). The pots were made for everyday use and for ritual purposes. The jade pieces were used as ornaments in life as well as in death (it was customary for aristocrats to be buried with their most precious possessions of carved jade). Recovered from tombs, the earliest surviving jade pieces are usually white or yellow; fewer are grey-green. The most finely-carved pieces of early Neolithic jade have been found in the eastern coastal region of China , at excavations in Zhejiang Province. Pottery from the Neolithic Period has been found in many sites throughout China—even as far west as present-day autonomous region of Xinjiang, long considered outside the orbit of primitive Chinese culture.

The painted pottery of the peoples of the Yellow River plain is best known to foreign visitors because of the famous excavation at **Banpo**, just outside the city of Xi'an. Banpo is the site of a large riverside village which, from 4000 to 3000 BC, had its own kilns producing distinctive decorated pots. The low-temperature fired red clay pots of Banpo are found throughout the Yellow River region, and are collectively known as 'Yangshao ware'. It is relatively easy to identify Yangshao pottery in a museum, since it is low-fired, unglazed and has rich decorative designs in red, black and occasionally white. Motifs can be bold swirling patterns, faces, fish or bird designs. 'Yangshao ware' is often referred to as Painted Pottery.

In the area around the Shandong peninsula on China's eastern seaboard, a different kind of pottery was produced in Neolithic times. Known as Black Pottery or 'Longshan ware', the pots have a distinctive black surface which has been polished after firing. Black pottery was wheel-made and, unlike Painted Pottery, has no surface decoration. The potter put all of his skill into creating subtle and elaborate shapes. The ritual vessels are paper-thin and are turned in the most elaborate and impractical forms. Archaeologists believe that the shape of the vessels of the Black Pottery people had an important influence on that of the bronze vessels of the later Shang dynasty.

During the Shang dynasty (c. 1600–1027 BC), the crafting of ceramic wares was eclipsed by the newly-discovered science of bronze casting. Bronze was more durable than clay and had important military applications. However, the development of bronze was shaped by the potter's skills—the moulds for the cast bronzes were made from clay, and many of the early shapes of Shang bronzes were again derived directly from the refined shapes of 'Longshan ware'. This was particularly true of the high-footed, trumpet-mouthed wine goblets known as *gu*, and the bag-legged, tripod wine heaters (the legs billow out like bags full of water) called *li*. Both shapes were to die out as the bronze-cast art evolved away from the traditions of the early potters.

The working of bronze was also influenced by the skills of the jade carver. One of the best-known features of Shang bronze art is the *tao tie*, an animal motif consisting of a monster head, and this pattern is found as early as 3000 BC, carved on the jade discs of the eastern coastal people. However, the discovery of bronze did not lead to the dying out of jade carving. Because of its translucent hardness, jade continued to be highly prized.

The Shang bronzes are famous for their vigorous shapes and bold designs. They are more like sculptures than decorated vessels. In the *tao tie* examples, a pair of savage eyes stare out of strong, swirling lines. Some vessels were formed in the contours of an animal, others in the mask of a terrified human face. It is not surprising that archaeologists have speculated that some of these ritual vessels were used at human sacrifices. The vessels were also cast in a large variety of shapes, each corresponding to a specific purpose in worship. For example, the *ding*, a rounded cauldron supported by three or four legs, was used for sacrificial food; the *zun*, a tall vase, was employed for offerings of wine.

With the overthrow of the Shang dynasty and the triumph of the Zhou in 1027 BC, the function of bronze vessels changed. During the rule of the Shang kings, bronze vessels had a religious function and were important in rituals and sacrifices. Under the Zhou rulers, bronze vessels also became symbols of rank and wealth. Zhou-dynasty patrons commissioned bronzes of refined shapes with swirling geometric patterns, such as the elegant 'thunder spiral' pattern (*leiwen*). Monster and beast shapes disappeared.

There has been much debate on whether the art of bronze casting evolved spontaneously in China or was transmitted from the ancient cultures of the Near East. Chinese bronzes are unique in incorporating lead in the bronze alloy of copper and tin—a fact that argues for the independent evolution of bronze casting in China. The addition of lead to the alloy gives the bronze a grey sheen much prized by connoisseurs.

It is from the bronzes of the Shang and Zhou dynasties that the earliest developments of the Chinese language have been studied. Sometimes the Shang and Zhou bronzes were inscribed with the maker's name and perhaps a short description of the occasion on which the new vessel was presented. These inscriptions have provided scholars with valuable material for their researches on ancient script—the bronze vessels are as much historical records as works of art.

*A Qing soldier with tiger's head shield,*
*sketched by William Alexander in 1793, and hand-coloured at a later date*

CHINA — PLATE 24.

Published Jan.ʳ 1814, by J.Murray, Albemarle Street.

Unlike bronze objects, jade did not appear to be used in ancient times for strictly religious purposes. Shang and Zhou jade pieces symbolized power; the jade discs and sceptres were the Chinese equivalent of the European royal sceptre and orb. Yet the Chinese invested the stone with protective qualities which could be said to have a religious significance, and it served an emblematic purpose in burials. The jade disc—or *bi*—was buried with rulers in the belief that it would help ease the passage of the soul to the afterlife.

Most of what is preserved from China's early dynasties has been excavated from tombs. Rulers and nobles of ancient China believed that they would need treasures, servants and animals in the afterlife (a tradition which still persists in contemporary Chinese culture, with the burning of paper money, paper houses and possessions for the dead). During the Shang dynasty, rulers took their wives and servants to the grave with them. In the Zhou dynasty, figurines of people mainly replaced live examples for these rites. The result was that, by the fourth century BC, the use of tomb figurines was widespread enough for Confucius to declare that the person who initiated the idea of going to the grave with figurines did not deserve to have descendants. In the 1960s, communist textbooks interpreted the comment to mean that Confucius was recommending the older tradition of human sacrifices. But it is clear from the context—and from other chapters—that Confucius had no interest in the possibility of the afterlife and disliked the tradition of tomb figurines as a reminder of earlier practices.

In the third century BC, Qin Shi Huangdi, China's first emperor, was buried in a tomb guarded by a complete, larger-than-life model army placed in pits nearby. These warriors and horses, excavated just outside Xi'an, are China's most famous archaeological treasure. The Han-dynasty historian, Sima Qian, wrote that Qin Shi Huangdi was also buried with fabulous treasures and members of his household. However, the tomb of the emperor has not yet been excavated, and despite being looted in the early years of the Han dynasty, it is widely believed to contain several undisturbed chambers. Archaeologists have made only exploratory digs around the site of the tomb, but they are concerned about the preservation of the contents and the possibility of booby traps—described by Sima Qian as being set up all around the imperial burial chamber.

The Han dynasty, which succeeded the short-lived Qin dynasty in 206 BC, also left a legacy of tomb treasures. However, the Han emperors did not make such elaborate tomb preparations as did the megalomaniac Qin Shi Huangdi. No living household members are believed to have been placed in Han tombs. In the early period of the Han dynasty, known as the Western Han (206 BC–AD 8), many precious objects were buried in the tombs of rulers and nobles. By the time of the Eastern Han (AD 25–220), this practice was officially prohibited, and—with some exceptions—bronze vessels were replaced by glazed earthenware or lacquerware, and valuable possessions by representational clay sculptures.

Jade burial suits are perhaps the most spectacular objects from early Han tombs. Made of a material that was hard, enduring and thought to be endowed with protective qualities, the jade burial suit was believed to prevent decay. Bodies of high nobles were encased in jade suits and their orifices sealed with jade discs.

One of the finest examples comes from the second-century BC tomb of Princess Dou Wan in Hebei Province. Also from that tomb is one of the finest small pieces of early Han sculpture yet excavated: a gilt-bronze oil lamp in the shape of a kneeling maid-servant. Its purity of form and the individuality of facial expression make the work a rare treasure amongst tomb figurines.

Han-dynasty tomb figurines are of great interest in providing information about daily life at that time. Miniature farms, houses, city gates, animals and utensils as well as models of favourite servants were placed in tombs. The painted bricks of Han tombs also tell much of daily life. They can depict anything from court ladies at leisure, nobles out hunting with their bows and arrows, to kitchen workers preparing a feast. Fragments of woven silk and lacquerware have also been found in many Han tombs. By the Han dynasty, lacquerware had completely replaced bronze vessels as household items, and thus many of the excavated Han tombs have revealed a wealth of red-and-black patterned lacquer boxes and utensils. One of the best exhibitions of Han tomb artefacts is in the Hunan Provincial Museum at Changsha. The museum has the complete collection of the Mawangdui excavation of a first-century BC (Western Han) noblewoman's tomb.

It was during the Han dynasty that the first contacts were made with Central Asia which would lead to the opening of the trade route later known as the Silk Road. After the introduction of Buddhism to China in the first century AD, missionaries and pilgrims travelling along the Silk Road to and from India left a rich legacy of religious art in the stretch of land formed by the narrow Gansu corridor and the fringes of the Taklamakan desert in present-day Xinjiang. To express their devoutness, they created, over many centuries, stupendous and beautiful frescoes and statuaries to adorn cave-shrines. Although much of the art was subsequently destroyed or removed by foreign archaeologists, some frescoes and sculptures remain, the most stunning of which are the Mogao Caves in Dunhuang. Nineteenth- and early 20th-century explorers and archaeologists also came upon a rich cache of manuscripts and paintings there. Other artefacts, including silk embroidery, jade carvings and pottery, have also been found in and around the cities of the Silk Road.

If the later period of the Han dynasty can be remembered by one object, it is surely the Flying Horse unearthed in Gansu Province, now on display in Lanzhou's museum. The small bronze sculpture has a lightness and fluidity of form far removed from the monumental grandeur of the earlier Zhou and Shang bronzes. Its spirited beauty brings to life the values and interests of a society which, without such works of art, may seem remote and alien.

# The Chinese Economy
### —Paul Mooney and William Lindesay

It is 8.00 am and Guangzhou's Qingping Market is already bustling as shoppers jostle each other in the narrow streets and pick through produce piled high on wayside stalls. In Shanghai, consumers crowd a department store examining the latest stereo equipment, TVs and home appliances, as their children push forward for a look at hand-held video games from Hong Kong. In Beijing's Zhongguancun 'computer street', a recent graduate buys a PC and plans to hook up to the Internet. Meanwhile, 'Avon ladies', knocking on doors around the city, sell a month's allocation of cosmetics in just five days.

## THE IRON RICE BOWL
The first-time visitor to China may take these everyday scenes for granted. Yet all this would have been unthinkable just 20 years ago, when socialism ruled unchallenged. At that time, the sight of a Chinese housewife queueing at sunrise, before the local market opened, to buy the ingredients for her family's dinner, was all too familiar. If she was lucky, she might come away with a scraggy bit of pork and some tired-looking vegetables. Many others often trudged home empty-handed.

The shelves of department stores were usually bare, while shoppers were conspicuous by their absence unless a shipment of coveted goods was expected. Then, crowds of hopeful customers would pile into the store, trying to squeeze their way to the counter before the few television sets or electric fans were sold out.

This was the aftermath of Mao's death and the Cultural Revolution, when the economy was still a slave to the Stalinist principles of central planning, which provided only the barest essentials of life. China, once a great and wealthy empire, found herself among the world's poorest nations. The communists, who won power in 1949, had promised a better future; but the socialist redistribution of wealth failed to deliver a significant improvement in living conditions.

In the early 1950s, though, such grim repercussions did not cloud the vision of China's new leaders as they pressed forward with their national plan. They went ahead with the collectivization of agriculture in the winter of 1955–56, organizing peasant households into co-operatives and turning over to them what had been privately owned property, including the means of production.

This was followed in 1958 by the 'Great Leap Forward', a campaign to accelerate rural and industrial development. A grand vision conceived by Mao, it was a disaster. It involved a nationwide mobilization of the masses, leading to a fever pitch of work. But under pressure to achieve near-impossible output targets, farms and factories took to reporting inflated production figures. Much of what was produced was of low quality or useless anyway, particularly the home-made steel from backyard furnaces. By the time the experiment collapsed, huge amounts of labour and raw materials had

*A statute of Mao Zedong gazes down Renmin Lu in central Chengdu, capital of Sichuan Province.
From head to toe the statue measures 12.26 metres,
a figure which corresponds to the Chairman's birthday—December 26th*

been wasted. In the ensuing economic havoc and famine, millions of people are believed to have died. One legacy of the first ten years of socialism was the 'People's Commune'. A form of organization intended to bring about social change in the countryside, the commune embraced several thousand households, and took responsibility for all the activities associated with farming, as well as providing security, education, health care, and even permission to have a baby. A commune was subdivided into 'production brigades', a grouping of several hundred households, and below that were the 'teams', made up of between 20 and 30 families.

Industry and commerce also passed into state ownership, and welfare measures were introduced to protect the worker. Most urban residents were assigned to a *danwei* or unit, the place of employment or study, which took care of just about all their basic needs. A worker lived in housing provided by his unit, which also guaranteed a certain level of rations, medical care, pensions and sometimes even schooling. Once attached to a unit, a person usually stayed for life. The trouble was he also lost his freedom of choice of jobs. Still, dismissal was rare, and when the time came for retirement, the job might go to one of his children. It was a cradle-to-grave welfare system which the Chinese themselves call the 'iron rice bowl'.

## THE REFORM DECADE

As against these benefits, the existence of the iron rice bowl also crushed incentive. The command economy functioned poorly—the years of apathy, wasted resources, arbitrary pricing and stultifying bureaucracy all added up to inefficient production and low standards of living for peasants and urban residents alike. Within two years of Chairman Mao's death in 1976, capitalism began slowly to poke its head out again.

China is still a predominantly agrarian country, so the shift to a market approach in agriculture had a profound impact on people's lives. Under the responsibility system implemented in 1979, peasant families were allowed to contract land for private farming. Farmers were no longer required to turn all their produce over to the state, but instead had to fulfil a quota and could then sell any surplus in the newly opened free markets for their own profit. Increasingly, family farming is the norm even though the vast majority of peasants are still tied to collectives.

With these changes, China, which has 22 per cent of the world's population but only 7 per cent of its arable land, began to make impressive gains. The gross value of agricultural production almost doubled in the 1980s, and productivity and farm incomes shot up too. The food shortages of the past faded from memory as markets around the country began offering ample supplies of meat, vegetables and fruit. Peasants became the new rich, able to afford new houses and a wide variety of modern comforts. For the first time in the history of China, urban dwellers, who had little opportunity of supplementing their income, began to look on their country cousins with envy. The agricultural reforms paved the way for sustained growth of agricultural output, which generated a surplus of rural savings which was used to boost industrialisation. The introduction of the management responsibility system into state-owned enterprises, brought market elements into the socialist economy. Enterprises began to enjoy a greater say in their own management, resulting in a new degree of efficency and productivity.

While people were previously unwilling to give up their iron rice bowls, millions, realizing they would never get rich working for the state, set up their own small businesses, becoming a new force in the economy. While state firms cut employment by 159,000 between November 1993 and June 1994, private firms increased it by 2 million. These entrepreneurs—in the early 1950s Mao labeled them 'capitalist tails that had to be cut off'—are now among the wealthiest people in China.

A provincial newspaper reported in June 1991 that official audits and secret checks had discovered 490 entrepreneurs who had put away more than a million yuan each, an amount that would take the average Chinese factory worker some 800 years to earn. These millionaires had clearly taken to heart one of Deng Xiaoping's utterances—that it was acceptable 'to make some people rich first, so as to lead all the people to wealth'.

Deng recognized that economic reforms could not be carried out in isolation—for China to catch up with the modern industrialized world she would need Western capital and technology. The 'open door' policy, launched in 1979, was designed to attract foreign investment and joint-venture projects. And the Special Economic Zones established along the southern coast were intended to be the focus for such investment.

The reform decade of the 1980s saw the economy expand at an average annual rate of about ten per cent, bringing improved living standards and a doubling of consumption. In China's large cities, some 80 per cent of households now own a colour television set and many also have video recorders. By 1990, foreign trade had more than tripled, and China had become the world's 13th largest exporter and a major participant in the international arena.

## CHAOS IN THE MARKETPLACE

The close of the decade, however, saw serious problems emerging. Rapid industrial growth had exacerbated shortages of energy and raw materials, and severely overstretched an outdated infrastructure, particularly the transportation network. The existing railroad and highway systems simply could not keep pace with demand, and telephone services remained among the worst in the world. The shortfall in energy production was forcing many factories to halt work one or two days a week.

There was a panic buying spree in the summer of 1988. For the first time in decades, prices got out of control and inflation reached 30 per cent. An austerity programme was imposed in 1988 to cool down the overheated economy. Bonuses, which by then accounted for as much as half of a worker's wage, were temporarily cut in most factories. Reforms were put on hold and in some cases even reversed. But some problems could not be solved by squeezing money out of the economy. The recession highlighted several areas of discontent. There appeared to be a diminishing number of jobs for young people and prospects were discouraging. In fact unemployment is likely to rise as industries become more capital intensive and arable land shrinks. It has been suggested that China may have almost as many peasants unemployed by the end of the century as the whole of the population of the United States at present.

Consumer demand remained unabated, despite propaganda urging restraint. To the horror of elderly communists, certain wasteful pre-revolutionary customs had been revived. Young urbanites were holding lavish weddings complete with rented Western wedding gowns, while at elaborate funerals, bereaved relatives were choosing burials that used up valuable land instead of opting for cremation as promoted by the state. In the shops, consumers had become more selective—those who considered radios, bicycles and watches luxury items a decade ago now had their eyes set on colour TVs, refrigerators, video recorders and home furnishings.

Corruption worsened. Even top communist officials or cadres began to 'xiahai', or jump into the sea of commerce. Some used their influence to set up relatives and friends in profitable private enterprises. The children of powerful cardres—dubbed princelings—are prominent on the boards of various local and foreign companies. Other officials, exploiting privileged access to scarce commodities, snapped them up at low state prices before reselling them on the free market at a premium. A number of officials even took low-interest loans for their own profit.

## Deng 'Retires', Jiang Rises

The growing public revulsion against corruption in high places and a keener aware-ness of the outside world through the 'open door' added to the pressures that were already building up for a faster pace of reform and greater freedoms. A crescendo of protests and demonstrations rose with students and workers converging and occupy-ing Beijing's Tiananmen Square in the spring of 1989. The government crackdown which followed unleashed universal condemnation, and the economy took a battering when sanctions and a freeze on much-needed foreign loans were imposed.

Despite the problems, China continued to plow ahead with its reforms. In the early 1990s, under its trial-and-error policy of 'crossing the river by feeling for the stones', stockmarkets were opened in Shanghai and Shenzhen, and futures trading markets sprang up around the country. A problem arose, however, when conservatives seized on the chaos of the 1989 demonstrations and stepped up their opposition to Deng's reforms. Despite having resigned from his last official office in 1989, Deng returned to the fore in early 1992, when he made his quasi-imperial southern journey to rally the support of local leaders. Deng was quoted at the time as saying 'there is no need to be afraid of capitalism... anyone who does not carry out reforms should be forced to step down, no matter who they are', the then 88-year old party patriarch warned.

The much heralded appeal worked as local officials took heart from Deng's exhor-tations to pick up the pace of reform. Hunan province, the birthplace of Mao and a hotbed of conservatism, is a good example. Heaven is high and the emperor is far away, goes a popular Chinese saying. But when the closest thing China had to an emperor made a 15-minute whistle stop at Changsha railway station to make a pitch for speedier economic reform, his message was heard loud and clear.

Hunan officials waited on the platform politely as Deng's train pulled out of the station. But as soon as the tiny figure disappeared waving in the distance, they raced back to their offices to rethink their economic plans. By the end of the year, Hunan's GDP had more than doubled, foreign trade jumped almost 50 per cent and foreign investors, once shunted off to a provincial backwater just a few years earlier, were being warmly welcomed to the province by the hundreds. The Hunan experience was repeated all over China.

The Chinese also moved faster with specific steps to promote economic liberalization. Price controls were liberalized. Dozens of inland cities were opened to the outside world and incentives were sweetened for foreign investment. With record amounts of foreign capital pouring into the country, coupled with a sharp rise in investments by local governments and enterprises, the economy began to overheat.

In the summer of 1993, economic czar Zhu Rongji launched a series of austerity measures aimed at reining in runaway economic growth, with limited effect. Despite vowing to tighten credit, the government, worried about killing off state enterprise and unable to pay wages and debts, continued to pour money into this sector.

How to deal with inefficient state enterprises remains a major problem for China's economic planners. State-run factories, which account for the bulk of manufacturing enterprises, continue to be unresponsive to the more sophisticated Chinese consumer; many still turn out shoddy, outdated products which end up unsold, having to be consigned to already large stockpiles of unwanted goods in warehouses.

If no political ideologies were involved, the appalling performance of the state industries would be ample argument in favour of privatization. Official reports say that as many as half are running at a loss and are only kept afloat by government subsidies, which run into tens of billions of yuan each year, accounting for 50 per cent of China's budget deficit. Yet they contribute about 50 per cent of industrial output and provide jobs for some 70 per cent of the nation's labour force. Worried about massive unemployment and the threat of social instability, until 1997 the government has been reluctant to bite the bullet and carry out effective enterprise reform.

'We would rather die in dignity than be taken over by a capitalist,' said the managing cadres of the Chongqing No. 6 Radio Factory to the owner of the Restar Group, the most successful electronics operation in the city, who had made an offer to take over the giant state enterprise. The rhetorical news, reminicent of the Mao era, came as a shock to the city's mayor, Pu Haiqing, who visited the factory himself in February 1997 to speak to its workers. He was surrounded by angry mobs who hadn't seen a wage packet for more than a year. 'We never said that!' they heckled, 'the leading cadres fabricated those quotes.' The workers said that they didn't mind who paid them, just so long as they got paid.

# Free to Choose

One day the new head of our factory showed me a machine costing several hundred thousand dollars that had been imported from West Germany years before and left to rust because no one could get it to work. He asked me if I could fix it. I told the truth when I answered that I didn't know. I had never seen anything like it, and to complicate matters, neither blueprints nor a manual could be found. 'Try,' he said. 'If you can get it working, I'll give you a sixty-yuan bonus.' My family needed the money badly; I was thrilled at the offer and eager to get started.

I ordered the machine moved to a large empty room. Then I surrounded it with barbed wire and a locked gate to prevent the curious from disturbing the expensive device. I alone was allowed within.

I soon discovered that whoever had ordered the thing had had no idea what he was doing; it was supposed to consist of two different components, and he had ordered two of one and none of the other. When I informed the boss, he was crestfallen. All the foreign exchange had been spent, and the factory could not possibly afford to import such expensive machinery for the foreseeable future. By now intrigued with the technology, I offered to try somehow to reproduce the missing half.

Painstakingly I drew blueprints of the component we had and then tried to imagine what the other must look like. Working every night until I could not keep my eyes open one second more, I became increasingly confident that my design was correct; it was time to put it to the test.

The construction took a whole year. I could concentrate on nothing else. I even dreamed of that machine. After a while I no longer had to refer to my drawings, for the placement of each nut and bolt had become more familiar to me than the placement of my own ears. By the time the missing half was completed and attached, there was absolutely no doubt in my mind that the contrivance would work. I was right.

After it had been functioning flawlessly for a week, I went to see my boss about the sixty yuan, but before I could remind him of his promise, he informed me that the two specialists from Shanghai he had engaged would arrive soon to fix the machine. Specialists? Fix it? There was nothing wrong with it. What was he up to? I immediately ran out of his office to destroy the blueprints. They were my creation, mine alone. The factory paid my salary and now had a sophisticated working machine, but no one had the right to my ideas. Who had sent me to school to learn about engineering? Who had given me books to study? Who had awarded me a trip to Germany to gain experience at German factories? Who had assisted me all those months? Not a damn soul!

When the specialists showed up, followed by a curious crowd of my co-workers, I was ready for them. The older of the two asked what the problem was. I switched the machine on at top speed and invited them to tell me. They looked puzzled, and then the younger one said there didn't seem to be anything wrong. The older one motioned for the younger to follow him below, into the servicing area, where they remained. Meanwhile the crowd looked on, humming with anticipation. I stared at my watch. Exactly twenty-two minutes later the two men climbed out. They had not touched a nut or a bolt.

The boss arrived and requested their report. The older one asked what qualified him to judge my work. The boss was speechless. Both specialists shook my hand with genuine admiration. They told me that between them they had fifty years of experience but would consider it a great honor to be my apprentice.

Still the boss refused to pay me the sixty yuan. I announced my resignation. 'No one ever quit before,' he shouted angrily. I replied, 'Good, I will be the first!'

When I walked out of that factory for the last time, I felt that at long last I had earned the right to hold my head high. It didn't matter that I had no real savings, that my family counted on my salary every month to survive, that others would never understand why I had left a job I enjoyed when they hated theirs and had had worse run-ins with their bosses. From then on I never again doubted that I was good at what I did, and I was confident that someone, somewhere, would always pay me for my services.

*Bette Bao Lord*, Legacies

(following pages) Built in the 1960s, the Yangtze River Bridge at Nanjing has a span of more than one and a half kilometres and is the longest double-deck road and rail bridge in China, and the only bridge to cross the river for hundreds of kilometres

This Chongqing incident shows that politics are still in command in the minds of many provincial officials, and it highlights contradictions which the government's ideologists are having to confront. The conservative 'old guard' point out that privatization of industry is a fundamental contradiction in a communist country: the individual is forbidden to exploit the masses. Interpreted in its strictest form, anyone who employs others to make personal profits, for example an entrepreneur, is exploiting the masses. But what is perfectly clear, not only to city mayors, but also in Beijing, is that the party must deliver the economic goods to remain in power.

Jiang Zemin knows that the biggest threat to the country's stability comes from unpaid workers in state enterprises. Hence many economists are urging the government to press on with *zhuada fangxiao*, which translates as 'seizing the large and freeing the small'. It is a policy which offers a lifeline to ailing, key state concerns, while giving the private sector considerable room for expansion.

Basically, the *zhuada* head of the policy allows the government to select 1,000 key state enterprises running in the red, and bail them out, while imposing fairly radical management reform upon them. That is the key. After all, who could ever have imagined that at the outset of Deng's reforms back in the late 1970s, minnow private companies—with no fixed assets nor privileges—would, in whatever sector they were allowed to operate, eventually outperform the state's goliaths. And the only difference is ownership. A private boss really cares and manges his factory well. In a state enterprise, everything is publically owned, and that in turn means that nobody cares about it.

Meanwhile, the *fangxiao* tail of the plan allows hosts of ailing enterprises to sink or swim—they will receive no state assistance. But with the freedom that comes with, *fangxiao* is actually an opportunity in a country with so much free capital and labour. Thousands of successful entrepreneurs are ready and willing to take over loss-making factories and capitalize on manpower with their available funds.

The criterium which will decide which enterprises are seized, and which are freed is strategic: the state will keep defence and infrastructural industries in its pocket— basically heavy and high-tech sectors including military, vehicles, transport, and telecommunications—while letting the light-industrial and consumer-goods-producing factories be taken over and flourish in private hands.

The willingness of the new leadership, with Jiang Zemin at its core, to press ahead with enterprise reform indicates the importance attached to adhering to the late paramount leader's greatest legacy: pragmatism, or in simple terms, to use Deng's oftquoted adage, not being concerned whether the cat is black or white, as long as it catches mice. With the 'old guard' on the wane, China's path is no longer a forked option between the policies of hardliners and reformers, but one between moderate reformers and more radical ones. Hence previous doubts about the momentum of reforms are now obsolete, with the main question being 'when?'—and the answer to that can only be sooner, or later.

# Cultural Capitals

## Xi'an

It is said of the famous English translator of Chinese literature, Arthur Waley, that he never wished to visit modern China, so as to keep intact his vision of ancient China—a vision he had built up carefully through his knowledge of classical texts.
It is also said that, in his mind's eye, he could take a walk through the Tang-dynasty capital of Chang'an—the city known today as Xi'an—and be familiar with all the city districts, their businesses and specialities. In modern Xi'an, the provincial capital of Shaanxi Province, it takes a major feat of the imagination to believe that this dusty, unassuming city was the site of 11 Chinese dynastic capitals, spanning over a thousand years. But in fact the loess plains around Xi'an and the River Wei, which flows close to Xi'an and empties into the Yellow River, lie at the heart of Chinese civilization and are a continual source of new archaeological discoveries, the most famous of these being the extraordinary terracotta army of the first emperor of China. It is these discoveries which have made—and will continue to make— Xi'an one of the most popular destinations for Western visitors to China today. (Some overseas Chinese, on the other hand, steer clear of Xi'an because they are superstitious about graves belonging to other people's ancestors.)

### Archaeological and Imperial Sites

A site near present-day Xi'an was the early capital of the Zhou Dynasty (1027–221 BC), the great period of bronze culture. However, archaeologists have unearthed even earlier settlements dating back to Neolithic times, as well as the bones of an early *homo erectus*, said to have originated about 800,000 BC at sites near the modern city. Enthusiasts of early archaeology can visit an excavated Neolithic village at **Banpo**, 11 kilometres (seven miles) to the east of the city, which is remarkable for its Painted Pottery (*see* page 63). More recent archaeological digs have uncovered Zhou sites, the most exciting being that of a Western Zhou (1027–771 BC) burial chamber at **Zhangjiapo**, south of Xi'an. The chamber yielded two bronze chariots and the remains of six horses, which can now be seen at a small museum west of the city at the village of Doumen.

Many Zhou artifacts are in the **Shaanxi History Museum** in Xi'an itself, which should be visited for its fine archaeological exhibits, ranging from Zhou bronzes to Tang coloured porcelain. Formerly located in a temple, the museum was moved in 1991 into a palatial Tang-style building near the Big Goose Pagoda. The famous 'Forest of Steles', which formed part of the museum's collection, remains at the old site, which has been renamed **Beilin Museum**. Steles are inscribed stone tablets; some of the ones in this collection date back to the Tang dynasty, providing a wealth of historical detail for the non-specialist visitor as well as the scholar. The Forest of Steles can easily be enjoyed with a well-informed guide and by taking a careful look at the carved illustrations on the steles—the maps and portraits, for example. A rubbing made directly from one of the steles can be expensive. However, the museum shop also sells rubbings made from copies of the steles, which are cheaper.

The feudal ruler of the state of Qin, who in 221 BC conquered his rival kings and unified China, is known as Qin Shi Huangdi, the first emperor of the Qin dynasty. During his reign, he undertook military campaigns to the far corners of the known world, a vast public works programme involving forced labour, the persecution of Confucian scholars, and the burning of books. Jia Yi, a Han-dynasty statesman born in 201 BC, five years after the fall of the Qin dynasty, wrote a famous discourse on the reasons for the rapid overthrow of the Qin. In it he concluded that the mighty Qin fell 'because it failed to rule with humanity and righteousness, and to realize that the power to attack and the power to retain what one has thereby, are not the same'—a very Confucian judgement on Qin despotism. The estimated 8,000 terracotta soldiers and the horses and chariots which lay buried for 2,200 years, guarding the tomb of the first emperor, are a testament to his power and megalomania.

The **Terracotta Army** was discovered in 1974 by peasants digging a well during a drought. The excavation site is in Lintong County, a few miles distant from the actual burial mound of the emperor. Visitors can climb the mound, but the burial chambers have not yet been excavated for fear of damage to the delicate treasures which are thought to lie within. History tells of the tomb being sealed with traps of poisoned arrows to deter violation. However, it is known that the tomb was looted during the Han dynasty, and one wonders how much is left inside. Archaeological work is taking place at the surrounding burial mounds.

Excavation has continued sporadically since the discovery of the Terracotta Army. All three pits are now open. Pit number one, larger than a football pitch, contains over 1,000 warriors beneath its hangar. Pit number three, though small, is thought to be the garrison headquarters of the Qin army. Excavations can be seen proceeding in Pit number two, another large site, which opened in October 1994. The soldiers are either standing or kneeling. A selection of the figures are displayed in glass cases, and you can see that each warrior is larger than lifesize and has different facial features, and that hairstyles and details of uniform vary according to rank. The figures were originally painted but the colours have leached away. Wooden implements have also rotted, but the original metal weapons have survived. The arrow heads do indeed have poisoned lead tips. Chariots of bronze with figures cast in bronze have also been unearthed in the vicinity.

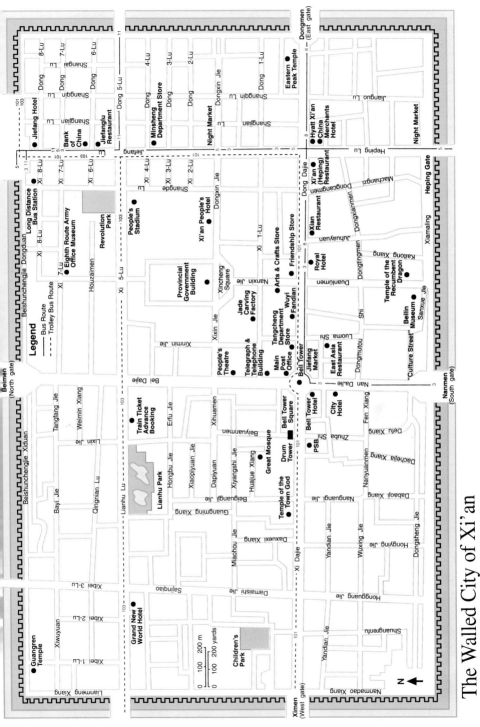

The Walled City of Xi'an

For those interested in other Qin excavations, a trip to **Xianyang** northeast of Xi'an is recommended, to see the site of the original Qin capital. Unearthed building materials of the Qin period, as well as a model of the first emperor's palace, are on display in the museum attached to the excavations. The Xianyang Museum, housed in a former Confucian temple, also has an impressive set of several thousand doll-sized painted terracotta figurines of soldiers and horses, dating from the Han dynasty.

The Qin dynasty lasted 12 years. At its demise, rival armies contended for control of the country, with Liu Bang emerging as the victor. He styled himself Gaozu (High Ancestor) and named his dynasty Han. The name of Han is now synonymous with China itself, Chinese people calling themselves *Han ren* (the Han people). During the first part of the Han reign, known as the Western Han (206 BC–AD 8), the capital was near modern Xi'an and known as Chang'an.

The best collection of Han artefacts is in the Shaanxi History Museum. However, there are also exhibits displayed in a museum at one of the Han tombs in the countryside. This is the **tomb of Huo Qubing**, a young general who served under Han Emperor Wudi (reigned 140–186 BC). It lies to the northwest of Xi'an, close to **Maoling**, the tomb of Emperor Wudi, and was built on the orders of the emperor himself, as a mark of imperial favour. Huo Qubing was killed at the age of 24 in one of the campaigns against the nomadic Xiongnu (Huns) from the northern steppes. To find allies against these nomads, who posed a constant threat to the security of China's northern frontier, Wudi sent his envoy, Zhang Qian, to Central Asia—and it was as a result of those expeditions that the route to the west was opened up, even-tually leading to the establishment of the Silk Road. The general's tomb has wonderful stone sculptures of horses, a tiger, a boar, an elephant and an ox, as well as two strange human figures which could be depictions of Central Asian gods or demons.

A small museum on site contains bronze articles, including money, agricultural implements and examples of the decorated building materials for which both the Qin and Han were famous.

To the northwest of Xi'an is the site, as yet unexcavated, of the most famous of the **Tang tombs**: that of the first Tang emperor, Taizong (reigned 627–649). However, some satellite tombs have been worked on, and the site—known in Chinese as **Zhaoling**—has a small museum, with a fine collection of funerary artifacts. The six stone horses, which once stood at the entrance to the imperial tomb, are no longer at the site. Four are at the Shaanxi History Museum, and the other two are in the Museum of the University of Philadelphia.

The other main burial site of the Tang imperial family is to the west of the city, and known as **Qianling**. It is the resting place of the famous Empress Wu Zetian

(624–705), the only woman sovereign in Chinese history. She was a concubine of Emperor Taizong and, on his death, flouted convention by marrying his son. Eventually she deposed her own son and usurped the throne. The main tomb of the empress and that of Emperor Gaozong have never been excavated, but of great interest is the excavated tomb of the Princess Yongtai, granddaughter of the Empress Wu, who is said to have been murdered on her grandmother's orders.

The tomb contains reproductions of murals showing Tang women in costumes heavily influenced by Central Asian dress. The composition of the murals is light and graceful, with draperies drawn in flowing lines and with figures depicted both in full face and in three-quarter profile. Also in the tomb are paintings of soldiers, grooms with horses, the Tiger of the West and the Dragon of the East. The tomb of the princess's brother, Prince Yide, also a victim of his grandmother's political ambition, is open and has fine paintings showing court attendants and a hunting scene. The nearby tomb of the Crown Prince Zhanghuai, forced to commit suicide by his mother, the Empress Wu, has a fine mural depicting a polo match. These tombs all show the influence of Central Asia at the court, at a time when trade along the Silk Road was flourishing under the protection of Chinese military outposts.

Close to the excavation of the first emperor's Terracotta Army are the **Huaqing Hotsprings**, originally a Tang-dynasty pleasure resort and now still used for bathing. The present buildings are late Qing, and the resort is set against an attractive mountain which is home to several Buddhist and Taoist temples. The resort became famous in recent times as the place where Generalissimo Chiang Kai-shek was captured in his pyjamas by a rebellious young general intent on forcing Chiang into an alliance with the communists against the Japanese. This episode, known as the Xi'an Incident, occurred in 1936 and ended with Chiang's eventual release, his reneging on the promised truce with the communists, and the execution of the young general as a traitor.

Huaqing is also associated with Yang Guifei, the seductive concubine of Emperor Xuanzong (reigned 712–756), who spent several winters here and so enthralled the emperor that he withdrew from his duties at court and nearly lost his throne to rebels. A new museum has been opened to display original Tang bathtubs, including a lovely petal-shaped one used by Yang Guifei.

Although the sights mentioned above are located outside Xi'an proper, they are easily accessible. CITS and most of the major hotels offer daily tours, either to the east or west of the city. An excursion to the east normally includes the Terracotta Army, Banpo and the Huaqing Hotsprings, while a tour to the west takes you to the tombs of the Han and Tang dynasties.

## BUDDHIST TEMPLES

In the Tang dynasty, Chang'an was not only a city of vast wealth but also a major religious centre, with Buddhist pilgrims from Central Asia and India arriving to teach and live in the capital. During this period, the monk Xuanzang went to India to bring back the Buddhist scriptures for translation. Scholars from Japan and Korea also came to Chang'an to study Buddhism, and much of the temple architecture that survives in Japan today was directly inspired by the buildings of the Tang era.

Sadly, little remains of Tang-dynasty architecture in modern Xi'an, or elsewhere in China, because of a major religious persecution undertaken by the Tang emperor, Wuzong, in the mid-eighth century. However, many fine Buddhist sites do remain, the most famous of which are the **Big Goose Pagoda** and the **Little Goose Pagoda** in the city centre, both of which formed part of large religious establishments which now no longer exist. The seven-storey Big Goose Pagoda was built in 652 at the request of the pilgrim monk, Xuanzang. It is adjacent to the **Da Ci'en Temple**, of which only a portion remains after the destructions during Wuzong's reign. The Little Goose Pagoda, built in 707, originally had 15 storeys, but the top two storeys collapsed in an earthquake in 1556. Both pagodas are fine examples of Tang masonry, displaying bold, simple lines on a square plan. You can climb to the top of both pagodas through the interior staircases, with the Little Goose Pagoda offering a particularly fine view over the city to the north.

Beyond Xi'an, in the surrounding countryside, are the remains of many Tang temples which have been rebuilt in later dynasties. Although they have been in a poor state of repair for many years, many of them are being restored, some with the help of funds from Japanese Buddhist foundations. The **Xingjiao Temple**, 22 kilometres (14 miles) southeast of Xi'an, is still a religious centre and has three pagodas, a white jade Buddha and several Ming-dynasty Buddhas.

The **Daxingshan Temple** is a 1950s reconstruction of a famous Sui and Tang temple. It lies in Xinfeng Park, south of Little Goose Pagoda.

Set in pretty countryside, the **Xiangji Temple** is 19 kilometres (12 miles) to the south of Xi'an. It has kept its fine eighth-century, 11-storey pagoda, and is the home of the Pure Land Sect of Buddhism—a sect which has a large following in modern Japan, but in China is nothing more than a part of religious history. Japanese donations have allowed for extensive restoration work. The shop on site sells rubbings including a superb one taken from a Tang carved illustration of the temple.

If time allows, there are other temples to be explored around Xi'an, with the help of a guide, a map and a hired taxi. The **Huayan Temple** is 19 kilometres (12 miles) to the south of Xi'an; **Caotang Temple** is further, some 56 kilometres (35 miles) to the southwest.

*Terracotta warrior, Xi'an*

## CITY SIGHTS

The city of Xi'an as it is laid out today dates from the Ming dynasty, and is much smaller in size than it was in Tang times. You can get an idea of its scale during the Ming by strolling along the ramparts of the **city walls**, which have been renovated in recent years; the best approach is at the East Gate (Dongmen). Other Ming sites worth visiting are all easily accessible and within close walking distance of each other: the Bell Tower, the Drum Tower and the Great Mosque. The **Bell Tower** and Drum Tower now face each other across a newly-built square. The bell in question was used to signal the dawn when the city gates opened, and the drum the dusk when they closed. Both towers are open daily. The **Drum Tower** overlooks the main Muslim quarter of the city. Around the corner from the Drum Tower is the **Great Mosque**, a fine place for a quiet walk, with its cool fountain and pretty Ming pavilion—the Chinese counterpart to the Arab minaret. The mosque is a repository of many Chinese Islamic artefacts and possesses a Qing-dynasty map of the Islamic world. The large prayer hall, which contains a name board given by the Ming emperor, Yongle, is always busy with visitors and worshippers.

There are scores of tourist and handicraft stalls clustering in the area between the Drum Tower and the mosque. Many visitors find it difficult to resist buying a piece or two of local embroidery brought to the city by the peasants from the surrounding countryside. For children, there are wonderful tiger padded shoes, pillows and hats, padded trousers with knee patches of embroidered frogs, and pinafores embroidered with scorpions and spiders to keep evil away from the wearer. If you are offered 'antiques', *caveat emptor*!

# Luoyang

The ancient city of Luoyang, which lies just to the north of the Yellow River in Henan Province, has a distinguished history as a dynastic capital second only to Xi'an. The Zhou dynasty established its capital on the present site of Luoyang in 1027 BC, and over the next 2,000 years the city served as the capital of nine dynasties.

Luoyang is best known for the Buddhist carvings of the **Longmen Caves**, which lie just to the south of the city. Work began on the caves in the fifth century, when the Northern Wei established their capital at Luoyang, and continued until the ninth century, when persecution of the Buddhist faith led to the closure of monasteries and the end of the patronage of Buddhist arts. However, the area around Luoyang is also famous for its rich heritage of archaeological treasures. Major art works, from

Neolithic times until China's early dynasties, have been unearthed in the region and put on display in the **Luoyang Museum**.

The modern landscape of Luoyang is heavily marked by industrialization, but the city's gardens are renowned for their peonies, grown in the region since peony cultivation began under imperial patronage in the Sui and Tang dynasties. Every year, a Peony Festival is held from 15 to 25 April. The best place to view the peonies is in the city's **Huangcheng Park**. The park is also notable for its lantern festival, held at the New Year (lantern-making is a traditional craft in Luoyang), as well as the two Han tombs which have been excavated beneath the park gardens. The tombs are open to the public and have fine wall paintings.

Visitors used to be taken to the **East is Red Tractor Factory** in Luoyang: the bright red tractors were an important symbol of China's reconstruction in the 1960s and the factory, with its model facilities for workers, was then considered a show-piece. In the present climate of economic reform, it is no longer an inevitable part of tour itineraries.

## OUTINGS FROM LUOYANG

Thirteen kilometres (eight miles) to the south of Luoyang, on the banks of the River Yi, lie the **Longmen Caves**. The craftsmen actually used the cliffs of the River Yi to create their monumental cave sculptures. There are in all 1,352 caves, over 40 pagodas, and some 97,000 statues.

Carving of the caves began in the Northern Wei dynasty, when the Emperor Xiaowen moved his capital to Luoyang in 494. The Wei emperors were devout Buddhists, and they manifested their piety by commissioning the creation of these large-scale shrines. The caves are scattered in various locations, but there are six which are the most frequently visited: the **Binyang**, **Lianhua** and **Guyang** caves of the Northern Wei dynasty, and the three Tang-dynasty caves of **Qianxi**, **Fengxian** and the **Ten Thousand Buddhas**.

Many of these caves have been badly damaged by earthquakes, water erosion and looters (both Chinese and foreign), but most of what remains is still impressive. The sculptures from the Northern Wei dynasty are highly textured and dynamic in form. They include beautiful flying *apsaras* (Buddhist angels) who float through flower- and cloud-filled skies, trailing fluttering ribbons. In the Sui-dynasty carvings, there is a more static feel to the sculptures, whose huge faces and foreshortened limbs create a deliberately imposing effect. In contrast, the Tang sculptures (particularly those in the Fengxian cave) have great freedom of form and a liveliness of expression. The sculptures seem to be independent of the rock face from which they are carved, and the torsos twist and move in dance-like postures.

Just over ten kilometres (six miles) to the east of Luoyang lies the **White Horse Temple**. This is considered to be one of the earliest Buddhist foundations in China, dating from the first century (Eastern Han dynasty), when the capital was at Luoyang. The surviving temple structures all date from the Ming dynasty, but many of the buildings have the original Han bricks. The temple is a centre for Chan—better known by its Japanese name, Zen— learning.

A half-day drive southeast from the Longmen Caves, in Dengfeng County, the **Songyue Temple Pagoda** looms on Mount Song. As the earliest surviving brick pagoda in China, it has obvious value as an architectural rarity. It was built around 520, in Indian style, and rises 40 metres (130 feet) in 12 storeys. It was once part of a thriving monastery founded in the Northern Wei dynasty.

Also in Dengfeng County is the **Shaolin Temple**, a place known to all *kungfu* enthusiasts. Set up at the end of the fifth century, Shaolin was the earliest Chan Buddhist temple in China. The style of martial art associated with it was developed by a band of 13 monks at the end of the Sui dynasty. Since 1988 there has been a martial arts training centre attached to the temple.

Eighty kilometres (50 miles) southeast of Luoyang lies the **Gaocheng Observatory**. Built in the Yuan dynasty, it is one of a series established throughout China. An imposing brick structure, it looks like a pyramid with its top chopped off. The Yuan-dynasty imperial astronomer, Guo Shoujing, worked here and in 1280 calculated the length of the year to be 365.2425 days—some 300 years before the same calculation was made in the West.

# Kaifeng

Kaifeng was the capital of the Northern Song dynasty (960–1127). Like Xi'an under the Tang emperors, it was the centre of power and learning in a glorious period of Chinese civilization. The city had previously served as the capital of several dynasties before the Song, but today, sadly, little of that imperial heritage has survived. The city has suffered from a number of disasters, one of which was a sacking in 1127 when the Jin Tartars moved into north China from Manchuria, causing the Song court to flee southwards; another was the deliberate flooding of the city in 1644 by Ming loyalists, desperate to push back the Manchu troops threatening the city. Kaifeng also suffered from periodic floods when the Yellow River—ten kilometres (six miles) to the north—overflowed its banks, so it is perhaps not surprising that the city has never developed into a major metropolis in recent centuries.

*Harvesting beans at the Three Pagoda Temple, Dali*

The original city walls still remain, however, revealing that the Song city was laid out in three concentric circles. The city architects of the later Ming dynasty built their cities on a rectangular plan.

Visitors to Kaifeng must include a stop at the Youguo Temple Pagoda, also known as the **Iron Pagoda**, which can be found in the northeastern part of the city. The exterior of the pagoda is inlaid with iron-coloured glazed bricks. Its eaves, pillars, and lintels are made from bricks glazed to resemble wood. The bricks have been carved in a very naturalistic style, with motifs of Buddhist immortals, musicians, flowers, plants and animals. Built in 1044 on the site of an earlier wooden pagoda which had been struck by lightning, the pagoda has an elegant octagonal shape and rises in 13 storeys. Its base was badly damaged in a flood in 1841, but its fabric has survived very well. Close to the pagoda stands a small pavilion which shelters a Song-dynasty bronze statue of a minor deity. It is considered to be one of the finest surviving masterpieces of Song bronze casting.

The **Xiangguo Monastery**, close to the city centre, was founded in the sixth century but came into its own as a major centre of Buddhist learning only in the Northern Song Dynasty. It was completely destroyed in the flooding of the city in 1644, and the present buildings date from the Qing dynasty. One of the temple halls is octagonal, with a small six-sided pavilion rising from the centre of the roof—a curiosity, since temple halls are usually rectangular.

Within the old city walls, **Yuwangtai**—sometimes known as the Old Music Terrace—can also be visited. It is set in landscaped gardens and is named after the legendary Emperor Yu, who tamed a great flood in prehistorical times—an appropriate tribute from a city bedevilled by floodwaters. (The bed of the Yellow River is several metres higher than the ground on which the city is built.) More recently, the temple was popular with poets of the Tang dynasty who came here to compose and carouse.

In an attempt to recreate its heyday as the Song capital, the city now boasts a Song-dynasty street, lined with buildings in the appropriate style. Kaifeng was the capital of the Northern Song for 167 years.

Northwest of the city, but close to the old walls, is the **Dragon Pavilion**. Set on a series of rising terraces overlooking lakes and gardens, it stands on the site of a Song-dynasty imperial palace and park. Like much of Kaifeng, the site was flooded in 1644, and all earlier buildings were lost. Prior to its redevelopment in the Qing dynasty, the site was known simply as Coal Hill. Its present name, Dragon Pavilion, is believed to be derived from the magnificent cube of carved stone which stands inside the pavilion. The four sides of the stone are carved with curling dragons.

# Nanjing

In its present form, Nanjing (Nanking) is a Ming-dynasty creation. It was the capital of the first Ming ruler, Emperor Hongwu (reigned 1368–98), who called the city Yingtianfu. He commissioned a magnificent palace as well as massive city walls, intersected by 13 gates, to enclose his 130-square-kilometre (50-square mile) city. In 1421, however, his son, Emperor Yongle (1402–24), moved the capital north to Beijing, for which he was to implement a design that would eclipse Yingtianfu in grandeur. Nanjing was then given its present name—the Southern Capital.

Unfortunately it has suffered more damage from war and rebellion than Beijing. Even though it is still the proud possessor of Drum and Bell towers, it has lost sections of the original walls and some of the gates. The Ming palace was destroyed in the 19th century. Nanjing no longer has the air of a proud imperial city, but rather the peaceful atmosphere of a provincial capital overseeing its fertile and wealthy hinterland. Jiangsu Province, of which Nanjing is the capital, is one of China's most prosperous regions and famous for its silk industry.

The location of the city is strikingly attractive, swept on its northern flank by the Yangzi River and surrounded by mountains. The river and mountains have made the city of strategic importance throughout history. It has been the capital of eight dynasties, and the setting of many bloody battles. The Rape of Nanking must be the worst example of these bloodbaths in recent times. In 1937 the Japanese occupied the city in the wake of the fleeing Kuomintang (Nationalist) army, which had made the city its temporary capital after the Japanese conquest of northern China. The occupation was followed by the brutal massacre of an estimated 340,000 people, both soldiers and civilians.

In the 19th century, Nanjing had already experienced tumult, for it served as the centre of a rebel regime which came very close to toppling the ruling Qing dynasty. The rebellion was led by a young scholar named Hong Xiuquan who believed himself to be the younger brother of Jesus Christ. Soon, the revolt—which had originated in the coastal province of Guangdong—turned into a tidal wave and civil war swept across southern China. After declaring the establishment of a new state, the Taiping Heavenly Kingdom, Hong and his followers captured Nanjing in 1853 and proclaimed it as their capital. Their creed was a form of messianic Christian despotism combined with an intolerance of the Chinese cultural tradition. Even while the Qing emperor was still holding court in Beijing, the Taiping Heavenly Kingdom leaders were attempting to redistribute land and putting their ideas into practice, such as allowing women an unprecedented amount of freedom. They failed to extend their control to the north of the country, however, and eventually the Qing army, helped by Western arms, crushed them in 1864. During the campaign, Emperor Hongwu's

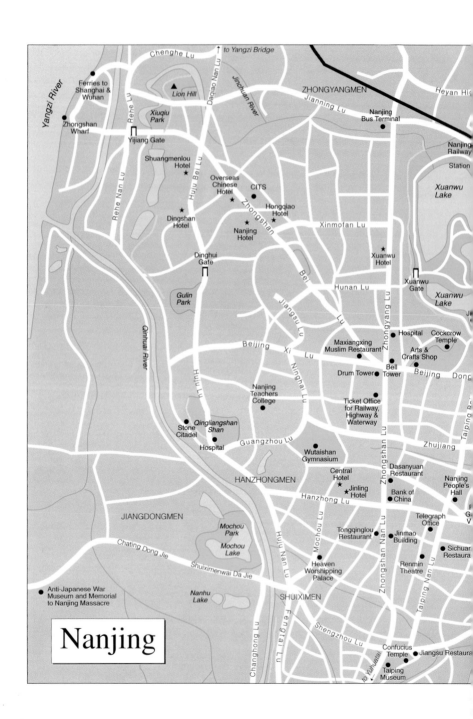

Chenghe Lu

↑ to Yangzi Bridge

ZHONGYANGMEN

Heyan Hig

Yangzi River

Ferries to
Shanghai &
Wuhan

Lion Hill

Daqiao Nan Lu

Jinchuan River

Jianning Lu

Nanjing
Bus Terminal

Nanjing
Railway

Zhongshan
Wharf

Rehe Lu

Xiuqiu
Park

Yijiang Gate

Station

Shuangmenlou
Hotel ★

Rehe Nan Lu

Huju Bei Lu

Overseas
Chinese
Hotel ★

CITS

Hongqiao
Hotel ★

Zhongshan

Xinmofan Lu

Xuanwu
Lake

Dingshan
Hotel ★

★ Nanjing
Hotel

Dinghui
Gate

Xuanwu
Hotel ★

Xuanwu
Gate

Xuanwu
Lake

Ji

Gulin
Park

Qinhuai River

Bei Lu

Hunan Lu

Jiangsu Lu

Beijing

Xi

Lu

Ninghai Lu

Lu

Zhongyang Lu

Hospital Cockcrow
Temple

Maxiangxing
Muslim Restaurant

Arts &
Crafts Shop

Drum Tower ●

Bell
Tower

Beijing

Dong

Huju Lu

Nanjing
Teachers
College ●

Stone
Citadel ●

Qingliangshan
Shan

● Hospital

Guangzhou Lu

Ticket Office
for Railway,
Highway &
Waterway

Taiping R

Zhujiang

Wutaishan
Gymnasium

HANZHONGMEN

Central
Hotel ★

★ Jinling
Hotel

Hanzhong Lu

Dasanyuan
Restaurant

Zhongshan Lu

Bank of
China ●

Nanjing
People's
Hall ●

JIANGDONGMEN

Mochou
Lu

Telegraph
Office ●

G
V

Chating Dong Jie

Mochou
Park

Mochou
Lake

Shuiximenwai Da Jie

Huju Nan Lu

Tongqinglou
Restaurant ●

Jinmao
Building ●

Zhongshan Nan Lu

● Sichuar
Restaura

Heaven
Worshipping
Palace ●

Renmin
Theatre ●

Taiping Nan Lu

Anti-Japanese War
Museum and Memorial
to Nanjing Massacre ●

Nanhu
Lake

SHUIXIMEN

Changhong Lu

Fengtai Lu

Shengzhou Lu

# Nanjing

to Xuhuatai

Confucius
Temple ●

● Jiangsu Restaura

Taiping
Museum ●

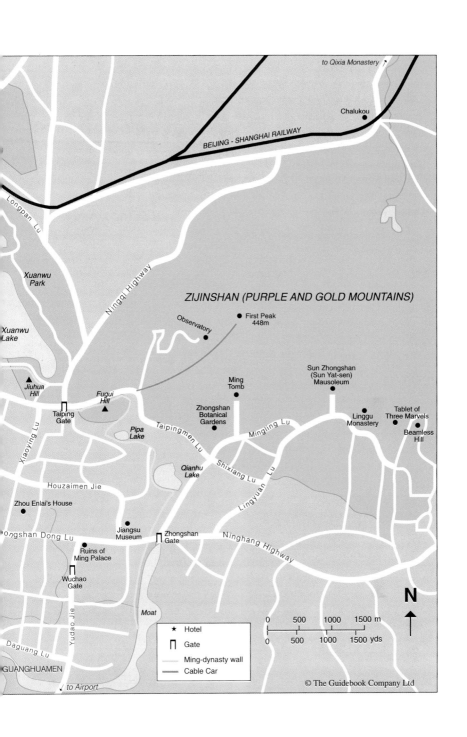

to Qixia Monastery

Chalukou

BEIJING - SHANGHAI RAILWAY

Longpan Lu

Xuanwu
Park

Ningqi Highway

ZIJINSHAN (PURPLE AND GOLD MOUNTAINS)

Xuanwu
Lake

Observatory

First Peak
448m

Jiuhua
Hill

Fugui
Hill

Ming
Tomb

Sun Zhongshan
(Sun Yat-sen)
Mausoleum

Taiping
Gate

Zhongshan
Botanical
Gardens

Mingling Lu

Linggu
Monastery

Tablet of
Three Marvels

Xiaoying Lu

Pipa
Lake

Taipingmen Lu

Shixiang Lu

Beamless
Hill

Qianhu
Lake

Lingyuan Lu

Houzaimen Jie

Zhou Enlai's House

Jiangsu
Museum

Zhongshan
Gate

Ninghang Highway

Zhongshan Dong Lu

Ruins of
Ming Palace

Wuchao
Gate

Yudao Jie

Moat

★ Hotel

Π Gate

Ming-dynasty wall

Cable Car

Daguang Lu

GUANGHUAMEN

to Airport

0    500    1000    1500 m
0    500    1000    1500 yds

N

© The Guidebook Company Ltd

palace was destroyed and his tomb looted. The Taiping Rebellion marked a turning point in the fortunes of the Qing dynasty, which never recovered from the blow dealt to it by such a forceful challenge to its authority.

Only two decades earlier, Nanjing had been the site of another tragedy—at least for the Chinese: the signing of the 1842 treaty with the English which was to end the first Opium War and lead to the opening up of China to trade with the West (on unequal terms). The Treaty of Nanking in 1842 foreshadowed later agreements which gave other Western powers a foothold in China, and heralded a new phase in China's relations with the outside world. It confirmed that the Qing government was totally incapable of defending the nation from superior Western navies and opium traders. The loss of sovereignty which resulted from granting concessions to foreigners was a source of profound humiliation to the Chinese.

Yet if the city has suffered in history, it has also seen days of splendour and fame as a centre of culture and Buddhist scholarship, particularly during the Tang dynasty. It was then that Nanjing was the home of the poets Li Bai (Li Po) and Bai Juyi (Po Chu-i), whose works are considered among the finest in Chinese literature.

## CITY SIGHTS

The **Nanjing Museum** houses an excellent collection representing over 30 centuries of Chinese history. Here you can see a jade burial suit, dating from the Han dynasty, which was believed to prevent physical decay. Small rectangles of jade were wired together to cover the body from head to foot, and a jade disc was then inserted into the corpse's mouth. Archaeologists discovered that the suit, alas, did not have the desired effect. The exhibits of the museum have been arranged chronologically, so visitors with little time can select the dynastic period in which they are most interested.

The **Museum of the Taiping Heavenly Kingdom** is fascinating for two reasons: its exhibits give a detailed picture of the rebel state set up by Hong Xiuquan, the 19th-century scholar who believed he could create the Kingdom of Heaven on earth, and it has a fine Ming-dynasty garden which has survived the political vicissitudes of the city.

The old **city walls**, more extensive than anything that remains in Beijing today, are worth exploring—perhaps as part of an evening stroll. In the 17th century, these walls were the longest in the world and today, even in a state of decay, they are still a magnificent sight. The **Zhonghua Gate** and the **Heping Gate**, built with a mortar mixture of rice-gruel, paste and lime, are the only two to have survived from the Ming Dynasty, and they vividly illustrate the insecure nature of those times—when the possibility of insurrection meant that hundreds of thousands of ordinary Chinese were made to undergo forced labour.

Within walking distance of each other, in the city centre, are the Ming **Bell Tower** and **Drum Tower**. The bell was used, as elsewhere, to sound the dawn, and the drum was rolled when the city gates were closed at dusk. Nanjing's two most well-known parks are **Xuanwu Lake Park** and **Mochou Lake Park**. In recent years, another scenic area has been developed around the **Confucius Temple** (Fuzi Miao), close to a stretch of the **Qinhuai River**. First built in the 11th century, the temple was destroyed in 1937 and reconstructed in 1986. It is flanked by shops and restaurants, and, together with the river, makes for a lively area to wander in.

Another recent addition to Nanjing's historical sites is the **Jiangnan Examination Hall**. The original examination hall, in which aspiring scholars of the region would gather in the hope of passing the civil service examination and winning an appointment to the imperial bureaucracy, has long since disappeared. During the Ming dynasty, it encompassed more than 20,000 individual cells in which the candidates would undergo their mental ordeal over three days of examinations. A new exhibition hall includes a reconstruction of some cells, and displays documents related to the history of imperial examinations, as well as inscribed tablets dating from the Ming, Qing and Republican periods.

## MODERN NANJING

A great achievement of Nanjing is its bridge over the Yangzi River, which was built despite the withdrawl of the Russian engineers who designed it. The **Yangzi Bridge** (*see* picture on page 76), with its road and rail platforms, is six-and-a-half kilometers (four miles) long, and was completed in 1968. The bridge is a symbol of national pride and is important in Chinese communications. Before its construction, all north-south traffic through China had to make the crossing by ferry.

In the city centre, at 30 Meiyuan Xincun, travellers interested in Chinese communist history can visit **Zhou Enlai's house**. Here the late premier lived and worked when negotiating with the Kuomintang after the defeat of the Japanese.

Another popular place to visit, particularly for Chinese tourists, is the **People's Revolutionary Martyrs' Memorial**. It stands on the original site of the Rainbow Terrace, a place of Buddhist pilgrimage. It is said to have won its name after the eloquent preaching of a sixth-century monk so moved the Buddha that he sent down a shower of flowers which turned to pebbles. These pretty agate pebbles are collected, polished and sold as souvenirs. They are at their most beautiful when they are wet—whether with rain or submerged in water in a small bowl. Traditionally, the glistening pebbles are displayed along with New Year narcissi or goldfish.

# High and Low

The rickshaw men in Peking form several groups. Those who are young and strong and springy of leg rent good-looking rickshaws and work all day. They take their rickshaws out when they feel like it and quit when they feel like it. They begin their day by going to wait at rickshaw stands or the residences of the wealthy. They specialize in waiting for a customer who wants a fast trip. They might get a dollar or two just like that if it's a good job. Having struck it rich they might take the rest of the day off. It doesn't matter to them—if they haven't made a deal on how much rent they'll have to pay to the rickshaw agency. The members of this band of brothers generally have two hopes: either to be hired full time, or to buy a rickshaw. In the latter case it doesn't make much difference if they work for a family full time or get their fares in the streets; the rickshaw is their own.

Compare the first group to all those who are older, or to all those who, due to their physical condition, are lacking in vigor when they run, or to all those who, because of their families, do not dare waste one day. Most of these men pull almost new rickshaws. Man and rickshaw look equally good so these men can maintain the proper dignity when the time comes to ask for the fare. The men in this group work either all day or on the late afternoon and evening shift. Those who work late, from four P.M. to dawn, do so because they have the stamina for it. They don't care if it is winter or summer. Of course it takes a lot more attentiveness and skill to work at night than in the daytime; naturally you earn somewhat more money.

It is not easy for those who are over forty and under twenty to find a place in these two groups. Their rickshaws are rickety and they dare not work the late shift. All they can do is start out very early, hoping they can earn the rickshaw rental and their expenses for one day between dawn and three or four in the afternoon. Their rickshaws are rickety and they run very slowly. They work long hours on the road and come out *short on fares. They are the ones who haul goods at the melon market, fruit market, and vegetable market. They don't make much but there's no need to run fast either.*

*Very few of those under twenty—and some start work at eleven or twelve—become handsome rickshaw men when older. It is very difficult for them to grow up healthy and strong because of the deprivations they suffer as children. They may pull a rickshaw all their lives, but pulling a rickshaw never gets them anywhere. Some of those over forty have been pulling rickshaws for only eight or ten years. They begin to slow down as their muscles deteriorate. Eventually they realize that they'll take a tumble and die in the street sooner or later. Their methods, charging all that the traffic will bear and making short trips look like long ones, are quite enough to bring their past glory to mind and make them snort with contempt at the younger generation. But past glory can scarcely diminish the gloom of the future and for that reason they often sigh a little when they mop their brows. When compared to others among their contemporaries, however, they don't seem to have suffered much. They never expected to have anything to do with pulling rickshaws. But when faced with a choice between living and dying, they'd had to grab the shafts of a rickshaw. They were fired clerks or dismissed policemen, small-time merchants who had lost their capital, or workmen who had lost their jobs. When the time came when they had nothing left to sell or pawn, they gritted their teeth, held back their tears, and set out on this death-bound road. Their best years are already gone and now the poor food they eat becomes the blood and sweat that drips on the pavement. They have no strength, no experience, and no friends. Even among their coworkers they are alone.*

*Lao She*, Rickshaw *(1936), translated by Jean M James*

## Outings from Nanjing

East of the city are the **Purple and Gold Mountains**, which are home to some of the most famous sights of Nanjing. One of these is the **Observatory**, built on the summit of one of the peaks. It houses a fine collection of astronomical instruments, including a Ming copy of a Han-dynasty earthquake detector. Also in the collection is a bronze armillary sphere, designed by the Yuan-dynasty astronomer, Guo Shoujing, in 1275.

The most visited sight in the Purple and Gold Mountains is the **Sun Zhongshan Mausoleum**. Sun Zhongshan, better known in the West as Sun Yat-sen, is considered the father of the Chinese Republican Revolution. He rose to prominence in the early years of this century as an activist in the anti-imperial movement. Prior to that, he lived in exile abroad (in 1896 he gained much publicity when he made a narrow escape after being kidnapped by Chinese secret service agents in London). In 1911, when news of the Qing overthrow reached him, Dr Sun returned to China and became the first president of the new republic. He did not have the support or personality to stop military leaders from taking power into their own hands, and he died a disappointed man in Beijing in 1925. You reach the mausoleum, which has a roof of brilliant, sky-blue tiles, after a spectacular climb up nearly 400 wide granite steps.

On the way to the mausoleum, visitors usually stop off at **Ming Xiaoling**, the tomb of the first emperor of the Ming dynasty. The tomb was looted during the Taiping Rebellion, but it is worth coming to see the pastoral site and its quiet Spirit Avenue, lined with stone warriors, scholars and beasts.

Also in the mountains is the **Linggu Monastery**, which is notable for its Ming **Beamless Hall**. This hall is made of bricks without any supporting pillars. It was constructed over a mound of earth which was subsequently scooped out on completion of the building, thereby leaving the hall standing in pillarless splendour.

The wooded **Qixia Mountain** lies 25 kilometres (16 miles) east of Nanjing, and is home to one of the oldest surviving monasteries in southern China. The present buildings of **Qixia Monastery** all date from this century, but there is a famous library with many ancient Buddhist scriptures. Within the monastic grounds there is an octagonal stone stupa, carved with images from the life of Buddha, which dates back to 601. A short walk from this stupa is a rock face carved with Buddha images. It is known as **Thousand Buddha Cliff** (a name used at many sites throughout China), and has carvings dating from the early seventh century.

One hour by car, to the northeast of the city, there are stone carvings from the fourth and fifth centuries. This was a period of political chaos in China, when a series of short-lived dynasties ruled different regions of the country, and the carvings reflect this. They are scattered over the fields at 31 different sites, and all are remains of aristocratic and imperial tombs of the period. They are known collectively as the **Southern Dynasties' Stone Carvings**.

# Beijing

Beijing lies just south of the rim of the Central Asian steppes and is separated from the Gobi Desert by a green chain of mountains, over which the Great Wall runs. The Great Wall was built and rebuilt by a succession of Chinese emperors to keep out the marauding hordes of nomads who from time to time swept into China—in much the same way as the wind from the Gobi still sweeps in seasonal sand storms which suffocate the city. The rocks beneath the city yield bitter water, which is barely drinkable, and only the presence of a few sweet springs made the growth of an imperial capital possible.

Modern Beijing lies in fact on the site of countless human settlements which date back half a million years. Visitors can see the site, outside the city at **Zhoukoudian**, where *Homo erectus Pekinensis*, better known as Peking Man, was discovered in 1929. The name Beijing—or Northern Capital—is by Chinese standards a modern term. It dates back to the 15th century, when the Ming emperor, Yongle, planned and built the city in its present form. One of the city's earlier names was the City of Swallows (Yanjing), a name given in the Liao dynasty (947–1125). The name is still appropriate, for in a land where few birds are seen in cities except in cages, Beijing boasts a large summer community of swallows, which make their homes in the capacious eaves of the ancient wooden buildings. At twilight, **Qianmen Gate**, which stands on the south side of Tiananmen Square, is circled by roosting swallows. This scene on a summer evening remains much the same as it must have been over the centuries, except that the gate now stands lonely and obsolete, no longer buttressed by the old city walls which have been torn down over the years.

Beijing first became a capital in the Jin dynasty (1115–1234), but it experienced its first phase of grandiose city planning in the Yuan dynasty under the rule of the Mongol emperor, Kublai Khan, who made the city his winter capital in the late 13th century. Kublai Khan's Beijing was known in Chinese as Dadu, but the Venetian explorer, Marco Polo, who visited the city at the time of Kublai Khan, knew it by the name of Khanbaliq. On his return to Europe, Marco Polo wrote a vivid account of his travels across Central Asia to China, which he called Cathay. However, his contemporaries did not believe his stories, and they nicknamed him *Il Milione*, saying his tales were thousands of lies. In fact, most of his descriptions of Cathay were accurate (despite some interesting omissions—chopsticks, for example), and his book can be recommended for an eyewitness account of 13th-century Khanbaliq.

Little of it remains in today's Beijing, except for the layout of **Beihai Park**, and remnants of Dadu's city wall between the northern legs of the third and fourth ring roads. The city of Beijing that visitors see today was the grand conception of Emperor Yongle, the Ming ruler who, having usurped the throne, moved the capital north

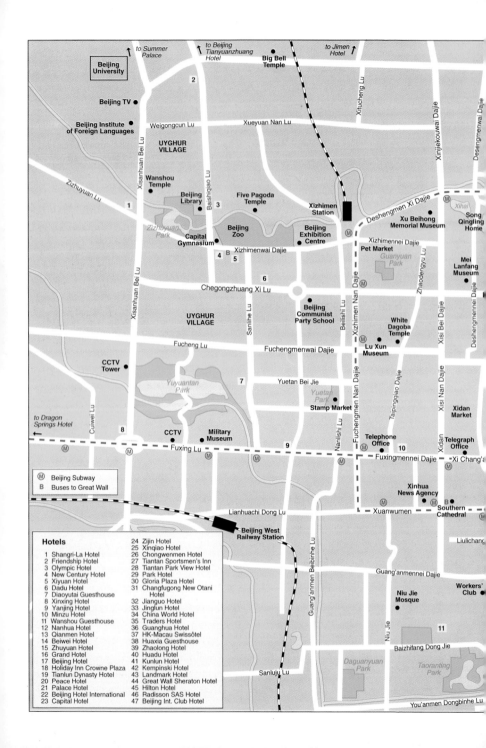

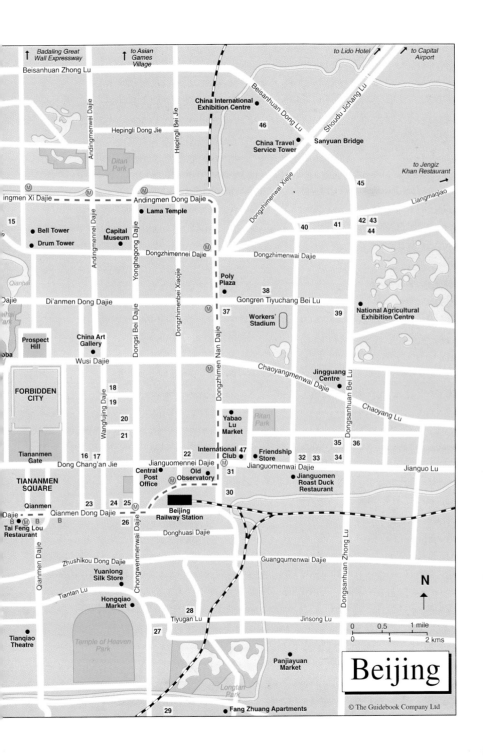

from Nanjing. Most of the major historical sites in the city date either from the Ming or later Qing dynasties. The major modern transformation of the city has been 'achieved' (if that is the word) by the present government, which on coming to power in 1949 decided to make Beijing its capital and to modernize the old city by demolishing the Ming city walls, destroying the commemorative arches (to widows and local dignitaries, among other honoured citizens), and replacing them with wide new roads and concrete housing blocks. The intimate network of *hutongs* —or lanes—was largely redeveloped, thus taking away the distinct pattern of neighbourhoods which had given the city such human proportions. A few of the old *hutong* districts remain north and south of the Forbidden City, but the city centre is dominated by the imposing Stalinesque buildings put up around Tiananmen Square in the 1950s.

The Cultural Revolution (1966–76) also caused the destruction of many of Beijing's historic and religious treasures in the name of revolutionary purity. During the anti-intellectual purges of the Cultural Revolution, there were many cases of famous scholars being killed or committing suicide. Perhaps the most infamous was the death by drowning of the writer, Lao She. Of all the writers of the 20th century, it is Lao She who writes with the most authentic voice about Beijing, its people, neighbourhoods and low life, especially before 1949.

The leadership of the present Chinese government is trying to make good the ravages of the Cultural Revolution with restoration work and rebuilding. One problem is that the skilled craftsmen, whose forefathers built and maintained the imperial city over generations, are a dying breed, and today's craftsmen often lack the necessary skills and knowledge of materials to save buildings, frescoes and carvings. Some restored murals have crude colouring and lines worthy of chocolate-box design. Even so, there is still enough to see in the city, and beyond, to keep an enthusiastic sightseer busy for a long time.

## City Sights

The **Forbidden City** (Imperial Palace) was the home of emperors from its creation by Emperor Yongle in 1420 until Puyi, who reigned briefly as the last Qing emperor, left it in 1924. The vast pageant of halls, white marble terraces and deep red walls is now used to display many exhibitions ranging from court costumes to the imperial collection of clocks and, in the dry autumn months, rare paintings. (Much of the imperial art collection was taken to Taiwan before 1949.) The entire complex of the Forbidden City, covering 74 hectares (183 acres), was designed to overawe the visitor while reinforcing the majesty of the Son of Heaven, as every Chinese emperor was known. The palace requires a visit of at least half a day, and it can be daunting in the heat of summer, the time at which the emperor and his court retreated to their cooler lakeside palaces.

The palace is at its most beautiful after a light winter snowfall. To see the golden roofs at their most brilliant at any time of year, try to get a view of the palace at dawn from an upper floor on the west wing of the **Beijing Hotel**, the **Grand Hotel**, or from Coal Hill.

Another stunning sight is the **Temple of Heaven** (Tiantan). This is actually a wonderful sequence of temples and altars set in a park as part of Emperor Yongle's grand design. Heaven—or *tian*—was considered the source of harmony and spiritual authority by Chinese philosophers, and so it came to symbolize the source of imperial power. The Temple of Heaven was the site of imperial sacrifices at the winter solstice to keep order and harmony on earth. The architecture reflects that sense of order: the northern wall of the complex is curved in a half-circle to symbolize heaven, and the southern wall is built as a square to symbolize earth. Whereas most imperial buildings have yellow tiles (the imperial colour) on their roofs, the blue tiles here are said to 'reflect' the colour of the sky. The main buildings and altars are also built in tiers of three to create nine dimensions of surface. Nine is the mystical number in Chinese tradition, and it also symbolizes heaven. At other times of the year, the emperor made additional sacrifices at the **Altars of the Sun, Moon and Earth**. These sites have been transformed into public parks and can be found in the east, west and north of the city, respectively.

The original water park of Kublai Khan is now **Beihai Park**. Nothing remains here from the Yuan-dynasty period except a vast, black jade bowl carved with sea monsters. Made for Kublai Khan in 1265, the bowl is displayed in the **Round City**, near the south entrance to the park. At the centre of Beihai Lake is a small hill on which stands a Tibetan-style **White Dagoba**, built in 1651 to honour the Dalai Lama's visit. The lake is actually only half of a larger one. The southern half lies hidden behind the high red walls of **Zhongnanhai**, once also part of the imperial park and now the residential complex of senior Communist Party leaders. No foreigner, unless he is a high-ranking dignitary, can visit the lakeside villas and steam-heated tennis courts used by China's privileged few. Ordinary Chinese and foreign tourists must take their pleasures on the north shores of the lake at Beihai, with boating in the summer and skating in the winter. Most of the buildings visited today date from the Qing dynasty. The park's **Fangshan Restaurant** is a popular place to host lunches and dinners. Indeed, its splendid setting and choice of recipes from the imperial palace kitchens make it *the* place to visit.

Directly to the north of the Forbidden City lies **Coal Hill**, also known as Prospect Hill, which offers a fine view over the Imperial Palace to the south and Beihai Park to the west. It played a sad part in Chinese history, since it was on its eastern slope that the last Ming emperor reputedly hung himself when his capital was overrun by rebel troops in 1644.

*(following pages) Snow covers the Forbidden City as the sun rises over Beijing. The Imperial Palace has occupied this site since the late 13th century, but the present layout was established by the Yongle emperor of the Ming dynasty in the early 15th century*

# The Trappings of Power

*Every time I went to my schoolroom to study, or visited the High Consorts to pay my respects, or went for a stroll in the garden I was always followed by a large retinue. Every trip I made to the Summer Palace must have cost thousands of Mexican dollars: the Republic's police had to be asked to line the roads to protect me and I was accompanied by a motorcade consisting of dozens of vehicles.*

*Whenever I went for a stroll in the garden a procession had to be organized. In front went a eunuch from the Administrative Bureau whose function was roughly that of a motor horn: he walked twenty or thirty yards ahead of the rest of the party intoning the sound "chir . . . chir . . ." as a warning to anyone who might be in the vicinity to go away at once. Next came two chief eunuchs advancing crabwise on either side of the path; ten paces behind them came the centre of the procession—the Empress Dowager or myself. If I was being carried in a chair there would be two junior eunuchs walking beside me to attend to my wants at any moment; if I was walking they would be supporting me. Next came a eunuch with a large silk canopy followed by a large group of eunuchs of whom some were empty-handed and others were holding all sorts of things: a seat in case I wanted to rest, changes of clothing, umbrellas and parasols. After these eunuchs of the imperial presence came eunuchs of the imperial tea bureau with boxes of various kinds of cakes and delicacies, and, of course, jugs of hot water and a tea service; they were followed by eunuchs of the imperial dispensary bearing cases of medicine and first-aid equipment suspended from carrying poles. The medicines carried always included potions prepared from lampwick sedge, chrysanthemums, the roots of reeds, bamboo leaves, and bamboo skins; in summer there were always Essence of Betony Pills for Rectifying the Vapour, Six Harmony Pills for Stabilizing the Centre, Gold Coated Heat-Dispersing Cinnabar, Fragrant Herb Pills, Omnipurpose Bars, colic medicine and anti-plague powder; and through-out all four seasons there would be the Three Immortals Beverage to aid the digestion, as well as many other medicaments. At the end of the procession*

*came the eunuchs who carried commodes and chamber-pots. If I was
walking a sedanchair, open or covered according to the season, would
bring up the rear. This motley procession of several dozen people would
proceed in perfect silence and order.*

*But I would often throw it into confusion. When I was young I liked to
run around when I was in high spirits just as any child does. At first they
would all scuttle along after me puffing and panting with their procession
reduced to chaos. When I grew a little older and knew how to give orders
I would tell them to stand and wait for me; then apart from the junior
eunuchs of the imperial presence who came with me they would all stand
there waiting in silence with their loads. After I had finished running
around they would form up again behind me. When I learnt to ride a bicycle
and ordered the removal of all the upright wooden thresholds in the palace
so that I could ride around without obstruction the procession was no
longer able to follow me and so it had to be temporarily abolished. But when
I went to pay my respects to the High Consorts or to my schoolroom I still
had to have something of a retinue, and without it I would have felt rather
odd. When I heard people telling the story of the last emperor of the Ming
Dynasty who had only one eunuch left with him at the end I felt very
uncomfortable.*

Pu Yi, *from* Emperor to Citizen, *translated by W J F Jenner*

Chinese science—astronomy in particular—developed very early on. A Chinese astronomer calculated the length of the year 300 years before it was discovered in the West. By the time the Jesuit fathers arrived in China in the 16th century, much of China's previous scientific knowledge had been lost, due to dynastic change and the resulting destruction and upheaval. In order to impress the Chinese emperors with the superiority of the Christian faith (a faith that had persecuted Galileo for his scientific discoveries), the Jesuit missionaries set about casting fine astronomical instruments and challenging the accuracy of the Chinese court astronomers' predictions. This was not a minor challenge, since the emperor—as Son of Heaven—was responsible for the accuracy of the calendar, and thus the harmony of the empire. The Jesuits' astronomical instruments are on display at the **Imperial Observatory**, alongside Ming and Qing pieces, on an open-air platform which was once a section of the city wall. Yet despite their great prestige at the Qing courts of Emperors Kangxi and Qianlong, and their work in the field of science, the Jesuits failed to achieve their objective of converting the imperial household.

**Tiananmen Square** is a vast 20th-century creation named after the Forbidden City's southernmost gate—the **Gate of Heavenly Peace** (*see* picture on page 1). In the centre stands the **Monument to the People's Heroes**, and behind that **Chairman Mao's Mausoleum** (open to the public only at limited times) was built in 1977. Previously the square gave an uninterrupted view from the city gate of **Qianmen** to the outer walls of the Forbidden City. On the west side of the square sits the Stalinesque **Great Hall of the People**, where party and national congresses are held. On the eastern side are the very worthwhile **Museum of Chinese History** and **Museum of the Chinese Revolution**. The square has long been a gathering place for every out-of-town visitor on a first trip to the capital. Groups and families like to have their photographs taken with the Gate of Heavenly Peace and a dour picture of Chairman Mao in the background. On a windy day, children old and young come into the square to fly kites. The square has been a stage for tumultuous events in China's modern history. Mao received millions of Red guards there in 1966 at the start of the Cultural Revolution, and ten years later it witnessed mass protests calling for the arrest of the Gang of Four.

Beijing is rich in museums. The Forbidden City is a vast museum in itself, besides housing several separate collections such as clocks and watches, ceramics, paintings and so on. There are also museums devoted to China's revolutionary history, and to special interests such as aviation and archaeology. Two other places are worth a visit if time allows. If an application is made in advance, permission is granted for a tour of the **National Library**, which has more than 13 million volumes including rare books and manuscripts. The **Beijing Art Museum** is the first major museum to open in 30 years. Located in the grounds of a Buddhist temple which for years had been

*Jugglers exhibiting in the court of a Mandarin's Palace*

occupied by the army, this museum displays an eclectic collection of Ming and Qing artifacts, as well as paintings from the Republican period.

Many of the city's old temples have been restored and opened to the public. There are many throughout the city—and they can be found with the help of a guide, a hired taxi and a good map. The **White Dagoba Monastery** (Baita Si) can be found in the Taipingqiao district, west of Beihai Park. Built in the late 13th century under the supervision of a Nepalese architect, it has a very fine collection of Tibetan *thangkas* (religious paintings), and is a quiet place seldom visited by tourists. Its white dagoba makes it easy to spot. To the northeast lies the **Lama Temple**, which is known in Chinese as Yonghe Gong—the Palace of Peace and Harmony—because it was originally the residence of a prince. When this prince ascended the throne as Emperor Yongzheng (reigned 1723–35), the complex of buildings was converted into a temple in accordance with custom. Under the next emperor, Qianlong, it became a centre of learning for the Yellow Hat sect of Tibetan Lamaism. It has a fine collection of Tibetan bronzes and paintings, but its most well-known treasure is a huge statue of Maitreya. Over 23 metres (75 feet) tall, this piece of sculpture is said to have been carved out of a single sandalwood tree.

# CHINESE OPERA

Peking Opera has its origins in southern China, but was adopted by the Qing court in the 19th century and thus came to be known as Jing Ju, meaning 'capital opera'. It is best known for its percussive style of music and the use of wooden clappers (rather like oblong castanets), which are used to mark the time of the actors' movements. There are only four tempos which set the mood of the scene: the slow tempo is used for scenes of reflection or when the actor is thinking out loud; the medium tempo is used during narrative; a fast tempo is used for moods of gaiety or excitement; and a free tempo is used for interludes between the action. Actors either sing in a falsetto style or in natural voice. The warrior characters have special techniques for singing, pushing their voice through the lower front part of their cheeks in order to create a deep, gruff effect. Chinese audiences love to applaud a particularly fine solo, which requires great voice control and range.

Chinese opera is different from its Western counterpart in many ways, but no difference is as striking as the painted faces seen on the Chinese stage. Ancient Greek dramas were performed behind masks for dramatic effect, but the Chinese opera demands that many of its characters have their faces painted in elaborate patterns to denote personality. Audiences, through their familiarity with the art, can tell the good and bad characters apart—they know that red faces belong to heroes and white faces indicate treachery. In the past the illiterate and poor learnt their history and legends through opera performances. Not all painted faces are elaborate and multicoloured. Some require only a layer of rouge over the face with white contours around the eyes and thick black eyebrows (the eyes are emphasized by the simple method of sticking tape at the corners to pull the eyes upwards). As a rough guide, the young female and male 'good characters' have unpatterned, rouged faces, while the warriors have elaborate face markings. Clowns are easy to distinguish with their white blob of paint in the centre of their faces. Maidservants and page boys wear little make-up and usually have two little jaunty topknots of hair. The faces of the gods are painted a brilliant gold, and the animal spirits have faces painted to resemble the animal in question.

The stage will have very few props; instead they will be suggested by the actors miming an action to tell the audience what must be imagined. For example, you may see an actor 'row' across the stage by bending his body as if balancing on a boat and sculling from the stern with one oar. A character who is about to ride a horse flourishes his tasselled whip and makes a mounting movement. A man who is leaving a room takes an elaborate step while pulling at the hem of his robe (all traditional Chinese houses have raised steps in their doorways). Great emotion is expressed by the shaking of the hands in the sleeves of the tunic. Shy love is shown by the woman turning her head behind her hand. These and other tiny gestures by the actors give important information to the audience, gestures which can be read after only a little experience of Chinese opera.

The stories of traditional operas usually have complex plots full of twists and turns. Plot rather than character development is the way in which suspense is injected into the drama. This is because there is no character development as we know it in the West; the painted faces of the characters are given at the beginning of the play and there is no change of either character or make-up in the course of the action. Bad characters are vanquished, not transformed. It is understandable that the plays most popular with foreign visitors are the acrobatic martial operas, which need little explanation. Yet even the martial spectacles are more exciting for having their plots unravelled. A particular favourite is *San Cha Kou* or 'Where Three Roads Meet'. This tale is of mistaken identity and includes a fight in the dark between two heroes and an innkeeper. The three actors mime a fight as if they were in the pitch dark. It is so convincing you forget the actors can really see each other. Their eyes never meet, and at one point one of the actors moves his sword into the air as if trying to catch the moonlight on its blade. It is thrilling stuff, so much so that it inspired the English playwright Peter Shaeffer to write *Black Comedy* after he saw a performance in the late 1950s.

Regional Chinese opera can be just as exciting and colourful as its metropolitan cousin. In Sichuan and Shaanxi operas you will often find the role of a comic dame sung by a man. In the Yue Ju style of opera of the Zhejiang region, all the parts are played by women and the music is softer, with more strings, wind instruments, and less percussion than northern opera. The classical Kunqu style, which originated in Suzhou, is still popular with older audiences in present-day China. There is a Kunqu troupe based in Beijing which performs quite regularly in the capital. They have one lively story in their repertoire concerning a wastrel husband who, as a young man, sold his wife. His punishment is to be taken into her service, on her secret instructions, and then to run errands while she pretends that she does not know who he is. He is filled with shame and heats her wine with trembling hands, dreading that she will recognize him. The story has a fine comic climax, in which the man is persuaded to marry an unknown bride, who turns out to be—yes—his wife, who has of course forgiven him. Chinese audiences delight in these tales of misfortune, forgiveness and reconciliation.

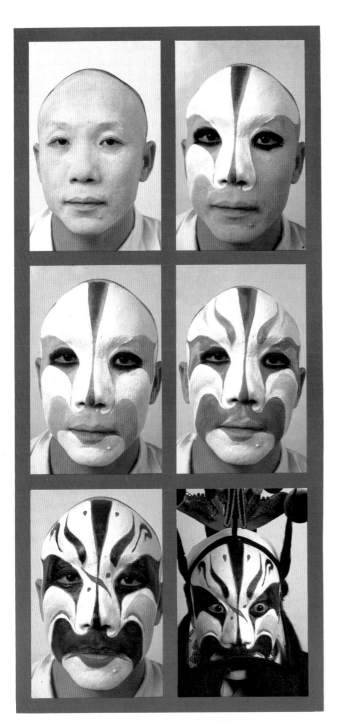

*Peking Opera requires elaborately painted faces to denote personality*

## Outings from Beijing

Legend has it that the Yongle emperor (reigned 1403–1423) picked the location for the **Ming Tombs** when out hunting to celebrate his birthday. While resting, local peasants came to wish him long life, so he renamed a nearby mountain Longevity Mountain and suggested to court geomancers that the valley be considered as a site for hosting the royal tombs. It satisfied the requirements of *fengshui*, literally 'wind-water' geomancy, a spiritual version of good vibes. It was sheltered from the evil-spirit bearing northern wind by mountains, while it possessed a wide-open aspect to the south, conducive to the approach of benevolent forces.

Royal parties would travel for two days from the Imperial City to perform ancestor worshipping rites at the tombs. Now the site can be reached in less than one hour via the new Badaling Expressway.

The entrance to *Shisanling*, meaning thirteen tombs, is announced by a towering marble *pailou*, or portico. At 33 metres (36 yards) in length and 10.5 metres (11.5 yards) in height it is said to be the largest in China. However, it is unique because ornate carving normally produced in wood has been achieved remarkably in marble. It has five arches and was erected by the Jiajing emperor in 1540. Only the emperor would pass beneath the central arch whose tablet bears no characters, as it was unfitting for anyone to write anything about the Son of Heaven. The six supporting column bases have superb symbolic reliefs on their four faces: lions for strength, *makara* for fertility, and five-clawed dragons symbolizing the emperor. Statuettes of *qilin* lions, symbolizing good admini-stration and peace, complete the arrangement.

A few hundred metres further on stands the Great Red Gate. Like all that follows, it was built as the approach to the Yongle emperor's tomb, **Changling**, but subsequently served the whole mausoleum. There used to be a pillar, *xiamamen*, or dismount (from horses) tablet here, but this has disappeared. Only the emperors body was allowed to pass under the central arch. Next is the stele pavillion serving the whole mausoleum. It is flanked by four *hua biao*, marble columns, on which fabulous dragons are carved. Inside the pavilion, the stele is mounted on a huge *ba xia*, a tortoise-like creature, said to be a descendent of the dragon and able to bear enormous burdens. The tablet has inscriptions on both faces: that on the south face, 3,500 characters long, praises the Changling tomb. It was composed by Yongle's son and written by a famous calligrapher. The north face inscription has a thirteen-line poem by Qianlong (reigned 1736–1795)—one for each tomb—whose dynasty, the Qing, maintained the mausoleum.

Beyond the tower beckons the avenue of statues comprising the Spirit Way (*see* picture on page 117). First come a pair of *wang zhu*, guiding posts, to show any wandering spirit the way back to its resting place. Twelve pairs of beasts follow, both mythical and real, providing a guard of honour for the spirits. Each beast appears first standing, then sitting, operating in a shift system to allow resting. The real animals, camels, horses and elephants symbolize the vast geographical extent of the great Ming empire with camels indigenous to Central Asia, horses to the northern grasslands, and elephants to the sub tropics of the south west. The elephant, or *da xiang* in Chinese, is also steeped with auspicion as it is a phononym for 'great universe'. Mythical *qilin* and *xiezi* represent the government's good administration and justice. Human figures begin with military officers to symbolize the empire's strength and security, while high civil officials, advisors to the emperor, make up the final four pairings. All hold an elongated *hu* tablet, on which they would have made notes during their audiences with the emperor. The symbolism combines to remind those entering the mausoleum of the magnificence of the Ming empire and dynasty. The end of the Spirit Way is marked by a protective screen: evil spirits were thought only able to travel in straight lines, hence the stone curtain thwarted their attempts at violating the sanctity of the mausoleum. Screens also appear in individual tomb courtyards.

Four kilometres (6.4 miles) ahead stands the red-walled, golden-roofed surface architecture of Changling, beneath which the Yongle emperor's body and treasures are thought to lie undisturbed. All 13 tombs have similar plans: a circular mound enclosed by a tumulus wall under which subterranean chambers were dug. This tomb head, the sole realm of the spirit, was adjoined by rectangular courtyards which made up the approach. The arrangement symbolizes a round heaven above a square earth.

Changling's main attraction is its massive Hall of Heavenly Favours, where the spirit received its living descendents. The massive roof is supported by 60 wooden columns, each one a single trunk of *nanmu* from the southwest. Jesuit Matteo Ricci recorded seeing similar timbers being transported along the Grand Canal on his own journey to Beijing around 1595 and estimated that they must have taken three years to be transported from their native place.

**Dingling**, the tomb of the great Wanli Emperor (1573–1620), is the only Ming tomb to have been excavated, from 1956–58. Its vaulted marble palace, deep underground, can be visited. It consists of six interconnected chambers, now bare except for original marble thrones and replica coffins. There are three of each: Wanli was buried with his empress Xiaoduan, and concubine Xiaojing. Most of the tomb's contents—garments, jewellery, jades—are exhibited in the Palace Museum and halls outside, including the Hall of Heavenly Favours at Changling.

Zhaoling, the tomb of the Longqing emperor (reigned 1567–1572), is being restored. However, those with more time would be well advised to visit some of the unrestored tombs. All have caretakers who readily permit those interested few to stroll around. By doing so, the construction of courtyard walls and stele-tower roofs can be better appreciated in tranquil, eerie surrounds which are now the haunt of birds nesting in thujas: trees planted around five centuries before to nourish the deceased in the tumuli beneath.

Further away from Beijing, and so less crowded with visitors, are the **Eastern Qing tombs** in Hebei Province. They are set in a peaceful farm landscape, backed with towering mountains. The carvings on their Spirit Avenues are notably different

from their Ming counterparts—the officials in the Qing avenues have pigtails in the Manchu fashion and wear Buddhist rosaries (the Manchus were very interested in this religion). The two long-lived emperors, Kangxi and Qianlong, are interred here—as is the infamous Empress Dowager Cixi who, at the end of the 19th century, took control of the government and was responsible for obstructing the necessary reforms that might have averted the fall of the Qing Dynasty.

A favourite haunt of the Empress Dowager was the wonderful series of lakeside halls and pavilions to the northwest of the city. These are poetically called in Chinese **Yiheyuan** (The Garden for the Cultivation of Harmony). We in the West know it as the **Summer Palace**. Here the Empress Dowager had a private opera stage built in the palace, as she did in the Forbidden City, so as to be able to enjoy whole days of theatrical entertainment. The marble boat on the north shore of the garden's Kunming Lake is also a folly associated with the Empress Dowager—she had it refurbished with misappropriated funds which should have paid for the modernization of the Chinese navy. The lake is a popular place for boating in summer, and is glorious for ice-skating in winter, with its willow-fringed shore and marble bridges. Overlooking the lake and close to the marble boat is a fine restaurant, Tingliguan, which is popular for banquets.

At one time there was another Qing imperial retreat, **Yuanmingyuan** (Garden of Perfection and Brightness). Foreigners often refer to it as the Old Summer Palace. It lies close to the newer Yiheyuan and is a romantic ruin of marble columns, broken

*(opposite page) Inside the Hall of Prayer for Good Harvests, Temple of Heaven, Beijing*
*(above) Twelve sets of stone animals guard a section of the seven-kilometre-long 'Spirit Way'*
*that forms the approach to the Ming Tombs, 50 kilometres north-west of Beijing*

fountains and scattered terraces. First bestowed on one of his sons by Emperor Kangxi in 1709, Yuanmingyuan was enlarged and restored under Qianlong. The ruins found at the site today are all that is left of the Western Mansions, a complex of palaces, halls and pavilions designed in European style by Jesuits for Qianlong. Yuanmingyuan was looted and blown up by foreign troops in 1860. Part of an expeditionary force sent by European governments to push the Qing government into greater trade concessions, the troops were under the command of Lord Elgin (self-proclaimed saviour of the Parthenon marbles, now in the British Museum). The site is still a popular place for summer picnics, and local people like to come here for painting, courtship and moon-gazing.

A similar day's outing can be made to the **Fragrant Hills** (also known as the **Western Hills**), particularly in the autumn months when the folds of the small mountains are burnt gold and red with the dying leaves. This certainly provides a serene contrast to sightseeing in Beijing. If you plan ahead, you can visit the **Temple of the Sleeping Buddha** (Wofo Si) and the **Temple of the Azure Clouds** (Biyun Si), since they are en route to the hills. As its name suggests, the Temple of the Sleeping Buddha houses a recumbent statue. In lacquered bronze, it measures five metres (16 feet). The Temple of the Azure Clouds is a lovely place to visit in spring, when the peach and apricot trees are in blossom. The Fragrant Hills was an imperial park at the time of the nomad emperors of the Jin and Yuan dynasties. They made it their own game reserve. Sadly, there is little wildlife left, but a series of small temples set amidst the trees makes the park a quiet haven for peaceful walking, reading poetry and a breath of fresh air. Of particular interest in the park is the 16th-century garden of the Study of Self Knowledge, with its circular pool enclosed by a walkway. A recent addition to the park is a cable car which takes passengers to the top of the hills in 18 minutes.

Close to the east entrance of park is the Fragrant Hills Hotel, designed by the celebrated Chinese-American architect I. M. Pei. It is a wonderfully simple design, inspired by classical Chinese architecture and interpreted in a modern way, but, under poor management since its opening, it has not fulfilled its potential of becoming one of the best hotels in China.

**Chengde** (formerly known to Europeans as Jehol) was another summer resort favoured by the Qing emperors. It lies beyond the Great Wall, a five-and-a-half hour train journey from Beijing. It was created by the cultured Emperor Kangxi, who planned a palace with lakes and parks in a sheltered river valley surrounded by mountains. Kangxi's grandson, Emperor Qianlong, doubled the number of landscaped beauty spots and had eight magnificent temples built, each of which was to reflect the different religious practices of the various domains of the Chinese empire. Only seven of these remain, since one was dismantled and removed by the Japanese earlier this century. One of the largest is a copy of the Dalai Lama's Potala Palace in Lhasa. Chengde fell from favour as a summer retreat in 1820, when Emperor Jiaqing was struck dead there by lightning.

# Cities Traditional and Modern

## Shanghai

By Chinese standards, Shanghai is a very modern incarnation. Although its antecedents go back to the Warring States period (475–221 BC), when it was just a small
fishing village on a tidal creek near the mouth of the Yangzi River, its transformation
into a flourishing and cosmopolitan trading city dates only from the late 19th century. It has since become the world's fourth largest and China's second largest city, as
well as the nation's biggest port and manufacturing base.

It was that very position at the mouth of the Yangzi, China's main trade artery
until well into this century, which made Shanghai so attractive to 19th-century merchants from Europe and America. Modern Shanghai owes its development, cityscape
and pre-eminence to that strange conjunction of Western traders and regional
Chinese entrepreneurs who flocked there to make their fortune in the late 19th and
early 20th centuries.

Shanghai was one of the five ports opened to foreign commerce and residence by
the Treaty of Nanking in 1842. Bound up with the idea of a Treaty Port was the prin-
ciple of 'extraterritoriality', which gave foreign residents immunity from Chinese
laws. As it was convenient for the self-governing foreign inhabitants to be grouped
together in specific areas, settlements or 'concessions' were set aside for them. At one
time Shanghai had British, French and American concessions, until the British and
American communities merged and became the International Settlement.

The communist government was not well disposed towards Shanghai when it
took over in 1949; it was suspicious of Shanghai's history of decadent prosperity,
entrepreneurial spirit and political independence. At the same time, the new leadership was keen to cash in on the city's wealth and business infrastructure. Yet it
starved the city of the funds needed for redevelopment and modernization, while
much of the money the city generated was creamed off to develop the poorer inland
regions. The Shanghainese have always resented this, especially as they are prone to
consider themselves more quick-witted and capable than the dour northerners in
Beijing.

In the new political climate where economics are increasingly in command,
Shanghai now finds itself being asked to take a lead role in spearheading the development of the socialist market economy. Just as Chinese society needs innovative individuals to get wealthy and act as catalysts to inspire others on the road from rags to
riches, the country needs entrepreneurial cities to do the same.

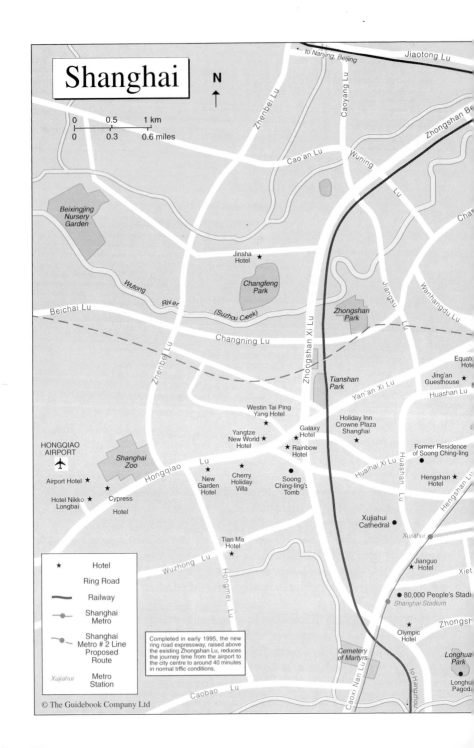

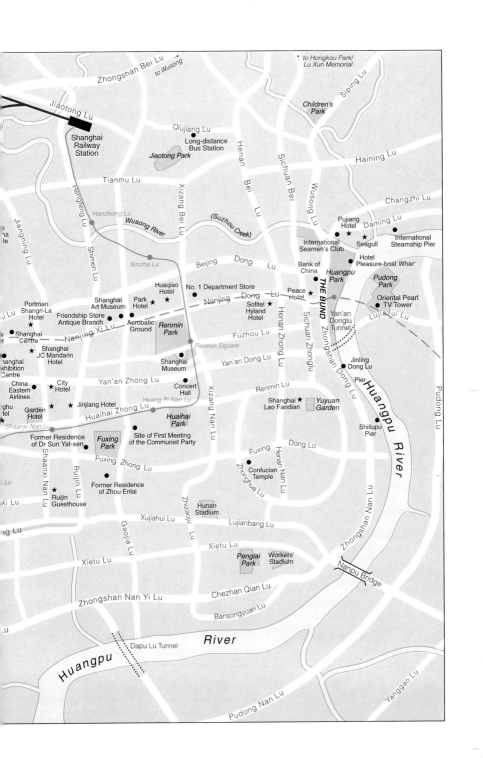

*Sungkiang Road, Shanghai early 1900s*

Shenzhen and other Special Economic Zones (SEZs) were established by Deng Xiaoping to do just that in the early 1980s. At that time Shanghai was overlooked by investors seeking footholds in China: it could not offer SEZ-type privileges. Deng equalized the ground rules after a tour of Shanghai in 1992, envisioning the development of 'Big Shanghai' with the construction of the Pudong New Area and Waigao-qiao Free Port. Moreover, the city's development augurs well by way of its *guanxi*, or connections.

Deng's successor, Jiang Zemin, the country's president and General Secretary of the Communist Party, was born near and educated in Shanghai, where he rose to the position of city mayor. Pragmatist and economic master Zhu Rongji, currently vice-premier, is also an ex-mayor and party chief of Shanghai and tipped to succeed Li Peng as China's premier.

Just as you don't go to New York to see colonial-style village America, so you don't go to Shanghai for a glimpse of China's imperial past. What the city does offer is a good view of treaty-port identity, modern Chinese life, and perhaps a look at the nation's future—in the new industrial areas, and in the emergence of a new generation of young people who, in all but name, have left behind their revolutionary heritage and are getting on with the good things in life.

*(preceding pages) The Bund, Shanghai, 1935; (opposite) the Bund at night*

## CITY SIGHTS: TRADITIONAL

Although Shanghai is a modern and industrial city, most Chinese and foreign visitors like to start their sightseeing with a trip to the old **Chinese city**, known as **Nanshi**. Here the streets are not built on an orderly grid system, as they are in the former International Settlement area, but run hugger-mugger in a mesh of lanes and alleyways. This is part of the charm of the place, but it is probably less picturesque for those who live here—the overcrowding means that homework, knitting, chess, preparing the dinner and even family quarrels often take place in the street.

It is also an area famed for its shopping. Unlike the large department stores of the famous **Nanjing Lu**, which sell anything from cameras to canned food, these small shops are speciality ones. Look out for shops with tea, fans, *bonsai* (miniature trees, known in Chinese as *penjing*) and singing birds. In the old city south of Nanjing Lu, you can add to your shopping list long cotton underwear for less than a few dollars, fans with Chinese opera characters, pot plants and patterned silks.

This quarter is popular with locals, too, thanks to its restaurants and the **Huxinting Teahouse**. This is set in the middle of a pond and is reached by a nine-turn, zigzag bridge. It has arched eaves and is painted red, making it a perfect setting for a leisurely cup of tea and traditional Chinese snacks.

On the other side of the pond is a slightly scruffier establishment, which serves delicious steamed dumplings known as Nanxiang dumplings. Made of minced pork, steamed in a thin pastry skin and dipped in vinegar and slices of ginger, they are so popular that the small restaurant can be identified simply by the sight of steam escaping from its windows and the crowds around its door.

A grander restaurant to visit nearby is the **Lubolang** (Walkway of the Jade Waves). This is famous for its steamed and baked Shanghai-style snacks, which include such lyrically named delights as Moth Eyebrow dumpling—a baked crescent of wafer-light pastry filled with shrimps and delicate vegetables. If you cannot get a seat in the restaurant—and it is always packed, especially near the windows which overlook the lake—you can buy snacks from the window downstairs to take away.

The **Yu Garden**, adjacent to the Lubolang restaurant, is a good place to walk off that lunch; it has marvellous vistas of pools, pavilions and rock gardens. The garden is attractive but it is often overcrowded with sightseers. It was laid out in the 16th century by a Ming official who made the garden to please his father. Only two hectares (five acres) in size, it recreates a wild landscape in miniature, with strange rocks, still pools, running water, meandering paths which offer changing vistas, and small pavilions in which to sit, dream or watch the moon. The garden also has an interesting history as the headquarters of the 'Society of Little Swords', an offshoot of the Taiping Rebellion in the mid-19th century. In fact, this association saved the garden from the destructions of the Cultural Revolution, since the 'Little Swords' were deemed to be early revolutionaries.

The city has some attractive temples, too. In the old quarter, there is the Taoist **Temple of the Town God**, but it is no longer used and stands merely as an architectural curiosity.

In the northwest of the city stands the **Temple of the Jade Buddha** (Yufo Si), named after its two exquisite milk-white jade Buddhas, which were brought from Burma in the 19th century. One of the Buddhas is seated, and the other is recumbent, the latter position symbolizing the Buddha's attainment of enlightenment. It is an active temple. The monks are used to visitors, who may, if they wish, attend the religious services here.

At the western end of the Nanjing Lu is the **Jing'an Temple**, dating back to the last century, when it was popularly known to foreign residents as the Bubbling Well Temple. It has a colourful history, and was once presided over by an abbot who was famous for his rich wife, seven concubines and White Russian bodyguard.

To the southwest of the city, near a small park, stands the **Longhua Temple**, with its seven-storeyed pagoda. The temple was founded in the third century, although the pagoda in its present form dates from the tenth century and the other buildings are all from the Qing dynasty. In a bid to attract tourists, the tradition of holding a temple fair here in spring—the season of peach blossom which can be seen in the adjoining Longhua Park— has been revived.

## CITY SIGHTS: MODERN

Modern Shanghai is largely a product of European colonialism, and much of the architecture, whether civic or suburban, reflects that heritage. The Bund and Xujiahui Cathedral are part of the Western legacy. The **Bund** is probably the most famous thoroughfare in China. Its present official name is Zhongshan Dong Yi Lu, though the Shanghainese call it Waitan. It stretches along a section of the Huangpu River, and is bounded on the other side by a row of colonial buildings. In the 1930s, those buildings housed the offices of foreign trading houses and banks, so the Bund was then Shanghai's equivalent to Wall Street. The same 1930s skyline remains, and appropriately the old Hongkong and Shanghai Bank building, with its broad facade, portico and dome is once again the bank's mainland headquarters after being vacated as the city's Communist Party HQ in 1996.

For all the changes since 1949, however, it is still exciting for the traveller lucky enough to arrive by ship. **Xujiahui Cathedral**, formerly the Cathedral of St Ignatius, is in the southwest of the city. Built by the Jesuits in 1906, the cathedral is still an active centre of Roman Catholic worship.

The port, the largest in China, is worth visiting just to gain an idea of the amount of traffic which flows through it. Shanghai's wharves stretch for 56 kilometres (35 miles) along the shores of the Huangpu River and, unlike the northern ports which

# A Society in Transformation

*For someone visiting Beijing for the first time in six years, the city is virtually unrecognisable. The quiet, tree-lined road to the airport is now a six-lane expressway. New office blocks and luxury hotels have sprung up amid the traditional low-rises, transforming the capital's skyline. Somehow the city looks incomplete. It reminds one of a snake that is in the process of shedding its skin: a sleek new look is emerging, but the old, dry and crumbling skin is still in evidence.*

Similarly, smartly dressed people mingle on Beijing streets with those who still wear the dowdy blue and gray outfits of the Maoist period. Bicycles vie for road space with Daimlers and Mercedes-Benz. The influence of Hong Kong, which provided the capital for much of the new opulence, is much in evidence, even in the language. Taxis are dishi, as they are in Hong Kong. No one uses the proper term, chuzu qiche, or "car for hire."

The biggest change of all has to do with the people. By and large, they are much better dressed, more confident — and much more money-minded. The term xiang qian kan, which ostensibly means "to look forward" but which can also mean "to look at money," aptly describes the national mood. This is evident the moment one arrives at the airport. Unscrupulous drivers try to charge you several times the going rate for a taxi — and curse you when you turn them down.

Also evident from the moment of arrival is the more relaxed mood of the country. Customs officials wave most people through without examining their luggage, while carefully filled forms detailing the amount of foreign currency being brought in, as well as the brand of one's camera, are not even collected.

Everything is now for sale. VIPs who wish to beat the Beijing traffic can rent military vehicles for Rmb 1,200 (US$140) a day — complete with flashing lights — that don't have to abide by traffic rules. And an evening stroll around the five-star Palace Hotel, partly owned by the People's Liberation Army, is not complete without a pimp offering the services of a young lady. According to a person in the know, any staff member who tried to interfere would be beaten up as soon as he stepped off the hotel premises. The tentacles of the underworld stretch into every nook and cranny. Sometimes they are indistinguishable from the long arm of the law because, very often, the two are one.

Just as the Cold War artificially submerged ancient enmities, so had tight control by the Chinese communists led to the virtual disappearance of old vices such as prostitution, drug addiciton and superstition, all of which have now resurfaced. The result is a far from perfect, but more normal, China.

The lust for money is also evident in Shanghai. At the airport, a young lady demands Rmb 9 for a luggage cart, despite a sign in both English and Chinese informing visitors the price is only Rmb 2. Travellers are told by security police, moreover, that check-in luggage must be locked. And, it so happens, those same people sell the locks — at several times their normal price.

For the vast majority of people here, life is without doubt more comfortable than before. Most people have benefited from the economic reforms instituted 15 years ago. Chinese can now afford to go on vacation, a luxury few enjoyed previously. Yet even though life is getting better for most, the pace varies greatly so that the gap between rich and poor is widening. The government, too, knows that there are still 80 million people living below the poverty line — a number larger than the population of many countries.

Traditional practices of all sorts have returned. Fortune tellers are consulted on everything, such as when to open a restaurant, whether to take a trip, and what direction a door should face. Mainlanders have even taken on board Hong Kong's fondness for auspicious numbers. In particular demand is the number eight, or ba, which sounds vaguely like the word for prosperity.

Officials take pride in the fact that their economy is doing so well, especially at a time when others are doing so badly. They are also proud that foreigners, such as Russians, are coming to China to look for jobs. Previously, the flow had been only in the other direction, with Chinese trying to better their lot by getting out of the country. Today, some who have returned after graduating from Western universities find that, in some cases, friends who have remained behind are better off, having become successful business people. Of course, many still want to go abroad, but the attractions of remaining in China are now much greater.

The Communist Party's abandonment of traditional concepts of socialism has led to an ideological vacuum, which accounts to a large extent for the new materialism evident everywhere. Many complain that traditional values, such as honour and respect and helping the weak and the elderly, have been jettisoned in the mad rush to make money. But while the current situation is undoubtedly abnormal and unhealthy, it is merely a reaction to the previous state-imposed straitjacket. Eventually, the pendulum swings will become less wild, and China will become more like other countries, with its own share of problems.

*Frank Ching, Features Editor*
*Far Eastern Economic Review, Hong Kong*
*(This article first appeared in the September 29, 1994 issue)*

ship more than they receive, the bulk of Shanghai's port traffic is incoming. Short rides on the Huangpu, as far as the mouth of the Wusong River (also known as Suzhou Creek), are offered from the Beijing Dong Lu wharf on the Bund.

The **Municipal Children's Palace** is as interesting for its setting as for its child prodigies. The palace is housed in the pre-1949 residence of the wealthy stockbroking family of Kadoorie. The Kadoories left Shanghai for Hong Kong, where today they are of considerable influence in the British colony's business community. Their former mansion is now a centre for children of exceptional abilities, who can pursue their studies or activities with special training facilities. Visitors can see athletic or musical performances given by the children.

For those who cannot resist pandas, even if they are in captivity, **Shanghai Zoo** in the western suburbs is of interest. There are also golden-haired monkeys, which once lived wild in the Yangzi gorges, and rare Yangzi River alligators.

Chinese revolutionary history was made in Shanghai with the founding of the Chinese Communist Party in 1921. The house where the founding members gathered, and the **site of the First National Congress of the Chinese Communist Party**, can be visited at 76 Xingye Lu, just north of Fuxing Park. In the Hongkou district north of the city, you can also find the residence of the writer Lu Xun (1881–1936). He was a pioneer of modern Chinese language and literature. A museum of his life and work can be found in the nearby **Hongkou Park**, where his tomb is placed at the bottom of a bronze statue of the writer.

Shanghai Museum, on People's Square, was opened in 1996 to exhibit one of the country's finest collections of cultural relics. The US$75 million building, shaped like an ancient bronze cooking cauldron, houses prime artifacts from all of China's dynasties.

## SHANGHAI NIGHTLIFE

If you prefer to eat, drink and listen to music, rather than sitting up in the evening with a book and a cup of jasmine tea, then Shanghai is the city for you. It has innumerable restaurants featuring cuisines of nearly all of China's culinary regions. The international hotels now offer anything from saunas and discos to English-style pubs, and the old hotels of the '30s have their own attractions—such as art deco interiors, shabby but grand dining rooms, and billiard tables. The **Dongfeng Hotel**, once the old Shanghai Club, is the home of the Long Bar, which in its day was the longest bar in the world. The hotel is past its best, and now one must go to the **Shanghai Centre** for a replica of the famous Long Bar. The **Peace Hotel** on the Bund features a jazz band which is almost legendary. Astonishingly, when China re-opened to tourism in the late '70s, the band was still able to play music from the '30s and '40s. Its members are said to have practised in secret during the Cultural Revolution, when all forms of Western culture were denounced as decadent.

On most tour group itineraries is the **Shanghai Acrobatic Theatre**. It is certainly worth obtaining tickets for its virtuoso performances of juggling, tumbling and plate-spinning. The local opera performed in the Shanghai region is known as *Yue Ju*. A more melodic relative of the Peking opera school, it has less percussion and more choruses than the northern style. The CITS office in the Peace Hotel can help you with bookings.

# Guangzhou

Guangzhou (Canton) is the capital of Guangdong Province, one of China's richest and—in the river plains—most fertile regions. With a sub-tropical climate, an extensive coastline and a mesh of tributaries of the Pearl River, which forms a rich alluvial delta, Guangdong Province produces an abundance of seafood. Indeed, the amount of fish, meat, vegetables and fruit available throughout the year makes the offerings of a northern Chinese table look poor by comparison. The Cantonese gourmet will eat an astonishing diversity of foodstuffs, some of which will never feature on a northern menu, such as pangolin, dog, snake, monkey, cat or even bear's paw. Such adventurous tastes both impress and appall Chinese from other regions.

The Cantonese have always been considered a distinct group in the Chinese world. All regions of China have their different dialects, but few are so difficult to master as Cantonese, with its imploding consonants and a more complex tone system than that used in the northern dialect of Mandarin or *Putonghua*. Separated from the Yangzi area by an east-west mountain chain and far from the early centres of Chinese civilization in the Yellow River basin, Cantonese culture has been relatively isolated, allowing the province to develop its own identity as well as its own distinctive dialect.

The sea has been part of the same process, endowing the people of Guangdong with their outward-looking and venturesome spirit. The long coastline facing out into the South China Sea, towards the islands of Southeast Asia and the shipping routes to India and the Middle East, means that Guangdong Province has always had better links with the outside world than other parts of China. It certainly has a history of being a conduit for new ideas and religions. Arab traders made their way up the Pearl River to the city of Guangzhou as early as the seventh century, leaving behind small communities of Moslems, with their mosques and imams. What they took away from China was more enduring than the porcelains and silks in their vessels. The Arabs absorbed Chinese ideas and inventions, most of which were ultimately to have a profound impact on the West. The Christian Crusades against the Arabs in the 12th century brought Europe into contact with such inventions as gunpowder, the magnetic

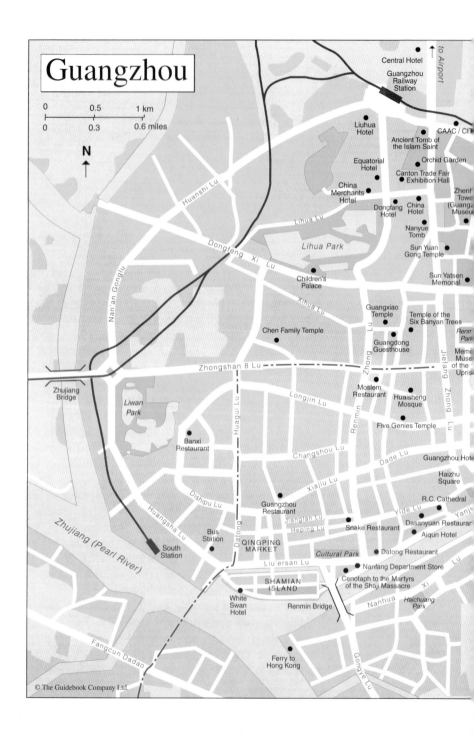

# Guangzhou

| 0 | 0.5 | 1 km |
| 0 | 0.3 | 0.6 miles |

N

*to Airport*

Central Hotel

Guangzhou Railway Station

Liuhua Hotel

CAAC / CIT

Ancient Tomb of the Islam Saint

Equatorial Hotel

Orchid Garden

Canton Trade Fair Exhibition Hall

China Merchants Hotel

Zhenh Towe (Guang Museu

Dongtang Hotel

China Hotel

Nanyue Tomb

Sun Yuan Gong Temple

*Huanshi Lu*

*Lihua Lu*

*Dongteng Xi Lu*

*Lihua Park*

Children's Palace

Sun Yatsen Memorial

*Nan'an Gonglu*

*Xihua Lu*

Guangxiao Temple

Temple of the Six Banyan Trees

*Renm Park*

Chen Family Temple

Guangdong Guesthouse

Mem Muse of the Upris

*Zhong Lu*

*Zhongshan 8 Lu*

*Jietang Zhong Lu*

Moslem Restaurant

*Zhujiang Bridge*

*Liwan Park*

*Longjin Lu*

Huaisheng Mosque

*Renmin Lu*

Five Genies Temple

Banxi Restaurant

*Changshou Lu*

*Dade Lu*

Guangzhou Hote

Haizhu Square

*Huagui Lu*

*Xiajiu Lu*

R.C. Cathedral

*Dishipu Lu*

Guangzhou Restaurant

*Jiangtan Lu*

*Yide Lu*

*Yanj*

Dasanyuan Restaurar

*Huangsha Lu*

*Heping Lu*

Snake Restaurant

Aiqun Hotel

*Datong*

*Zhujiang (Pearl River)*

Bus Station

QINGPING MARKET

*Cultural Park*

Datong Restaurant

South Station

*Liu'ersan Lu*

Nanfang Department Store

Cenotaph to the Martyrs of the Shaji Massacre

SHAMIAN ISLAND

White Swan Hotel

Renmin Bridge

*Nanhua*

*Haichuang Park*

*Xi*

*Fangcun Dadao*

Ferry to Hong Kong

*Gongye Lu*

© The Guidebook Company Ltd.

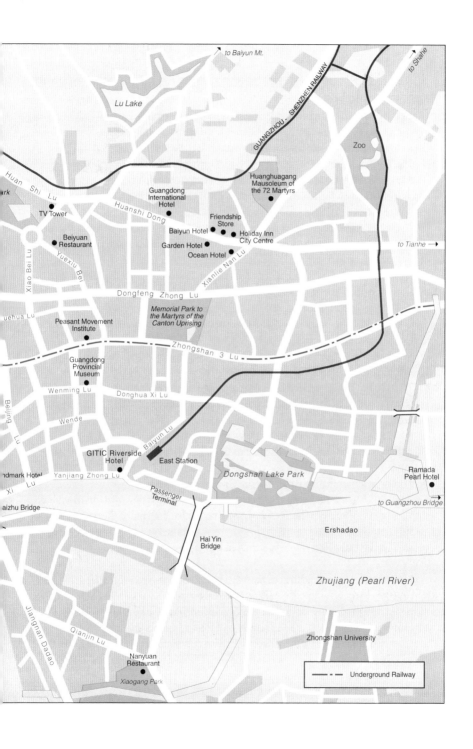

compass, the stern-post rudder and papermaking, all of which had originated in China, unknown to the Europeans who learnt these new sciences from the Arabs.

In economically lean times, the sea has also offered an escape: the waves of emigration of the Cantonese over a long period have resulted in the establishment of Chinatowns in many Southeast Asian, North American and European cities.

In the 15th century, the Portuguese traders who arrived in Guangzhou—guided by compasses which had been invented long before in China—found a wealthy, cosmopolitan city which already had centuries of experience in trading with foreigners. Indeed the Portuguese were shocked that they were viewed as just one more contingent of barbarians who were after Chinese silks and porcelains. English ships came in the 17th century and were followed by Christian missionaries. For a time, these European merchants and missionaries behaved in accordance with Chinese law and customs. The law required all foreign trade to be confined to Guangzhou. But as trade expanded, Western traders began to find this restriction increasingly irksome and started pressing for freer conditions of commerce than were allowed by imperial regulations. Their moment came when they possessed the arms and warships to offer a military challenge to the Chinese: By this time, the British had also established an extensive mercantile empire in India. This was the setting for the arrival of Guangzhou on the stage of international history.

In 1839 the British opened fire on Guangzhou after the British Parliament had voted to go to war in order to sustain its lucrative opium trade with China. This trade in Indian-grown opium had developed as an easy means of exchange for Chinese silks and teas. It was, however, considered pernicious by many Chinese government officials, who persuaded the Qing court to put a stop to the trade in 1839. The British responded by adopting Palmerston's 'gunboat diplomacy'. The subsequent Opium War brought a humiliating defeat for the Qing troops whose weapons and tactics were too outdated to deal with the superior firepower and the highly manoeuvrable ships of the British navy. The Treaty of Nanking, which concluded the war in 1842, opened four other Chinese ports to foreign trade and thus broke Guangzhou's monopoly. By the early 20th century, Shanghai had eclipsed Guangzhou as China's major port.

Nonetheless, the late 19th century was a period of prosperity for Guangzhou. It remained a city of great intellectual and political ferment. By the 1890s, an anti-Qing movement was gathering momentum in Guangdong Province, fuelled by the Qing government's inability to curb the activities of foreign traders and missionaries—activities much resented by the Chinese. This resentment erupted in 1900 in the form of the Boxer Rebellion, which swept over North China and left hundreds of foreigners and Christians dead. The turmoil temporarily masked the activities of anti-imperial revolutionaries in the south. Under the leadership of Cantonese Dr Sun Yat-sen, they were busily forming cells and soliciting overseas Chinese support for their planned revolution. In fact, it was in Guangzhou itself that the October 1911 Revolution, which overthrew the Qing Dynasty, was foreshadowed. In April of that year, an uprising led by anti-Qing activists was defeated by imperial troops at the Battle of Canton. Over 100 young revolutionaries died in the fighting. When the October Revolution came, the city quite peacefully went over to the Republican side, and there was little bloodshed.

Guangzhou was badly damaged and suffered a large loss of civilian life during the Japanese occupation of the 1940s. There was much resistance to the occupation, and many communist-led cells organized sabotage operations in the area. Yet it was only after the 1949 Revolution, when the Communist Party came to power, that political struggle became an everyday reality in Guangzhou. In the 1950s, the anti-landlord movement led to mass executions of peasants who were rich enough to have rented out land or to have employed workers. And in common with other major cities, Guangzhou experienced severe disruption during the Cultural Revolution (1966–76).

Much urban renewal has been accomplished since then, although the city still gives an impression of sprawling untidiness. Still, the shabby, impoverished atmosphere of the 1970s has been converted into a bustle and brashness by the unprecedented prosperity that has come with the economic reforms of the last decade. Guangzhou's great advantage has been its proximity to the former British territory of Hong Kong, which provided the city with an invaluable link to the developed West. With the territory's return to Chinese sovereignty, it remains to be seen whether the link with the new Special Administrative Region of China will remain largely unique to Guangdong Province, or exert a wider, weaker influence.

Almost the entire Chinese population of Hong Kong either migrated from Guangdong Province or are descended from natives of the province. A familiar sight in the early 1970s was Hong Kong people thronging the railway station on the eve of holidays or festivals, scrambling to get to Guangzhou and beyond to visit their relatives. Nowadays the traffic between the capitalist haven of Hong Kong and the communist port of Guangzhou is more hectic than ever. Hong Kong businessmen and manufacturers have relocated entire factories to Guangzhou and its surrounding towns. Many of these factories are in Guangdong's three Special Economic Zones, **Shenzhen**, **Zhuhai** and **Shantou**, which were opened to attract foreign trade and investment, and which offer lower labour costs than in the more developed Asian countries.

*(following pages) A flagstone path leads through terraced rice paddies in the mountains of northern Guangdong Province. Much of the fertile farmland amongst the 11,000-square-kilometre network of the Pearl River Delta to the south, is under serious threat from industrial development*

## City Sights: Traditional

The oldest and least visited temple in Guangzhou is **Guangxiao Temple**. For those with an interest in Zen (Chan in Chinese) Buddhism, the Guangxiao Temple is of great historical significance. It was here in the Tang Dynasty that the Sixth Patriarch of Zen Buddhism, Hui Neng, was initiated into the monkhood. Hui Neng taught that enlightenment can be attained in a flash of illumination, and does not necessarily have to be earned through systematic discipline and study. That doctrine is the core of Zen Buddhism. The temple is also of architectural interest. Despite frequent repairs and rebuilding over the centuries, the Great Hall retains its Song-dynasty dimensions. In the temple compound you can find an early Song iron pagoda, which was originally built for another temple and moved to its present site in 1235. At the entrance to the temple is a small antique shop.

More popular on tourist itineraries, however, is the **Temple of the Six Banyan Trees**, with its nine-storey pagoda, the Huata. Founded in the fifth century, some time after the Guangxiao Temple, it is also associated with the Sixth Patriarch. Its present name dates from the Song Dynasty, when the poet and calligrapher, Su Dong-po, came south to Guangzhou and, impressed by the trees of the temple, wrote two characters meaning 'Six Banyans' as an inscription. The two characters are engraved on stone in the poet's calligraphy, and this tablet (or stele) can still be seen near the temple entrance. Here is also a Song bronze statue of the Sixth Patriarch, as well as several fine Qing brass Buddhas.

An interesting example of an ancestral temple, few of which have survived in modern China, is the **Chen Clan Temple**. Built in the 1890s, it is a splendid example of traditional southern architecture of the late Qing period. Chen (Chan in Cantonese) is a very common surname in the province; members of the Chan family from 72 counties in Guangdong founded this temple to give a proper setting for ancestor worship and Confucian studies. In the moral order expounded by Confucius, education, loyalty and filial duty were all stressed. The spirit tablets of the ancestors are no longer in the central hall at the back, and in fact the clan temple now serves as the Guangdong Provincial Folk Arts Museum, which displays examples of carving on a variety of materials, such as walnut shells, ivory and wood. Carving is the most striking feature of the temple halls: the surfaces of its window frames, doors and pillars are all elaborately decorated with carving and sculpture. Even the eaves and roof ridges are floridly ornamented with clay figurines.

The arrival of the Arabs in the seventh century also brought a new religious centre to the city. The **Huaisheng Mosque** is one of China's earliest mosques, and is believed to have once stood at the edge of the Pearl River. The river has shifted its course, and the mosque now lies in the city centre, just south of Zhongshan Lu on Guangta Lu. It has a fine, plain, stone minaret, known as the Guangta, indicating the early date of the mosque's foundation—most late mosques having small pavilions in place of the minaret. Visitors can climb the minaret for a view of the city.

## City Sights: Modern

In order to gain an impression of how European traders once lived, it is worth visiting **Shamian Island**, a one-kilometre (two-thirds of a mile)-long sandbar in the Pearl River. The Chinese authorities gave the land to Europeans in the 19th century, to be their residential base, along with extraterritorial rights. Once on the island, the Europeans were no longer subject to Chinese law or supervision. Shamian was made an elegant enclave with large mansions, churches, a yacht club and tennis courts. Now the area is far from elegant, though it is an interesting place for a leisurely walk. A five-star hotel, the **White Swan**, with a glass atrium lobby, waterfalls, trees and swimming pool, has been built here and makes a convenient place to relax and enjoy a cool drink.

These days traders from all over the world come annually to the spring or autumn **Canton Export Commodities Fair** sponsored by China's foreign trade corporations. The Fair, established in 1957, used to provide the only opportunity for business exchanges between China and the capitalist West. Today, each session of the fair is still attended by some 30,000 businessmen even though more direct exchanges at factory and provincial levels are now the norm.

For locals, just as much bargaining and trading goes on daily at the **Qingping Free Market**, where over 2,000 stalls sell all sorts of farm produce from fish, meat and fruit to goldfish and Chinese herbal medicine.

Just west of Haizhu Square on Wende Lu lies the **Roman Catholic Cathedral**, open to worshippers again after serving for many years as a warehouse. It was built in granite by a French architect and was consecrated in 1863.

The **Mausoleum of the 72 Martyrs** is a memorial to the young revolutionaries who lost their lives in the Battle of Canton. Donations for the memorial, which was built in 1918, came from patriotic overseas Chinese as far away as Canada and Chile. The mausoleum is constructed in a bizarre blend of styles, with a miniature Statue of Liberty, an Egyptian-style obelisk, and two traditional Chinese guardian lions!

The founding father of the Chinese Republic is commemorated in the **Sun Yat-sen Memorial Hall**, with its brilliant blue tiles. Inside there is a 4,700-seat auditorium used for concerts, operas and other shows.

The city's earliest contribution to communist revolutionary history is remembered in the **Peasant Movement Institute**, which was once the headquarters of such activists as Mao Zedong, who set up a school to educate young cadres. The Institute is housed in a Ming-dynasty Confucian temple, and is therefore both historically and architecturally interesting.

# The Invisible Hand

*Old T'ung-pao felt his being reassert itself. His years had indeed not been lived in vain! It would be a plentiful year. He walked among the tall stalks and caressed them. There would be a four-picul harvest! Sometimes when his fingers felt of the heavy, drooping ears, he half-imagined there might even be five piculs out of every mow. Every ear was so full! He began to calculate the future. No exaggeration to count on four and a half piculs. Surely not. That meant he would be able to reap forty piculs altogether. Six and four-tenths piculs went to the tax collector. He would still have over thirty piculs. Figuring conservatively at ten dollars a picul, that meant three hundred dollars! That would pay off the best part of his debts. He couldn't imagine a price of less than ten dollars a picul! He and all his neighbors would be relieved of their burdens by one good harvest. Heaven surely had good eyes!*

*But while Old T'ung-pao contemplated his grain and his rosy dreams, the rice merchants in town, like Heaven, had eyes in their heads, and their eyes were only for their own profit. Before the rice was even cut, the price began to fall. During the reaping—the villagers were cutting down the fruits of months of toil, and piling their grain in neat stacks—the price in town fell to six dollars a picul. While they were grinding out the grain, the price fell further to four dollars. Finally, when they packed their coarse, plentiful rice into market, they could barely sell it at three! The rice merchants looked coldly at their outraged faces.*

*"That's today's price," they said coldly. "It'll be lower still tomorrow."*

*Debt collectors were busy in the village pursuing their debts. Would they take rice for the debts? Well, yes. The coarse rice at two-ninety. White rice at three-sixty.*

*Old T'ung-pao stood confused and silent amid the ruins of all his rosy calculations.*

Mao Tun, 'Autumn Harvest', 1932

Another incident in communist revolutionary history was the so-called Canton Uprising of 1927. The uprising, led by the Chinese Communist Party, resulted in the establishment of a soviet government, the Canton commune. This took place just before the Kuomintang army pushed northwards to unify the country. The Kuomintang or Nationalist Party was founded shortly after the 1911 Revolution. It ruled China, often in name only, until 1949, after which it established on Taiwan what it claims to be the legitimate government of China. In the early 1920s, the Kuomintang had formed an uneasy alliance with the communists, who then proceeded to infiltrate Kuomintang ranks. The situation was highly unstable, as the radicals and conservatives within the party continued to compete for control of policy. In 1927 the alliance collapsed and Chiang Kai-shek, leader of the Kuomintang, moved quickly to suppress the radicals and communists. In reaction, the Chinese Communist Party in Guangzhou revolted and took over the city with much bloodshed and destruction. However, the Canton commune was just as bloodily crushed, with about 5,000 suspected communist activists or supporters put to death. This event is remembered in the **Memorial Park to the Martyrs of the Canton Uprising**, where local people now go boating or strolling. A fine chrysanthemum fair is held here every autumn.

Botanists and amateur gardeners will also enjoy the **South China Botanical Garden**, the finest of its kind in China. Founded in 1958, it is administered by the Chinese Academy of Sciences and is set in 300 hectares (750 acres)—large enough to find a quiet spot, even in hectic Guangzhou.

Finally, the **Municipal Museum** is worth visiting for three main reasons. It is housed in a Ming-dynasty watchtower, the Zhenhai Tower, built by a general in 1380; it gives a fine view over the city; and it has an interesting collection of historical documents. Even better is the **Nanyue Museum** and **Royal Mausoleum**, with burial treasures from the tomb of a king who ruled here in 200BC.

## OUTINGS FROM GUANGZHOU

Many adventurous travellers explore the countryside of Guangdong Province by bus. This is quite easy to do, since there are now good bus services to the towns and villages. Those with less time to explore by themselves can join a tour to one of the farming centres outside Guangzhou, such as **Dali**. Dali town, formerly a People's Commune encompassing 19 villages, is surrounded by paddy fields, vegetable plots and orchards. Another standard tour from Guangzhou is to **Foshan**, 28 kilometres (17 miles) southwest of the city. Foshan has a famous ceramics industry, and is also well known for its folk arts such as paper-cutting, lantern-making and carving. The town has retained many fine old temples which, like most Cantonese temples, are brightly decorated with roof figures, colourful murals and carved doors. The Foshan Ancestral Temple, dedicated to a Taoist deity, was first built in the 11th century.

An excursion can also be made to **Conghua Hot Springs**, 80 kilometres (50 miles) to the north of the city. If you wish to stay, there are hotels and guest villas on the spot. A bath in the mineral water from the 12 hot springs in the area, which varies in temperature between 30°C (86°F) and 70°C (158°F), is meant to help those suffering from such ailments as arthritis, hypertension and digestive disorders. The resort is set in a pleasant green landscape along the Liuxi River.

Overseas Chinese are sometimes interested in visiting the **former residence of Sun Yat-sen**. The father of the Republic was born in Cuiheng Village, in Zhongshan, in 1866.

Across the Pearl River delta from Cuiheng is **Shenzhen**, the first Special Economic Zone to be established in China. These zones are interesting if you have a desire to see what economic progress is taking place in China today, but Shenzhen has also tried to attract tourists by offering other amenities. Its most successful venture is the 'Splendid China' exhibition. (Visitors to Hong Kong who have only one day to spare for a quick side trip to China will find it well worth their while making that their destination.) Splendid China is a heritage park in which all the most renowned monuments and scenic sights in China are reproduced in miniature. You will see a Temple of Heaven, for example, reduced to a tenth of its real size, or the cliffs of the Three Gorges of the Yangzi River rising just 2 metres above a shallow stream. The exhibits have been made with great attention to detail and authenticity, and laid out in pleasant grounds studded with kiosks selling light refreshments and souvenirs.

Next to this park is the **China Folk Culture Village**, where you will find superb, full-sized reproductions of buildings from all over China, with an emphasis on the minority areas. People from these areas work here and give regular folk dance performances.

# Tianjin

Tianjin (Tientsin), a leading commercial centre on the River Hai in northern China, has municipality status but is not a major destination for foreign travellers unless they are in China on business. A short train- or car-ride from the capital, the city with its large artificial harbour, is the port for Beijing. In recent years it has come to be considered by foreign businessmen as more go-ahead than Shanghai (the other major Chinese port) in its efforts to attract overseas capital.

A European trading community was established here in the 19th century. The Western powers which had been pressing for trading privileges saw Tianjin's importance as the gateway to North China and were eager to gain a foothold in the city. They were able to achieve this at the conclusion of the second Anglo-French war against China in 1858, when the Treaty of Tientsin was signed authorizing the establishment of French and British concessions in the city. From the end of the 19th to the beginning of the 20th centuries, more concessions were given to Japan, Germany, Russia, Austro-Hungary, Italy and Belgium. As a result of these settlements, Tianjin inherited a mixture of architectural styles as well as improved shipping facilities.

Severely damaged by the catastrophic Tangshan earthquake of 1976, Tianjin has had to redevelop its urban infrastructure on a massive scale. Nevertheless, some of the buildings from its treaty-port days have survived, most notably those on the west bank of the Hai River, clustering round the two main throroughfares, Heping Lu and Jiefeng Lu.

Visitors to Tianjin usually go to one of the city's famous **carpet factories**. Woven by hand from painted patterns placed on the weaver's loom, the carpets are made in a variety of patterns and sizes, the most popular still being the classic designs using traditional motifs. The weaver is responsible for interpreting the pattern and matching the colours of the wool to be used. After being woven, the carpets are hand-trimmed with electric scissors to create an embossed effect.

Two handicrafts from the Tianjin region—kites and New Year posters—are famous throughout China. The kites are made in fabric or paper, and are stretched over thin bamboo frames. Designs can range from a basket of peonies to a goldfish. The New Year poster workshops—located outside the city centre, in Hexi district—produce the brightly decorated pictures which the Chinese like to paste up in their homes during the lunar New Year. The posters traditionally feature fat babies, the god of longevity, maidens plucking lotuses (lotus seeds being symbols of fertility), and door gods. After the overthrow of the so-called 'Gang of Four', when Mao's widow, Jiang Qing, and three others were arrested for political crimes, the poster workshops produced jolly pictures of small children sticking knives and spears into caricatures of the famous four. Recently these political themes have disappeared from the posters—perhaps forever.

Tianjin's traditional arts and crafts can be purchased at a recently created **Ancient Culture Street** along the River Hai close to the city centre. The street incorporates the renovated 14th-century temple to the local goddess of fishermen, which contains a folk museum. While exploring Ancient Culture Street, try the famous Tianjin steamed dumplings called *goubuli baozi*. The name means, disconcertingly, 'dogs won't touch them'. Yet despite their name, they are delicious. These *baozi* are also sold in **Food Street**, a complex of 110 restaurants and snack shops in the south of the city.

Businessmen whose itineraries demand extended stays in Tianjin would be advised to make a trip to **Shanhaiguan** where the Great Wall meets the Bohai Sea in a pleasant coastal town. Other such day trips can be made to the lakeland region of **Baiyangdian** to the south, in Hebei Province. Here, tourists make water tours of the lakeside villages, which thrive on fishing, ducks and reed weaving. To the north of the city, within the municipal boundary, is the **Temple of Singular Happiness** (Dule Si), in Jixian district. This Buddhist temple was founded in the seventh century and is famous for the 11-headed Guanyin (Goddess of Mercy) statue. The eastern gate of the temple is the earliest of its kind extant in China.

*Baochu Pagoda, originally built in AD 968 during the Song dynasty, overlooks the city of Hangzhou and West Lake (see map on page 153). Part of Bai Causeway is visible on the right*

*Tianjin docks*

# Cities in a Landscape

## Wuxi

Three thousand years ago two fugitive princes from the north arrived in the area close to the present-day location of Wuxi and settled there. They and their descendants set up a new state and called their capital 'Mei'. In around 200 BC, the town was renamed 'Youxi'—which means 'with tin'—when reserves of the metal were discovered nearby. Later, when the deposits ran out, the city's name was changed to Wuxi or 'without tin'.

Since the seventh century Wuxi has benefited from the fact that the Grand Canal runs through its centre. The Grand Canal was built by the Sui emperor Yangdi to link the north and south of his realm, and to transport grain from the fertile Yangzi valley to the arid north. Visitors can stand on any of the city's many bridges and watch boats pass by, just as they have done for over a thousand years. Yet despite the city's strategic position on the canal, Wuxi did not prosper—as did neighbouring Yangzhou—until the early part of this century. It was then that Wuxi burgeoned as a centre of silk-reeling and weaving (although silk production had long been a major industry of Jiangsu Province, in which Wuxi is located).

The great attraction of Wuxi is Taihu, a lake about seven kilometres (four miles) outside the city. Its expanse of shining water set between soft hills mirrors the sky in all its moods, and fishermen trawl its waters for the fish which play such an important part in the cooking of Wuxi. Along the shores are orchards growing the best of sweet oranges, peaches and Chinese plums. The shallow edges of the lake are harvested for their freshwater shrimps, lotus roots, seeds and water chestnuts. The lotus seeds are ground into a sweet paste for buns or simmered in a sugary soup; the water chestnuts are used in savoury dishes to create a crisp, light contrast to the meat. And beyond the orchards are the mulberry fields, supplying the leaves which go to feed the countless silkworm larvae whose cocoons will be spun into silk thread for the factories of Jiangsu Province.

### City Sights

The **Plum Garden** is a particularly popular place in spring, when thousands of plum trees are in blossom. The best time to eat the plums themselves is in late summer. Another sylvan pleasure is the **Li Garden**, which is modern by neighbouring Suzhou standards. Yet it is well worth seeing, since it contains all the elements of a classical Chinese garden in an idyllic setting.

Chinese visitors to Wuxi invariably come away with one or two *ni ren* or clay dolls, made at the **Huishan Clay Figurine Workshop**. The tradition of making clay figures dates back to the Ming Dynasty. At the workshop, which may be visited, you will find brightly painted figures in traditional round shapes of dozing monks, fat babies and smiling children holding fish, coins or lotus flowers (the symbols of plenty, prosperity and fertility). In recent years, new shapes have been introduced which reveal the influence of Western cartoons. Look out for a Chinese 'Snow White and the Seven Dwarfs', as well as some very blonde nymphs.

Much of Wuxi's surrounding arable land is patterned with groves of mulberry bushes, so it is hardly surprising to learn that there is a thriving silk industry here. Visitors are often taken to the **Number One Silk Reeling Mill** or the **Number One Silk Weaving Factory**. The **Zhonghua Embroidery Factory** is also open to visitors. (During the Cultural Revolution, the traditionally lyrical names of shops and businesses were considered a 'feudal' relic and all factories were renamed by their size, be it Number One or Two, or by some patriotic label such as Red Flag or East is Red. Sadly, these names have stuck.)

## OUTINGS FROM WUXI

**Lake Taihu** has 90 islands in all. The visitor can enjoy them and their related sights either by taking one of the shallow-draught ferry boats or by cruising across the lake in a grander dragon boat (in fact, a gaily decorated barge). **Turtle Head Island** is the most popular destination for pleasure craft on the lake. Here visitors can walk through bamboo groves and paths lined with flowering shrubs, or climb to get a view of the entire lake from **Deer Peak Hill**. Chinese holiday-makers like to savour the peace of the island by finding a quiet spot on the rocky foreshore to read, chat and enjoy a family picnic. The lake is equally popular with government officials from neighbouring cities, who can come for a rest at one or other of the many sanatoriums and government holiday villas built along the shore.

From Wuxi, a trip on the **Grand Canal** can be arranged through the CITS office. This can be either a short three-and-a-half-hour excursion which incorporates a meal on board the boat, or a tour of several days covering 220 kilometres (136 miles) and including visits to Changzhou, Zhenjiang and Yangzhou. Similar tours are offered at all the Jiangsu towns on the Grand Canal.

When first constructed the canal linked the northern city of Luoyang, which the Sui emperor Yangdi chose as his capital, with the southern town of Yangzhou in Jiangsu Province. Later it was extended as far as Beijing in the north and Hangzhou (in Zhejiang Province) in the south. The canal's construction was completed in an astonishing six years, bringing great suffering to the conscript labourers who excavated the canal and lined it with vast slabs of stone. During the six years, bridges were also constructed across the canal and its embankment was paved to make roads. The canal was of economic, political and military importance, ensuring the emperor a constant supply of rice and other products from the river-washed farmlands of the Yangzi basin to the arid lands of the north. It was also important for the speedy despatch of troops to the south. However, the vast public works scheme undertaken by Emperor Yangdi undermined the popularity and finances of the dynasty. The result was that in 618, only one year after Yangdi died, the country was swept by a rebellion bringing the Tang Dynasty to power. Today, the canal is no longer a strategic artery, but it does function as a commercial route. Barges ply between canal cities, carrying agricultural produce and bulk goods expensive to transport by the overworked rail system.

Finally, a day trip to the neighbouring city of **Yixing** is highly recommended, both for its teapots and its tea. The simplest way is by car, as Yixing is only 60 kilometres (36 miles) from Wuxi. Yixing is the home of the famous **Purple Sand Pottery Factory**, where you can see traditional clay teapots being made. The dark, reddish-brown and blue teapots are unglazed, their fame resting on a sophisticated simplicity of form. Older versions of Yixing ware can be seen in the **Pottery Museum**. Modern craftsmen can turn out teapots shaped as pumpkins with a dragon's head on the lid—when the tea is poured the dragon's tongue protrudes! Other designs include small squirrels running across branches carved from the clay sides of the pot, or a handle shaped as a simple twist of bamboo.

# Suzhou

Suzhou is notable for its intimacy of scale as a city and its tradition as a centre for refined garden design. If Hangzhou can be described as a city set within a landscape (see page 152), Suzhou is a series of landscapes set within a city. (The beauty of both cities was extolled in the well-known saying, 'In heaven there is paradise, on earth Suzhou and Hangzhou'.)

A casual stroll around Suzhou will not immediately reveal the gardens; they are hidden behind high walls. The gardens were the creations of scholar-artists, who made their own private, landscaped retreats from the cares of the outside world. They are not simply areas for tending and planting, but are also artistic conceits designed in harmony with rocks, pools, plants, decorative windows, pebble mosaics, walkways and carefully devised vistas. In addition, they are laid out as settings in which to entertain as well as retire, to observe the changing moods of the seasons as well as the light and shade of the passing day.

Suzhou's fame dates back to the Tang Dynasty, when its beauty and affluence were praised in poetry. Yet its origins can be traced to a very much earlier period. It is believed that a settlement was first built on the present city site during the sixth century BC, when the marshlands of the region were reclaimed. From these earliest times, Suzhou was known for its canals, which crisscrossed the low-lying land. The canals had steep humpbacked bridges, under which sailed the river craft which carried the city's traffic. During the 13th century, when Marco Polo visited the city, he claimed the city canals had 6,000 stone bridges. Most of those canals have disappeared with the need to reclaim more and more land for building, so that only 168 of the original thousands of stone bridges are left standing. Nevertheless, Suzhou remains an attractive and graceful city, with its low-eaved, whitewashed houses and tree-shaded streets. In the old city quarters, there is even a flavour of traditional village life, now that the economic reforms of the last decade have allowed families to set up their own stalls, selling anything from dumplings to handmade inkstones.

According to Chinese tradition, Suzhou women are among the fairest of their sisters, and their local dialect is so charming that even a quarrel is attractive to overhear. Suzhou women are also famed for their skill at needlework.

## CITY SIGHTS

The great period of garden-making in Suzhou was during the Ming Dynasty (1368–1644), when it was recorded that the city contained over 250 gardens. Today, it is known that over 100 still remain, but only a handful of the more famous ones have been renovated and opened to the public.

One of the smallest and yet most remarkable is known as the **Garden of the Master of the Fishing Nets** (Wangshi Yuan). A garden was first built here in the Song Dynasty, but its present form and name date from the late 18th century, when the scholar, Song Zongyuan, bought the property. A walk through the garden with its bridges and carefully devised views is particularly rewarding. Some visitors may recognize the Hall for Eternal Spring, which has been recreated in the Metropolitan Museum of Art in New York. A song and dance entertainment is held every evening during the tourist season.

The larger and more open garden known as the **Garden of the Humble Administrator** (Zhuozheng Yuan) is part park and part a restored Ming garden. In the park section, visitors can stroll by the small pond and enjoy hot snacks served at a nearby stall. The classical Ming garden has a pool patterned with islands and bridges, one island of which—the Xiangzhou—is said to suggest a moored boat. In the small enclosed Loquat Garden are a series of decorative pebble pictures.

The oldest extant garden in the city is reputed to be the **Pavilion of the Blue Waves** (Canglang Ting), dating back to the Song dynasty. The garden was

re-landscaped in the Ming dynasty and then destroyed in the Taiping Rebellion of the mid-19th century. It was restored in 1873. The garden has an imposing artificial hill and an open vista to an adjacent, willow-fringed canal.

Another seductively named garden is the **Lingering Garden** (Liu Yuan). With stylized landscapes in an ornamental setting, this large 16th-century garden is famous for its classical round doorways known as moon gates. These and other geometrically-shaped doorways provide natural frames for viewing the plants, pools and rocks beyond. The garden pool is framed by vast rock formations, which create the impression of mountains.

For the connoisseur of rocks, the **Forest of Lions Garden** (Shizi Lin) is a favourite. It was laid out in the Yuan dynasty (1279–1368) under the supervision of the painter Ni Zan, and is thus one of Suzhou's most admired gardens. It has a fine collection of rocks, one of which is so large and eroded that it has small caverns and grottoes through which you can actually walk. Oddly shaped rocks were an indispensable feature of Chinese gardens; they were regarded as aesthetic objects and the most ornamental and coveted ones were those dredged from the bottom of Taihu Lake near Wuxi.

The **Garden of Harmony** (Yi Yuan) is a Qing-dynasty garden which has been modelled on earlier Ming ones. It too has a number of rocks dredged from Taihu Lake, which have been arranged as a mountain frame for the pond. It is interesting to note that this, like other classical Chinese gardens, does not have the dynamic, fluid quality of the Japanese garden. In the Chinese version there is a pleasure in the composed harmony of elements and the appreciation of devised contrasts.

East of the city is the quieter **Plough Garden** (Ouyuan), which is recommended if you want to escape the crowds. This is an important consideration, since in the warmer months the crowds in Suzhou's gardens almost obscure the view. The best idea is to visit the gardens just as they open in the morning or—if you want to take special photographs—go to your guide and see if you can arrange a visit before opening time.

As far as temples are concerned, staying in Suzhou would be incomplete without a visit to the **Cold Mountain Monastery**. This monastery has been immortalized in a Tang-dynasty poem by Zhang Ji, copies of which are painted on fans or carved on inkstones and sold as Suzhou souvenirs. The temple was founded in the fifth century and is adjacent to a small, attractive canal, spanned by a high-arched bridge which is featured in the name of the poem, 'Midnight at Maple Bridge':

> *The moon sets, a crow calls in the frosty air,*
> *Under dark maples and fishermen's lamps, I toss in troubled sleep.*
> *Cold Mountain Monastery stands outside the city walls,*
> *And the chimes of its midnight bell are wafted to my boat.*

The monastery's bell has disappeared and the Ming replacement was taken to Japan and lost. The present bell, cast in 1906, was given by a Japanese Buddhist delegation. Cold Mountain Monastery is also famous for its association with the Tang-dynasty Buddhist monk-poet Han Shan, who stayed here at one time.

Opposite the Lingering Garden, you will find the **West Garden Temple**, designed by the scholar, Xu Shitai, in the Ming dynasty. The main curiosity is a pond where a reputedly 300-year-old turtle lives.

Of the many stone bridges remaining in Suzhou, the most famous lies in the southeast of the city and is known as the **Precious Belt Bridge**. It is over 1,000 years old, built in 816, and it has 53 arches. In its present form, it is a 19th-century restoration of the original. The bridge is so named because an early governor of the city is said to have sold a precious belt in order to raise funds to build it.

The **North Temple Pagoda**, easy to find because of its height, is a prominent landmark of Suzhou. It was built in 1582 and has been restored so that visitors can safely climb up to get a good view of the city. In the central district of the city stand the **Twin Pagodas**, which were built in the Song dynasty. They are all that remain of an earlier Tang temple.

The **Folk Custom Museum** and the **Drama and Opera Museum** are fascinating places to visit for those interested in Chinese culture. The city's old Confucius Temple now houses a **Museum of Stelae** (stelae are inscribed stone tablets). The most interesting of these is a Song-dynasty constellation chart and a Yuan city map, which shows Suzhou as it was in the early 13th century.

In common with several other towns in Jiangsu Province, Suzhou has long been an important centre of silk production; the industry had certainly become highly organized by the 16th century. It is not surprising that the art of embroidery developed too. The **Research Institute for Embroidery**, set up in 1957, is well worth a visit. It has its own museum showing the development of embroidery stitches and motifs, and there is a shop. Some of the most outstanding examples of embroidery show perfect stitching on both sides of the silk, and the reversed image is made to stunning effect. One popular double-sided piece features fluffy white cats with one blue and one brown eye. The Institute regularly accepts commissions to produce portraits by embroidery. The embroiderers are also able copy from photographs.

Suzhou also has a tradition of making intricately carved sandalwood fans, which can be bought at the **Sandalwood Fan Factory**. The fans keep their fragrance for years, and traditionally were dowry gifts.

## OUTINGS FROM SUZHOU

To the northwest of the city is **Tiger Hill**. It is a wonderful sight, with its leaning pagoda, waterfalls, spring, rocks and landscaped paths. The hill was built in the Zhou Dynasty (1027–256 BC) as a burial mound for a local ruler, the King of Wu. Legend has it that a tiger guards the tomb—hence the name of the hill.

For another half-day outing, the **Dongshan** area, 40 kilometres (25 miles) southwest of Suzhou on Taihu Lake, and **Changshu**, about the same distance to the north, both offer a glimpse of rural life. Both places are located in the midst of rich farmland. Several types of crop—including rice, rapeseed and tea—are produced. Changshu also has a thriving lace industry.

# Hangzhou

Although Hangzhou was once an imperial capital in the Southern Song Dynasty (1127–1279), the city is better known as a pleasure resort. Specifically, it is best known for its West Lake, which has been celebrated over the centuries in both song and verse. Marco Polo, who visited Hangzhou in the 13th century, wrote lyrically of the pleasures of the lake and concluded, 'indeed a voyage on this lake offers more refreshment and delectation than any other experience on earth'.

Without West Lake, Hangzhou would have been just another prosperous city thriving on its position as the southern terminus of the Grand Canal, and on its two agricultural industries of tea and silk. But with West Lake, Hangzhou has gained a status not far short of paradise. To quote a much-repeated saying: 'In heaven there is paradise, on earth Suzhou and Hangzhou'. If Suzhou's loveliness as a city of gardens is almost entirely man-made, Hangzhou has little need of artifice to enhance its natural beauty. The city skirts the shore of a wide, shallow lake rimmed by green and gentle hills, on the slopes of which are grown the famous Longjing tea of the region and mulberry leaves for the silkworm larvae.

The modern city is, alas, less prepossessing. It was virtually destroyed during the Taiping Rebellion in the mid-19th century, and underwent extensive modernization and industralization after 1949. Walking around Hangzhou today gives the visitor little idea of the glories of its time as the capital of the Southern Song, a period famous for great cultural achievements. Little remains, too, of its later imperial heritage. It is only when contemplating the lake that one understands why, in the Yuan, Ming and Qing dynasties, Hangzhou was an imperial resort, and why the two famous long-lived Qing emperors, Kangxi and Qianlong, each made six visits to the city.

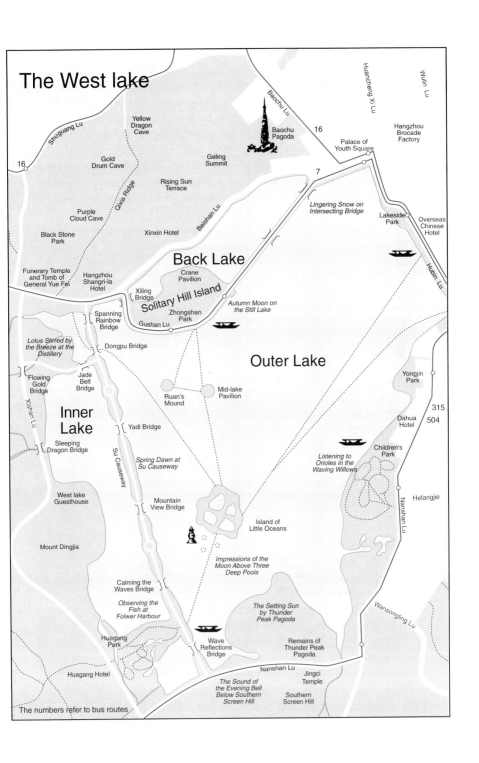

# The West lake

Huancheng Xi Lu

Wulin Lu

Baochu Lu

Shuguang Lu

Yellow Dragon Cave

Baochu Pagoda

16

Palace of Youth Square

Hangzhou Brocade Factory

Gold Drum Cave

Geling Summit

16

Qixia Ridge

Rising Sun Terrace

7

Lingering Snow on Intersecting Bridge

Lakeside Park

Overseas Chinese Hotel

Purple Cloud Cave

Xinxin Hotel

Beishan Lu

Black Stone Park

Hubin Lu

## Back Lake

Crane Pavilion

Funerary Temple and Tomb of General Yue Fei

Hangzhou Shangri-la Hotel

Xiling Bridge

## Solitary Hill Island

Zhongshan Park

*Autumn Moon on the Still Lake*

Spanning Rainbow Bridge

Gushan Lu

*Lotus Stirred by the Breeze at the Distillery*

Dongpu Bridge

## Outer Lake

Flowing Gold Bridge

Jade Belt Bridge

Yongjin Park

Ruan's Mound

Mid-lake Pavilion

315

Xishan Lu

## Inner Lake

Dahua Hotel

504

Yadi Bridge

Sleeping Dragon Bridge

Su Causeway

*Spring Dawn at Su Causeway*

Children's Park

Listening to Orioles in the Waving Willows

Hefangjie

West lake Guesthouse

Mountain View Bridge

Nanshan Lu

Mount Dingjia

Island of Little Oceans

*Impressions of the Moon Above Three Deep Pools*

Calming the Waves Bridge

*Observing the Fish at Folwer Harbour*

*The Setting Sun by Thunder Peak Pagoda*

Wansongling Lu

Huagang Park

Wave Reflections Bridge

Remains of Thunder Peak Pagoda

Huagang Hotel

Nanshan Lu

Jingci Temple

*The Sound of the Evening Bell Below Southern Screen Hill*

Southern Screen Hill

The numbers refer to bus routes

Hangzhou has a rich literary heritage. The city and West Lake have been the setting of numerous folk-tales and scholars' stories. In one tale recorded by a Ming collector of folk legends, Feng Menglong, a white snake maiden, aided by her blue fish maidservant, falls in love with an ordinary mortal during a rainstorm on West Lake. The story ends tragically when the white snake and blue fish are captured by a Buddhist monk, made to revert to their original animal forms, and then imprisoned under a pagoda. The pagoda is said to have been the Thunder Peak Pagoda, which once overlooked the lake from its southern shores but tumbled down in 1924.

This is not the only such tale. In an earlier story, told by a Tang scholar, the Qiantang estuary to the south of West Lake—which once joined it as part of the same tidal basin—was reputed to be the home of a hot-tempered dragon. It is no wonder then that the estuary is famous for its tidal bore, which can reach six metres (20 feet) in height. Such a phenomenon would be easy to associate with mischievous dragons who are known to make their homes in lakes, rivers and clouds.

West Lake's two most renowned literary associations are with the Tang poet, Bai Juyi (Po Chu-yi), and the Song poet, Su Dongpo. They both served as governors of the city, and both were responsible for major earthwork projects designed to safeguard West Lake from flooding. The lake has two major causeways named after the poet-governors who commissioned their building. The causeways now have attractive lakeside walkways, planted with willows and flowering trees.

## City Sights

Many scenic places in China traditionally have a number of famous vistas, and the **West Lake** is no different. Some time in the Song Dynasty, ten 'prospects' were selected for the lake, but their original locations are not known. The sites now designated as the Ten Prospects were marked in the Qing Dynasty, during the reigns of the two emperors—Kangxi and Qianlong— who liked the West Lake so much they each made six visits to it. Fanciful names given to the views were carved on stone tablets and placed at the sites. Today, with the help of a map and a guide, the visitor can still see 'Spring Dawn at Su Causeway', 'Observing the Fish at Flower Harbour', 'Listening to the Orioles in the Swaying Willows', 'Lotuses Ruffled by the Breeze at the Distillery', 'Setting Sun by Thunder Peak Pagoda' (the pagoda has gone), 'Autumn Moon on the Still Lake', 'Impressions of the Moon above Three Deep Pools', 'Lingering Snow on Intersecting Bridge', the 'Sound of the Evening Bell below Southern Screen Hill' (the bell has disappeared, as has the Jingci Monastery in which it hung), and a little way from the lake, 'Twin Peaks Piercing the Clouds'.

The best way to start a visit to the lake is to take a boat from the northern shore to the central **Island of Little Oceans** (from where can be seen 'Impressions of the Moon above Three Deep Pools'). The island is man-made and has been cleverly contrived to enclose four small lakes, which creates the effect of lakes within a lake.

Here a small pavilion serves refreshments, including the famous West Lake lotus root simmered into a sweet broth. Three stone lanterns jutting out of the water close to the island are sometimes lit with candles at night to create the impression of three moons reflected in the water.

The **Su Causeway**, named after the poet Su Dongpo, is an excellent place to stroll and enjoy a view of the lake. Small bridges intersect the causeway, and thus it is sometimes known as Six Bridge Dyke. The causeway is particularly beautiful in spring when the willow, peach, camphor and horse-chestnut trees are in bud and blossom. At the northern end of the Su Causeway is a prospect— 'Lotus Ruffled by the Breeze at the Distillery'. It is here that visitors come in summer to see the deep pink lotus blossoms.

**Solitary Hill Island**, the largest of the lake's islands and easily found near the Hangzhou Hotel, is linked to the shore by Xiling Bridge as well as the famous **Bai Causeway**, named after the poet Bai Juyi. On the island is the **Xiling Seal Engraving Society** where visitors can order a seal carved with their name in Chinese. The **Zhejiang Museum** and its adjacent botanical garden on the island are also worth exploring. Another of the Ten Prospects can be seen from the southeast corner of the island— 'Autumn Moon on the Still Lake'. It was here that Emperor Qianlong of the Qing Dynasty had a pavilion built so as to be able to enjoy the prospect. On the north shore of the lake stands the **Tomb and Temple of Yue Fei**, a popular place to visit for Chinese tourists because of Yue Fei's reputation as a patriot. Yue Fei, a general who served the Southern Song Dynasty, led several successful campaigns against the Jin nomads, who had conquered North China and driven the Song emperor southwards to a new capital in exile at Hangzhou. General Yue Fei incurred the jealousy and distrust of the prime minister, Qin Hui, who had the general murdered in 1141. When Yue Fei's reputation was restored, his remains were interred in Hangzhou and the temple was established.

Also on the north shore of the lake is the slender **Baochu Pagoda** (*see* picture on page 144), which was first built in the tenth century. The present structure dates from 1933. A small adjacent teahouse offers an attractive view over to the south of the lake, where there are the remains of the seven-storey brick **Thunder Peak Pagoda** which fell down in 1924.

Overlooking the nearby Qiantang estuary is the impressive 13 storeyed, dark red, wood-and-brick structure of the **Pagoda of the Six Harmonies** (Liuhe Ta). It was first built in 970 on the site of an earlier pagoda which had served as a lighthouse. The pagoda's name refers to the six codes of Buddhism—to strive for the harmony of body, speech and thought, and to renounce physical pleasures, personal opinions and wealth. Visitors can ponder on these codes as they climb the pagoda for a view over the river.

There are other reflective spots in Hangzhou. Of the several parks in Hangzhou,

*A sign of the general growing affluence amongst the population of China—department stores like this one in Hangzhou stock a wide range of modern consumer goods, from karaoke machines to motor cycles*

the best for gardening enthusiasts is the **Botanical Garden** on the western outskirts of the city. It has a fine medicinal herb section and is in a peaceful rural setting. North of the Hangzhou Hotel are three caves, which are open to visitors: Purple Cloud Cave, Gold Drum Cave and Yellow Dragon Cave. They are crowded on rainy days, when sightseeing below ground becomes an attractive option.

Not far from the Botanical Garden is the tea-growing area that takes its name from the 'Twin Peaks Piercing the Clouds' prospect. Another tea plantation is found on the road past the Pagoda of the Six Harmonies, at Meijiawu. Both cultivate Hangzhou's famous Dragon Well (Longjing) tea. To learn about Hangzhou's other important industry, it is worth arranging a visit to the **Silk Printing and Dyeing Complex** or the **Du Jinsheng Silk Weaving Factory**.

## OUTINGS FROM HANGZHOU

If your plans allow an extended stay in Zhejiang Province, there are several short or day outings to be made from Hangzhou. To the west lies the **Lingyin Temple**, notable because of its woodland setting next to the **Peak that Flew There** (Feilai Feng). The peak is actually a limestone outcrop which, according to a Buddhist monk from India who founded the temple in the fourth century, was a section of Mount Grdhrakuta in India. The Peak that Flew There is famous for its Yuan-dynasty Buddhist carvings, but earlier carvings in the rock-face date back to the tenth century. The open-air teahouse next to it is an excellent place to sit and drink a cup of pale green Longjing tea and look at the Buddhist carvings. The temple buildings have been destroyed several times since its founding in the fourth century; the present ones are restorations from the 1950s. Close to the temple is the Taoguang Hermitage, offering walks through bamboo groves and, at the top of the path, a fine view over the city.

Longer outings from Hangzhou offer a chance to see the neighbouring towns of **Shaoxing** and **Ningbo**. Neither of the towns features on the standard tourist circuit, but both of them are interesting. Shaoxing is only a 70-kilometre (43-mile) ride away from Hangzhou, to the southeast. It is a canal town, surrounded by many lakes, and has old and attractive buildings and temples. Besides fishing, Shaoxing people also live by the town's traditional industry of making rice wine—visitors can ask to go to a tasting at the Shaoxing Winery. Another famous site in Shaoxing is the old home of Lu Xun, the 20th-century writer, and a museum dedicated to him. Ningbo is further—the train from Hangzhou takes three and a half hours. Being a coastal port, Ningbo's fortunes have long been tied to trade and shipping. It was one of the five Treaty Ports established in 1842, and it is one of the 14 coastal cities opened by the Chinese government to foreign investment in 1984. Apart from its seafaring traditions, Ningbo also has a reputation for producing tough mercantile inhabitants who are particularly hardheaded in business. Its most famous son was, however, the Kuomintang leader, Generalissimo Chiang Kai-shek. From Ningbo, there is a steamship service to **Putuoshan** (*see* page 262), an island off the Zhejiang coast, which has one of China's nine sacred mountains.

## Guilin

Guilin is one of China's best-known cities on account of its beautiful landscape of limestone mountains, likened in a Tang poem to jade hairpins. The city has been popular with sightseers for over 1,000 years, and many famous poets and painters have lived and worked here, celebrating its river and mountain scenery.

Once the capital of Guangxi Province (the capital was moved south to Nanning in 1914), Guilin has always been a prosperous commercial centre, profiting from its proximity to the Ling Canal which links the two major river networks of the Pearl and the Yangzi. This canal was built in the second century BC, during the reign of Qin Shi Huangdi, the first emperor of China, who used it to link the middle regions of his empire around the Yangzi with the far south. But central government control of Guangxi was only intermittent, and the province remained a frontier region of the Chinese empire until the time of the Tang dynasty (618–907). Many Guangxi people are not ethnic Chinese. Around 35 per cent of the population are Zhuang, the most populous minority group of the province. However, the land they occupy covers over 60 per cent of the province, and thus the province has been designated a Zhuang Minority Autonomous Region.

# King of the Pedants

When I was twelve, I got a job as a waiter in the Prosperity for All over on the edge of town. The boss said I was too young and stupid-looking to wait on the long-gown crowd in the side room, but he could use me to help out behind the bar. Now the short-jacket crowd was easy to deal with, but even so there were quite a few of them who would run off at the mouth and stir up trouble there was no call for, just because they couldn't keep things straight in their own heads when they ordered.

So I'd ladle the yellow wine out from the big earthenware crock and into a pot, and they'd watch like hawks to make sure I didn't slip any water in. They never felt at ease until they'd seen the pot safely placed in the hot water. Under supervision like that, cutting the wine wasn't easy. And so it wasn't long before the boss decided I wasn't cut out for that job either. Luckily the person who'd gotten me the job had a lot of prestige, so the boss couldn't just up and fire me even if he'd wanted to. And so he made me into a specialist. From then on I would tend to nothing but the boring business of warming the wine.

From one end of the day to the other there I'd be, standing behind the bar. Though I performed my assigned task to the best of my ability, it was downright monotonous. And what with the stern face of the boss and the unfriendliness of the customers, I was never able to loosen up. The only time I could relax a bit, and even have a laugh or two, was when Kong Yiji came around. And that's why I still remember him even now.

Kong Yiji was the only customer in a long gown who drank his wine standing up. A big tall fellow with a scraggly grey beard, he had a face that was pale and wrinkled. And every so often, sandwiched in between those wrinkles, you'd see a scar or two. Kong wore a long gown just like the gentry, but it was so raggedy and dirty you'd swear it hadn't been patched or washed in at least ten years. When he talked, he always larded whatever he had to say with lo, forsooth, verily, nay and came out with a whole string of such phrases, things that you could half make out, and half couldn't. Because his family name was Kong, people nicknamed him Yiji. They got the idea from the first six words of a copybook that was used in teaching children how to write characters: ABOVE—GREAT—MAN—KONG—YI—JI, a string of words whose meaning you could half make out, and half couldn't.

One day he came to the wineshop and all the regulars, as usual, started to eyeball him and laugh. Somebody yelled, "Hey there, Kong Yiji, you've put a few new scars on that old face of yours!"

Without responding, Kong looked straight toward the bar and said: "Warm two bowls of wine and let me have a saucer of fennel beans." He set out nine coppers all in a row.

Someone else kept the fun going by shouting, "You must have been caught stealin' again!"

Kong Yiji opened his eyes wide in indignation and replied, "How dare you, without a shred of evidence, besmirch a man's good name and even—"

"What good name? Wasn't it the day before yesterday I saw you trussed up and beaten with my own eyes?"

Kong's face flushed red and the veins stood out on his temples as he began to defend himself. "The purloining of volumes, good sir, cannot be counted as theft. The purloining of volumes is, after all, something that falls well within the purview of the scholarly life. How can it be considered mere theft?" Tacked onto that was a whole string of words that were difficult to understand, things like The gentleman doth stand firm in his poverty, and verily this and forsooth that. Everyone roared with laughter. The space within the shop and the space surrounding the shop swelled with joy.

*Lu Xun, 'Kong Yiji'(1919), translated by William A Lyell*

Guilin lies along the west bank of the Li River, and was once a walled city. However, widespread destruction during the Japanese occupation in the Second World War, along with a recent modernization and industrialization programme, have left the city drab and undistinguished amidst its mountains. In the 1980s tourists began coming here in increasing numbers, both Chinese sightseers who had been made prosperous by the economic reforms, and foreign visitors encouraged by the expansion of hotels and air services. The city was inundated with tourists, with the result that prices rose higher and higher. So why come to Guilin at all? The answer is simple—its landscape of abrupt mountains amidst verdant river plains still has the ability to refresh and enchant the senses.

## City Sights

The city sights of Guilin are of nature's rather than man's making. However, the small mountains which punctuate the river plain have been embellished with delicate pavilions, winding paths and carvings. It is great fun to climb one of these mountains and gaze out over the city and the **Li River**, where fishermen pole their bamboo rafts through the lazy current while their cormorants dive for fish.

In the city centre, the best-known peak is **Solitary Beauty Peak** (Duxiu Feng), which was once part of a 14th-century palace of the Emperor Hongwu's nephew, Zhou Shouqian. The calligraphy on the peak's rock-face dates from the Tang and Ming dynasties.

Close to Solitary Beauty Peak is **Fubo Hill**, named after a famous general of the Han Dynasty. Halfway up the hill is a cave where the Goddess of Mercy, Guanyin, was worshipped. Fubo Hill has many fine stone inscriptions and carvings; those outside the Cave of Guanyin are attributed to the Qing painter, Li Pingshou.

Another interesting hill, this time with four peaks, is the **Hill of Piled Silk** (Diecai Shan). It offers sweeping views over the Li River and the city to the south. It also has many fine stone carvings, some again from the hand of Li Pingshou. The hill has several Buddhist altars, which were built between the tenth and the 13th centuries.

The small group of peaks which make up **West Hill** (Xi Shan) was once famous for its Buddhist statuary. They are all but gone after Red Guards smashed them in the 1960s. However, when the more popular hills in the centre of town are crowded, this is a good place to wander in quietly and enjoy a view over the countryside.

South of the city centre are two hills which cannot be climbed but are interesting for their resemblance to animals—**Camel Hill** and **Elephant Trunk Hill**. The latter juts out into the Li River at its junction with Peach Blossom River, and at dusk looks extraordinarily like a larger-than-life elephant drinking from the river. Camel Hill is found on the eastern bank of the Li River, past Seven Star Park. The park, so called because of its peaks arranged as the stars of the Big Dipper, contains the attractive

*Cormorant fishermen at dawn, Guilin*

covered Flower Bridge. It is in the environs of the park that you find the **Seven Star Hill** and **Cave**. Underground caves are often found in limestone areas, since the rock easily erodes in water, forming vast caverns below ground level. The Seven Star Cave contains dripping stalagmites and stalactite pinnacles, all illuminated with coloured lights. Other caves worth visiting are Reed Flute Cave, White Dragon Cave (beneath South Creek Hill), and Returned Pearl Cave (beneath Fubo Hill).

## OUTINGS FROM GUILIN

The **Li River** boat trip is undoubtedly the highlight of most people's visits to Guilin. It is not too hard to understand why, for even the most well-travelled visitor finds the quiet, pastoral landscapes along the river enchanting. Setting out downstream just beyond the city (return journeys upstream are also available), the boat passes a landscape of manicured fields shaded by leafy bamboo groves and punctuated with steep, bizarrely-shaped hills. The hills have fanciful names, which are in the Chinese tradition of making a picture when looking at landscapes— Crown Rock, Conch Hill, Jade Lotus Peak and Snow Lion Peak are examples. These limestone or karst formations evolved thousands of years ago, when the area was under the sea. The process of erosion of the rock over a long period created the strange shapes we see today. On the river, you may see the well-known cormorants who fish for their masters.

The boat ride downstream usually stops at the village of **Yangdi**, but the karst scenery can be seen all the way to **Yangshuo** County, a small market town that has been heavily marked by tourism in recent years. When the water level drops in the winter, the cruise may start at Yangdi and go downstream as far as Yangshuo. The stretch of the Li River from Guilin to Yangshuo is 83 kilometres (52 miles). On the way back to Guilin by bus, there is usually an opportunity to stop at the village where the **Thousand Year Banyan Tree** grows. Nowadays, it shelters a mini-market of hawkers' stalls. The village lies at the foot of a limestone peak, and small pigs run amidst the dirt paths alongside hens and children. The tree is an astonishing sight, with its massive spread of branches and house-like trunk.

You can visit the **Ling Qu Canal** by going to the small county town of **Xing'an**. Over 2,000 years old, the canal symbolizes the extent of the military power of China's first dynasty, the Qin, which had its capital at Xi'an, over 1,000 kilometres (620 miles) to the north. The canal joins the two major river systems of the Pearl—which flows into the sea south of Guangzhou—and the Yangzi, which joins the ocean just north of Shanghai. The joining of these two river systems was of great strategic and economic importance. By means of the inland water route, the government could transfer grain from the rice-growing areas to feed the less well-endowed north, while at the same time it could despatch troops to the south to quell the rebellions of the traditionally troublesome minority peoples.

# Expeditions

## Inner Mongolia

The grasslands of China's Inner Mongolia Autonomous Region are relatively little visited by tourist groups. This is a shame, since the region offers some of the most tranquil, undeveloped landscapes in the whole country. With a northwesterly wind blowing off the Siberian steppes, winters are harsh in the region but summers are warm and glorious. From May to September, herds of cattle, sheep, goats and camels roam the grasslands, and Mongolian herders follow their animals, using as a home the decorated felt tents which we know as *yurts*, but which the Mongolians themselves call *ger*.

The Mongolian people are the descendants of the armies of Genghiz Khan, who conquered the entire land mass of Central Asia, from the Caspian Sea to the present borders of North China, in the early 13th century, and who—under Kublai Khan—went on to conquer the whole of China and to found the Yuan Dynasty. Their original homeland was the northeast corner of what is now the Mongolian People's Republic, the highland country sandwiched between the Soviet Union in the north and the People's Republic of China in the south. Known as Outer Mongolia, this vast area was at one time controlled by the Qing empire until, in the early part of the 20th century, it gained independence with Soviet help. The territory remaining within the People's Republic of China—Inner Mongolia—has since been administered as an Autonomous Region. The Mongolian people are thus divided by an international boundary between the People's Republic of Mongolia, and Inner Mongolia within the People's Republic of China.

During the reign of Kublai Khan, Tibetan Lamaism had gained favour among the Mongol aristocracy, and the Mongols remain followers of this form of Buddhism to this day. The influence of this religion can be seen in their arts and temple architecture.

Latent Mongolian nationalism has made the Chinese government acutely sensitive about their northern border, shared with the Soviet Union. In the 1960s, during the Cultural Revolution, the use of the Mongolian language, dress and customs was prohibited. Today, the teaching of Mongolian in schools and universities has been reintroduced, but the Mongolians of China believe their culture is doomed because Chinese is now the language of education—and thus of privilege. They fear the destiny of the Manchus, whose language ultimately became a relic of their nomadic past. Migration of Han Chinese into the territory has diluted the proportion of ethnic Mongolians in the population, who now account for less than 15 per cent compared with some 80 per cent of Chinese.

Most foreign travellers come to Inner Mongolia to visit the high-altitude grasslands and experience the nomadic lifestyle. However, the model yurts laid on for foreign guests are usually situated in pastoral areas which provide permanent winter dwellings for the herders and their families. These are a welcome innovation for the Mongolian nomads, although they do not reflect the hardships of a traditional nomadic lifestyle. On the other hand, this lifestyle has undergone radical changes anyway, as a result of increasing cultivation of forage crops.

There are three such places open to tourists outside Hohhot, the capital of Inner Mongolia. **Xilamulunsumu** can be reached as part of a day trip from Hohhot. Visitors can stay here in yurts specially set aside as a 'motel', complete with washing facilities. The more distant communities of **Huitengxile** and **Baiyinhushao** require an overnight stop. All offer traditional Mongolian hospitality of a yurt 'At Home': butter, tea and mutton ribs. You may also be offered fermented mare's milk and even a Mongolian-style singalong. The Mongolians are enthusiastic singers and, when there are no Chinese around, they enjoy singing of those 13th-century battles when they conquered the Chinese.

A visit to a yurt 'motel' offers you the chance to dress up in Mongolian costumes and pose for photographs alongside tasselled camels. Some travellers prefer, however, to strike out across the grasslands on horseback or by jeep. The rolling hills and

*(opposite page) Inside a yak-hair tent, a Tibetan family's summer home on the grasslands of northwest Sichuan. The fire is fuelled by yak dung, while yak meat hangs from a line to dry and acquire a smoky flavour; (above) Mongolian family outside their tent, known as a yurt*

limitless expanse of undulating meadows may seem monotonous at first glance, but if you travel quietly, you will be pleasantly surprised. You can catch glimpses of wild-fowl bathing in the shallow pools which lie in small hollows. Wild irises grow amidst the grass, and skylarks rise from the pastures, singing into the clear blue heavens. Lone herdsmen watch their flocks grazing, occasionally moving them on with a flick of their lasso whip. Sometimes, by the verge of a track, you will see a white arrow pointing seemingly to nowhere. These are used by.aircraft pilots to help them find their bearings.

## HOHHOT

The present capital of Inner Mongolia was founded in the 16th century by a group of nomads known as the Tumet. The city grew and prospered under the Qing Dynasty, and with the founding of the People's Republic of China in 1949, it was renamed Hohhot—meaning 'Green City' in Mongolian.

The city is not green, but it does have a liveliness imparted by the outgoing nature of its Mongolian inhabitants. City-dwelling Mongolians are hard to distinguish from the Chinese because they wear the same clothes. But the Mongolian is more gregarious and spirited in his outlook on life than his Chinese cousin.

The history of the region is well documented in the **Museum of Inner Mongolia**. The museum cannot be missed, since a white statue of a prancing horse rises from its roof. During the Cultural Revolution, Chinese officials turned the statue so that it faced Beijing. Now the statue once again faces north towards the grasslands.

Popular on tour itineraries is a visit to the **Tomb of Wang Zhaojun**. Wang Zhaojun was a Han-dynasty princess who, in the first century, was married off to a barbarian chieftain to seal an alliance. Most Chinese consider her marriage an act of self-sacrifice—a potent reminder of how the Chinese have traditionally viewed their nomadic neighbours.

The Mongolians adopted the Tibetan Buddhist faith in the Yuan dynasty, and Inner Mongolia had many fine lamaseries before the Cultural Revolution. Some of those damaged lamaseries are now being restored. Of particular interest in the city is the **Dazhao Lamasery**, founded in the 16th century. Nearby, the **Xilitu Monastery** is the home of a Living Buddha. The man who was designated as the present incarnation of the Living Buddha is sometimes introduced to foreign journalists.

For many, the most attractive sight of Hohhot is the **Five Pagoda Temple** (Wuta Si). In fact, it is not really a temple but just a stupa with five small stupas on its roof, which was once part of a long-destroyed monastery. The main stupa contains the Buddhist treasure of the Diamond Sutra, written in Mongolian, Tibetan and Sanskrit. A wealth of finely worked carvings cover the exterior of both the main stupa and the five roof stupas.

Inner Mongolia has a large community of Chinese Muslims (known as 'Hui'). Their **Great Mosque** (Qingzhen Si) of Hohhot is open to visitors. It was built in the 17th century and, like all late mosques built in China, it has no minaret. In imperial times there was an order for minarets to be replaced by pavilions, in which were placed inscriptions reminding the Muslims of their loyalty to the emperor.

In the eastern suburbs of Hohhot stands a rare piece of architectural history. The **Wanbuhuayan Pagoda** dates from the tenth century and has survived with little change, despite a series of renovations over the centuries. The pagoda is a beautiful brick and wood structure in seven storeys.

## BAOTOU

Baotou, Inner Mongolia's only major industrial centre, is very much the creation of the town planners of the 1950s. It is the site of major iron, steel and coal industries. Located to the west of Hohhot and connected to it by railway, the city offers very little for the sightseer, but beyond the city are several interesting destinations.

A two-hour bus ride into the Daqing Mountains takes you to the **Wudang Monastery**. (A more expensive, and rather more comfortable, option is to hire a jeep for the day.) Once one of the most important lamaseries of the region, this monastery is still an important spiritual centre for Mongolian Buddhists today. It is a Tibetan-style lamasery of the Yellow Hat sect, and it is said to have been modelled on the Potala Palace in Lhasa. In the main halls are richly coloured murals dating from the late-18th century. The largest monastery in the region, it encompasses accommodation for monks and continues a tradition of Buddhist festivals and ceremonies, sending monks out to pray for rain when the grasslands are dry.

South of Baotou is the **Tomb of Genghiz Khan**. Since he is father of the Mongolian people, his tomb has become a focal point for Mongolian festivities. In spring every year, a *suduling*, very similar to the Highland Games in Scotland, is held near the tomb. Young Mongolian men gather to test their prowess in the skills of wrestling, spear-throwing and riding.

From Baotou, visits to a part of the **Ordos Desert** can be arranged. The tours take visitors to a place known as **Noisy Sands Bay** (Xiangshawan), where the sands have such a high metallic content that they literally rumble when you slide across them.

*(following pages) Monks in Inner Mongolia*

# The Silk Road

Beyond the western fringes of China stretch the gravel and sand deserts and barren mountain ranges of Central Asia. This vast expanse of barely inhabitable land was once home to nomadic tribes and small pockets of settlers, who farmed the land wherever oasis springs watered the earth. Depending on their own military strength and organization, these tribes were sometimes able to pose a considerable threat to the border regions of the Chinese empire. In the second century BC, the Han emperor—as a defensive measure against further incursions by some of the nomads—sent large expeditionary forces into Central Asia to find allies among other tribes to help him in his border campaigns. It was through such diplomatic activity and contacts that Chinese influence was extended westwards. The power of the Han dynasty brought an era of stability to those Central Asian lands—and from this balance of forces arose the opportunity for establishing that great trade route known as the Silk Road. In fact, the route from the settled lands of China to the **Karakoram Mountains**, which separate the modern borders of China's Xinjiang Uygur Autonomous Region, Kashmir and Pakistan, was well known to a few intrepid traders of even earlier times. The Chinese love of jade, much of which comes from the Karakoram range, made the hard journey across the deserts and mountains worth the effort for the high premiums paid in the palaces of China. By the time of the Han Dynasty, it was Chinese silk—prized in the noble homes of the Near East and the Roman Empire—that gave the major impetus to the development of the routes which we now call the Silk Road. The Road was in fact a chain of caravan trails, reaching north across the Gobi Desert, west across the Taklamakan, then as far south as present-day India and Iran, before leading to Antioch on the eastern shores of the Mediterranean. China controlled these trade routes to the west, while drawing in great wealth.

Along with trade came travellers—and with them, ideas. The Silk Road may have seen the exchange of small but precious gems, porcelain, furs and silk, but in the long term the greater exchange was of science, religion and art. In the Han dynasty, the Silk Road brought Buddhism to China, and by the Tang dynasty, Islam, Nestorian Christianity and Zoroastrianism were to find roots in Chinese soil. The two latter faiths never flourished beyond the Tang dynasty, but Islam was to grow to be a major force in Chinese culture, particularly in the areas spanned by the Silk Road. It remains the dominant religion in Xinjiang.

The modern traveller, journeying through regions which were once part of the Silk Road, will find it easy to conjure up images of those early wandering imams and monks, bringing their faith to Central Asia's oasis towns. Large communities of Muslims continue to flourish, and vast Buddhist cave shrines mark the passage out from China to the beginning of the Taklamakan Desert. But it should not be forgotten that

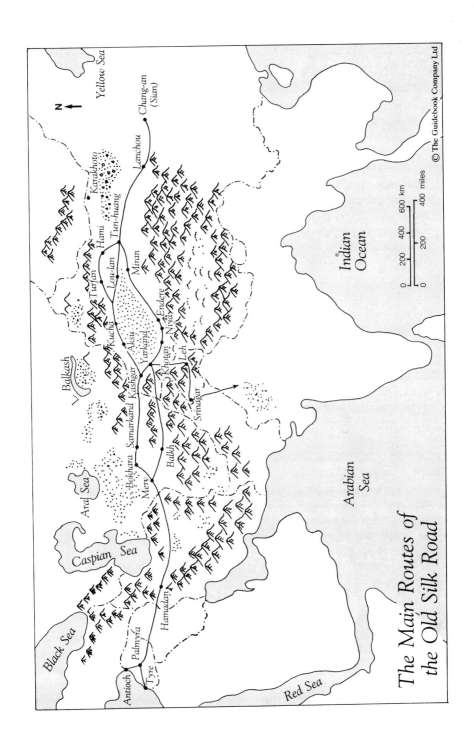

# The Main Routes of the Old Silk Road

it was along this route that the Chinese inventions of the compass, gunpowder and paper were carried westwards—inventions which were eventually to unleash the forces which would bring about the demise of the Silk Road. Advances in navigation first made by the Arabs, and later by the Iberian nations of Spain and Portugal, were to lead to a flourishing maritime trade with China. And it was this opening of the sea routes that in turn brought ruin to the oasis kingdoms and cities built on the wealth of the caravanserai.

Today, a journey along the entire length of the Silk Road is more feasible than at any other time since the 1930s. Within China, betwen Xi'an and Kashgar, scores of cities, towns and counties directly on the Silk Road have opened up to foreign travel. Moreover, land borders previously closed between China and the USSR, are now open crossings between China and Kyrgyzstan. Beyond, travel into Uzbekistan is totally welcomed, while crossings into Iran are expected to be possible soon. While it would be optimistic to say an unbroken overland odyssey to Turkey is possible, it is quite within the bounds of reality, especially for the determined with visa-hunting time, to go most of the way. Others may be forced to take to the air. Such is the challenge of Silk Road travel in the late 1990s.

## FROM XI'AN TO LANZHOU

Xi'an (see also page 79), formerly Chang'an, marked the traditional starting point of the Silk Road in the journey to the west. Modern Xi'an is much smaller than it was in the Tang dynasty, but it still holds reminders of its former glory. The **Shaanxi History Museum** has many treasures of Silk Road days—Tang figurines depicting hook-nosed merchants from Western Asia, steles with Nestorian Christian inscriptions, and coins from as far afield as Greece.

In tracing the Silk Road, many modern travellers choose to fly or take the direct train from Xi'an to Lanzhou, the capital of Gansu Province and the best place to begin an organized tour of the Silk Road. However, for the visitor with time to spare, a series of train and bus trips between the two cities is recommended because of the wealth of archaeological sites which can be visited en route. The journey yields as many side-trips as the traveller can afford—to the small towns along the route to Lanzhou, and to the southern grasslands of Gansu where Tibetan and Mongolian communities of herders live interspersed with the Hui (Chinese Muslim) people.

**Xianyang** is the site of the capital of the Qin dynasty which unified China in 221 BC. The Afang palace of the first emperor has been excavated, but little now remains. We are left only with the descriptions of its grandeur recorded in the Shi Ji, a history compiled in the Han dynasty. It is said that the megalomaniac Qin emperor had replicas of the palaces of his defeated rivals built within his own palace, and brought artifacts from the conquered states to be used in his own household. Indeed, in the exca-

*(preceding pages) A golden eagle perches on the arm of a Kirghiz horseman. Each autumn in western Xinjiang, groups of Kirghiz men like this set out in hunting parties. Their eagles and falcons are trained to hunt for animals like gazelles, foxes and rabbits*

vations at Xianyang, coins from the distant southern state of Chu were uncovered.

West of Xi'an lies **Baoji**, the home of the early Zhou-dynasty culture. For those interested in the extraordinary bronzes of this era, the Zhou Yuan Cultural Relics Exhibition Hall should be visited.

A once important city for Silk Road traders, Baoji is now a major rail junction. The city, set on the banks of the River Wei, has a quiet and prosperous air. Its most striking sight is the Ming-dynasty **Jintai Monastery**, built high on a hill overlooking the city and the surrounding mountains. In the monastery is a stele carved in the calligraphy of the famous scholar-general Cao Cao, a prominent military leader during the Three Kingdoms period. This general was the ruler of the state of the Northern Wei from 220 to 265, and is famous for his poetry as well as his calligraphy. The inscription in the Jintai Monastery is in the 'melon-skin' style (and barely legible even to the Chinese).

**Tianshui** is the first town you reach after crossing the border between Shaanxi. and Gansu provinces. Famous for its carved lacquerware, the town has been little touched by modern development schemes. It is here that the traditional one-storey houses and memorial arches so common in 19th-century cities can still be seen. Tianshui was the birthplace of Li Guang, the famous 'Flying General' of the Western Han dynasty. He was sent by his emperor to fight the Huns (Xiongnu) of Central Asia, and helped bring peace and prosperity to the region. His tomb, where only his possessions could be buried after his death in battle, can still be visited.

Just beyond the city of Tianshui is the major Buddhist cave complex of **Maijishan**. The name, which means 'Wheat Rick Mountain', refers to the shape of the small mountain, which rises in a blunt-ended cone of soft yellow stone. Maijishan is one of the five most important Buddhist cave centres, the others being Yungang in Datong, Longmen at Luoyang, the great Dunhuang caves also in Gansu, and Dazu in Sichuan (*see* also pages 87, 178, 204). Many of the caves are almost inaccessible, but the outer face of the mountain is carved with magnificent Buddha images. The interior of the caves is decorated with frescoes and clay statues.

A few miles to the north of Maijishan rises **Xianren Cliff** (Immortal Cliff). Many of the carvings here date back to the fifth century. Within the caves there is an eclectic mix of statues: Buddhist and Taoist figures as well as Confucian sages stand side by side.

Northwest of Tianshui, on the northern bank of the River Wei, stands a whole complex of caves and temples. These caves, situated in Wushan County, are little visited and floods sometimes cut off access. On one cliff face, known as **Lashao Temple**, are carved the three figures of the Sakyamuni Buddha and his two disciples. The Buddha is sitting serenely in the lotus position and his two disciples stand on either side, holding lotus blossoms. These carvings were originally painted and some of the colours still remain. Beneath the Buddha's feet is a series of bas-reliefs featuring strange animals, some of which bear a close resemblance to the carved lions seen in Persian sculpture.

Sprawling along the banks of the Yellow River, Lanzhou, the capital of Gansu Province, is an industrial centre for the northwest. The city's main attractions are the treasures in the **Gansu Provincial Museum**. It is in this museum that the visitor can find the famous cast-bronze flying horse which was sent on a cultural tour of major world capitals in the 1970s. The horse, a magnificent representation of the new breed of horses that had been brought along the Silk Road from Ferghana (Uzbekistan) to the Han court of China, dates from the second century. The Ferghana horses had greater speed and stamina than the native breeds, qualities which made them extremely valuable. The bronze sculpture vividly portrays the speed of the Ferghana steed, with its flared nostrils, windswept mane and tail, and one of its hooves poised on the back of a flying swallow. Fine examples of Neolithic pottery, known as Yangshao ware, are also in the museum, along with Zhou ritual bronzes and a reconstruction of a Han tomb.

## Expeditions from Lanzhou

**Binglingsi** is an important Buddhist cave complex dating from the fifth century and added to for the next 1,500 years. It lies upstream on the Yellow River from Liujiaxia Dam, which is 70 kilometres (43 miles) southwest of Lanzhou. Between spring and autumn, when the water level of the river is high enough, you can get to it by taking a two-hour boat ride from the dam. The hundreds of caves with their statues and frescoes depict the life and works of Buddha and his disciples. Some of the carvings show Indian influences. When the dam was built, the lower-level caves were submerged although the best statuary was saved and moved to higher sites.

The **Labrang Lamasery** is one of the most important Tibetan Yellow Hat Sect monasteries in China. Situated southwest of Binglingsi, close to the small town of Xiahe, it is the focal point of the local Tibetan community. Labrang was founded in 1709 under the patronage of the Qing Emperor Kangxi. It became an important centre of worship and religious instruction due to the continued benefaction of the Qing emperors, who were much attracted to the Buddhist faith. Labrang is also the home of a Living Buddha—believed to be a reincarnation of a Bodhisattva returned to earth to teach. Labrang now houses 1,000 lamas, but previously it had more than 4,000. Originally, too, it owned most of the surrounding farmland, but the communist regime confiscated the land and destroyed part of the monastery. Since the lamasery is an important spiritual site, it maintains the traditional calendar of Buddhist festivals. It is likely that visitors will see part of the religious life of the lamasery and, if lucky, may even see one of the great debates held publicly by the lamas. At New Year, the lamas perform demon mask dances to usher in good fortune for the coming year.

Xiahe itself offers a glimpse into a semi-nomadic Tibetan community which lives by farming and herding. Many of the small traders in the town are Muslim, though they sell the paraphernalia associated with Tibetan lamaism such as prayer wheels and sutras.

On the road to the Labrang Lamasery lies the small town of **Linxia**, the capital of the Hui Autonomous Prefecture. The Hui people are Chinese Muslims, whose ancestors adopted the faith during the Tang dynasty when Arab and Central Asian merchants travelled to, or even settled in, China. As a reminder of the region's Arab connections, the tomb of an Arab missionary stands on the summit of a local hill. In Chinese, the imam was known as Han Zeling, but his Arab name is believed to have been Hamuzeli. The Dongxiang minority people also live in this area. They too are Muslims, like the Hui, but their bright blue eyes and aquiline noses betray more Western antecedents. Linxia is a lively town with a muted Han Chinese presence. Numerous teahouses, restaurants and small shops line the narrow streets. Here you can try sanxiangcha (three-flavoured tea), a delicious blend of green tea, rock sugar and 'dragon eyes' (the fruit known most widely as 'longan'), or browse among the carpets, prayer mats, knives and Tibetan jewellery offered for sale. From the top of Wanshouguan, a Taoist temple built in the Ming Dynasty and recently restored, there is a sweeping view of the town's 20-odd mosques.

## FROM LANZHOU TO URUMQI

After leaving Lanzhou, the inhospitable nature of the old Silk Road and surrounding landscape becomes increasingly evident. To the south lie the barren slopes of the Qilian range; to the north, the Gobi Desert stretches beyond the western limits of the Great Wall. The winds in this region are fierce. Crops are grown in the crevices of flat stones laid out across the fields to keep the earth from blowing away. Except where streams and springs give life to patches of vegetation, the land is bone-dry. With a little imagination, the modern traveller can readily understand the difficulties faced by the Silk Road merchants who travelled by foot with a camel caravan. Today, train and bus make the journey far easier.

After the railway leaves Lanzhou, it turns northwestwards towards **Wuwei**, a city in the Gansu or Hexi Corridor. It was at Wuwei that the famed Flying Horse of Gansu was discovered. Continuing westwards, the track reaches **Jiayuguan**, the pass which marks the western limit of the Ming Great Wall (*see* special section on Great Wall pages 289–304) . Many people break their train journey here to see the Ming fortress, built to guard the strategic pass between the Qilian Mountains to the south and the Black Mountains to the north. It is also here that some of the earliest segments of the Great Wall can be seen. Much of the wall, which has crumbled to an undulating earth mound, dates back to the Han dynasty and bears no resemblance to the Ming sections which can be seen north of Beijing.

From Jiayuguan, the journey to **Dunhuang** is usually by bus or train. However, visitors on a tighter schedule fly in, as Dunhuang does have an airport.

The Buddhist caves of Dunhuang are one of the Silk Road's most impressive landmarks. Located at **Mogao**, which is served by a twice-daily bus service from Dunhuang, the caves are found in the Minsha Hills 25 kilometres (16 miles) away. Although the caves were first worked in the fourth century, no carvings from that era have survived. The earliest caves that can be seen date from the fifth century. Monks and craftsmen lived and worked in Dunhuang for over four centuries, and the many caves reflect the changes of style during that period.

Besides carvings, the caves also contain numerous murals. The early frescoes, dating from the Northern Wei dynasty, take their theme from the Jataka stories of Buddha's life. The execution is dynamic, with swirling clouds and apsaras (Buddhist angels) trailing floating ribbons. This was to give way later, during the Sui dynasty, to paintings which show a greater stillness of composition. These paintings include fewer illustrations from the Jataka tales and more serene iconographic Buddha and Bodhisattva figures.

In the early 1900s, a succession of orientalists came and carried away thousands of the paintings and documents stored in the caves, among whom were Sir Aurel Stein (whose collection can be seen in the British Museum in London and the National Museum in New Delhi) and Paul Pelliot (who took his finds to Paris).

Close to the caves is a small, sickle-shaped lake, set amidst sand dunes. A walk to the **Crescent Moon Pool** makes a refreshing break after the dark interiors of the cave.

Northwest of Dunhuang, the railway crosses into the **Xinjiang Uygur Autonomous Region**, an extensive territory sharing international boundaries with India, Pakistan, Afghanistan, Tajikistan, Kyrgyzstan, Kazakhstan, Russia and Mongolia. The oasis town of **Turpan** (pronounced *Tulufan* in Chinese), on the railway line to Urumqi, is an extraordinary contrast to the barren gravel desert on all sides. Where the line of fields and trees ends, the desert begins with a brutal abruptness. An important way-station on the northern section of the Silk Road, the Turpan oasis was a centre of Buddhism in the early centuries. Later, as a result of migrations by the Uygur people, the region came under the influence of Islam. Making up the largest ethnic minority group in Xinjiang, the Uygurs are a Turkic-speaking people originally from Siberia. In the tenth century they adopted Islam.

Turpan, lying in a depression well below sea level, has extremes of temperature which can swing from a high of 43°C (109°F) in summer to a low of -32°C (-26°F) in winter. The water for Turpan comes from underground channels, which bring the snowmelt from the nearby Tianshan range. This system distributes water from the base of the mountains along channels that slope less than the geographical depression, thus

*Murals from the Mogao Grottoes, Dunhuang*

# No Way Out

During the long summer Turfan is undoubtedly one of the hottest places on the face of the earth, and the thermometer registers around 130° Fahrenheit in the shade, but it is not hot all the year round and in winter the temperature falls to zero Fahrenheit. The heat is accounted for by its geographical location, which is in a depression watered by no river of any size, and lying below sea-level. Between May and August the inhabitants retire underground, for the mud or brick houses, even though they have deep verandahs and spacious airy rooms, are intolerable by day. In each courtyard there is an opening which leads by a flight of steps to a deep dug-out or underground apartment. Here are comfortable rooms and a kang spread with cool-surfaced reed matting and grass-woven pillows which help the people to endure the breathless stagnation of the midday hours; they eat and sleep underground and only emerge at sunset. The shops, which have been closed during the hot hours, are opened by lamplight, and all necessary business is done then, but people avoid the living and sleeping rooms of their houses because they are infested with vermin. There are large and virulent scorpions which creep under sleeping-mats, drop on to the unconscious sleeper from the beams or hide themselves in his shoes. One jumping spider with long legs and a hairy body as large as a pigeon's egg leaps on its prey and makes a crunching noise with its jaws. Turfan cockroaches are over two inches in length, with long feelers and red eyes which make them a repulsive sight. All these creatures know how to conceal themselves in sleeping-bags and rolls of clothing, so that man is handicapped in dealing with them. Apart from these virulent monsters, the inns provide every variety of smaller vermin such as lice, bugs and fleas, and each is of an order well able to withstand all the patent nostrums guaranteed to destroy them. On account of these pests the people of Turfan sleep on wooden beds in the courtyards, but the constant watering of the ground results in swarms of mosquitoes, which torment the sleeper almost beyond endurance.

Mildred Cable, The Gobi Desert

ensuring that the water flows closer to the ground by the time it reaches the town. In the fields surrounding Turpan are grown sweet grapes and the famous Hami melon. Some of the grape harvest is dried in the open in the town (Turfan's seedless white raisins are exported). Besides raisins, the brightly-coloured fabrics worn by Uygur women and Moslem caps are also found in the main market of the town. Small restaurants on either side of the market serve mutton kebabs, rice pilaf as well as pastries and noodles. Behind this area is a sheep and goat market.

One of the city's most famous sights is the **Emin Minaret** at the Suleiman Mosque, founded in the late l8th century. This circular minaret, built in the Afghan style of unglazed mudbricks arranged in bold geometric patterns, is much photographed.

Beyond the city rises the **Flaming** or **Fire Mountains**, whose deep-red rocks absorb the sun's heat and create furnace-like temperatures. Travellers walking in the mountains have found the soles of their shoes melting in the heat. Set amidst these mountains is the Buddhist cave centre of **Bezeklik**. The complex is also known, like many others on the Silk Road, as Thousand Buddha Caves. Carved between the fifth and l4th centuries, they have been very badly damaged, but some fine Tang frescoes have survived.

Turpan is close to the ruins of two ancient cities which were abandoned when trade along the Silk Road fell into decline at the end of the Yuan dynasty. **Gaochang** (Karakhoja) was a first-century walled city of which very little now remains save for massive crumbling walls and foundations. The cemetery of Gaochang, known as **Astana**, has had some of its tombs excavated, one of which—from the Tang dynasty—contains fine murals. The smaller abandoned city of **Jiaohe** (Yarkhoto) has an incredible setting on the top a cliff, an island at the confluence of two rivers.

**Urumqi**, the capital of the Xinjiang Uygur Autonomous Region, has no historical connection with the Silk Road. However, it is an important transportation hub for modern travellers. Xinjiang has 11 airports, the highest number for any region in China, and so travellers can choose to reach the more remote destinations by air in preference to road journeys, which can be dusty, hot and tiring, not to mention time-consuming. Most travellers make an air connection to Kashgar (known as Kashi in Chinese), which is the westernmost city within China's borders. Kashgar is the starting point for the trip along the Karakoram Highway to Pakistan.

The city of Urumqi is modern and, by and large, wholly lacking in attractive architecture—except for a few sections where traditional Russian design has survived. Its standard government offices and cinemas were built in the 1950s by the People's Liberation Army Construction Corps. Though Urumqi may have a uniformity common to most major Chinese cities, its inhabitants are widely dissimilar. The majority of the people in Xinjiang are Uygurs and Khazakhs. Uygurs are Muslims, but

*(following pages) Riders show off their steeds in a horse market, part of the huge Sunday bazaar just outside the town of Kashgar—an ancient oasis town on the Silk Road*

they are also well known for being heavy drinkers, and street brawls in Urumqi are quite common. The Uygur men dress like most of the Han Chinese, but Uygur women cut a more colourful figure, with braided hair, veils and bloomers peeping out below their dresses. There is little to see within the city, but the **Xinjiang Regional Museum** contains an interesting exhibition of the region's early history and much material on the ethnic minorities. From Urumqi, most visitors take trips to the surrounding mountain ranges.

## Expeditions from Urumqi

The most popular, and perhaps the most overrated of these, is to the **Tianshan** (Heaven Mountain) and the **Tianchi** (Heaven Lake). The journey up into the cool alpine meadows of the Tianshan is a welcome relief after the heat of the desert, but the trip is crowded on weekends and holidays, so be warned. Cruises on the lake, which lies some 1,900 metres (6,300 feet) above sea level, are available.

The day-trip to the **Nanshan** (Southern Mountains) is a more attractive alternative, since fewer people make the journey. The Khazakh people live amidst the mountain pastures. They enjoy equestrian sports and are often quite happy to put on a display of local polo. Tour group visitors are usually invited into the local yurt for a meal of home-baked bread, cheese and mutton kebabs.

The newly completed Urumqi-Moscow railway started passenger service in late 1991. Travellers with valid USSR visas can buy tickets in Urumqi.

Rising in the Tianshan Mountains, the Yili River gives its name to the Yili Kazakh Autonomous Prefecture, with its capital at Yining. An interesting side-trip can be made from Uxumqi to **Yining**, not so much for any Silk Road associations but because it has flourished in recent years as a result of increased trade across the Chinese-Soviet border. The city was opened to foreign visitors only in 1990, and is accessible by either bus or plane from Urumqi. A frontier atmosphere still clings to Yining, which is 60 kilometres (35 miles) from the international border. Many of the buildings are constructed in Russian style, and painted in colours not often seen in Chinese cities. Khazakh herders live mainly on the grasslands surrounding the city. As one would expect in a pastoral community, yogurt and cheese are widely available. The Kazakhs like a hard goat's cheese called *kurut*, which is available in the markets; and yogurt as well as a home-brewed beer made from honey and wheat is sold from ubiquitous refrigerators around the city.

## From Urumqi to Kashgar

Along the northern fringe of the Taklamakan lies **Kuqa**, formerly an important trading post along the Silk Road. The old city, centred on the main mosque and bazaar, retains much of the flavour of medieval Central Asia. Small teashops serve *qwxira*, a spicy soup of dumplings made with mutton, turnips and red peppers. The Friday market is a huge melee with donkey carts, horses and thousands of Uygurs all involved in the selling of saddles, melons, silk, rugs, embroidered caps and other wares. Some 65 kilometres (40 miles) northwest of Kuqa, the **Kizil Thousand Buddha Caves** are located in an attractive setting on the bank of River Muzat. First hewn in the fourth century, the caves were abandoned with the spread of Islam in the l4th century. Of the 236 caves, only 75 have remained intact. The statuary has all disappeared, but strange murals depicting man-beasts, double-headed birds and Buddhist immortals remain. The chief interest here are a number of frescoes which show a strong Indo-Hellenistic influence.

**Aksu** lies southwest of Urumqi and is usually a refuelling stopover for flights to Kashgar. It is a uniformly grey Chinese city with little to interest the tourist.

**Kashgar** (Kashi) has a long history stretching back over 2,000 years. Situated at the foot of the Pamir Mountains, the city stands at the point where traffic along the great trade routes crossed over the high passes into what is today's Pakistan and beyond. In the Han and Tang dynasties Kashgar was under Chinese control, but the indigenous people of the region are believed to be Indo-European in origin (blue eyes and aquiline noses are common among the people of Kashgar). At the end of the l9th and beginning of the 20th century—during the struggle between Britain and Russia for control of Central Asia which was later referred to as the 'Great Game'—Kashgar with its foreign consulates was a listening post in the intrigues and intelligence-gathering activities of the two powers.

Despite its earlier role as a meeting point for Buddhists monks and craftsmen, the city is now thoroughly Islamic in character, little touched by Chinese attempts at modernization. It is smaller than Urumqi and easy to explore on foot or bicycle. Because of Kashgar's trade with Pakistan, its bazaars are full of goods from the Indian subcontinent. There is a choice of hats of every description: fur-trimmed, embroidered and plain. Silks from China are also on sale, as are semi-precious stones and the beautiful hand-woven rugs of the region. The Sunday market is particularly exciting—colourful, lively and an occasion for joining the Uygurs in consuming huge quantities of nan bread, kebabs, mutton dumplings and bitter black tea, or for watching the Tajik and Kirgiz horsemen showing off their riding skills (*see* picture on pages 182–183).

In May 1986, when the Karakoram Highway was opened, Kashgar once more became an important city for foreign travellers between China and South Asia.

## THE ROAD TO PAKISTAN

The route from Kashgar to the Pakistani border over the **Khunjerab Pass** may be one of the most spectacular and exhausting road trips in the world.

As the road heads south, travellers pass through the small town of **Gez**, which has a large community of Kirgiz people. The Kirgiz are nomadic herders, whose women have a liking for elaborately embroidered head cloths, heavy silver jewellery, and waistcoats decorated with buttons. From Gez, the road sweeps past the two great peaks of Mount Kongur and Mount Muzagata. Around **Taxkorgan** in the foothills of the Pamir Mountains, live the Tajik people. The Tajiks are pastoralists descended from Persian stock. The Tajik women are also colourful, using buttons, tassels and silver discs to decorate their plaits. The nomadic Tajiks live in houses built of earth and grass, and many of their tombs are constructed in the shape of a saddle—reputedly because of their love of being on horseback.

From Taxkorgan, it is approximately a two-and-a-half hour journey by road to the border crossing into Pakistan. In earlier days, the route was extremely hazardous and entire camel caravans could be frozen to death on the passes when a snow storm swept in. Luckily, the modern traveller on the Silk Road is better insulated against such dangers, and the route is only open in the summer and autumn months, from 1 May to 30 November.

# Tibet

There are many mountains in the world, but few have contained such a uniquely spiritual civilization as the Himalayas of Tibet. Tibetan history began to be recorded in the seventh century, when Buddhism took root in the country. Buddhism blended with the ancient indigenous animistic beliefs of Bon and became the core of Tibetan culture. In time the people of these mountains created a society in which monasteries acted as the centres of learning, of medicine, and ultimately of economic and political power. Thus a group of warrior tribes was transformed into a theocratic state.

Yet the peaceful doctrines of Buddhism did not always prevent the Tibetans from warring with each other, or with their neighbours. Due to the high altitude and scarce soils, farming was limited to a few river valleys, where only barley could be grown successfully. Tibet therefore could not develop a social system of settled farming communities in the manner of its Chinese neighbours to the east. The young men of Tibet could only herd, trade or join a monastery. Up until the middle of this century, the term 'monk' covered the widest possible range of character and activity. Some monks were cooks, others were the craftsmen of the brotherhood, and a chosen few were educated to become lamas—those who, in turn, transmitted Buddhist teachings and the traditions of Tibet's culture and medical knowledge to others.

The great unifier of Tibet, King Songsten Gampo, patronized the establishment of Buddhism in the seventh century, along with the development of a Tibetan script in which the scriptures themselves could be written. He also made tactical marriages to two Buddhist princesses, one Nepalese and one Chinese. The king's descendants ruled Tibet until the middle of the ninth century, when the monarchy came into conflict with the monasteries. After the last king was assassinated by a monk, rival monasteries created power bases, and the country was divided into regional spheres of influence. Tibet's earliest monasteries were controlled by rival sects, the most powerful of which were the Red Hats. In the 14th century, a scholar named Tsong Khapa founded the Yellow Hat Sect, which subsequently eclipsed the older Red Hat Sect and proved to be a force for reunification.

From the Yellow Hat Sect evolved a line of master monks known as Dalai Lamas, a title meaning 'Ocean of Wisdom'. In the 17th century, during the tenure of the fifth Dalai Lama, his ascendancy over all other lamas was established, and he was proclaimed to be the reincarnation of Chenrezi, the Bodhisattva of Compassion (the Tibetan version of India's Avalokitesvara, and China's Guanyin). The fifth Dalai Lama ruled from Lhasa but brought Shigatse, the second city of Tibet, under his control by enhancing the power of that city's Yellow Hat monastery, Tashilhunpo. Tashilhunpo's abbot had been the Dalai Lama's tutor and, in honour of his wisdom, the Dalai Lama had him named the Panchen Lama, meaning 'Great Scholar'. The Panchen Lama was then proclaimed to be a reincarnation of the Amitabha Buddha, thus making his status in Shigatse unchallengeable.

The theocratic government of Tibet ruled for the following two centuries with no interference from China, though it exercised a little of its own influence at the Qing court. The Qing rulers, who were Buddhists, often invited high-ranking Tibetan lamas to Beijing to teach and advise their court. However, by the late 19th century, the British in India and the Russians had become alert to the possibility of using Tibet as a pawn in their power game for control of Central Asia. This scheming in turn reminded the Qing rulers of the importance of Tibet in Chinese political concerns. In 1904, the British sent the Younghusband Expedition into Tibet to force a treaty of trade and friendship on the Tibetans. In 1910, it was China's turn to invade Tibet, seeking political concessions. The 13th Dalai Lama fled to Darjeeling and requested British aid to oust the Chinese. But it was the newly unified Chinese communist government which finally gained control of the country, sending in its own army to 'liberate' Tibet in 1950.

The traditional way of life continued for over a decade until an abortive uprising in 1959. After this the 14th Dalai Lama fled with 80,000 followers over the Himalayas

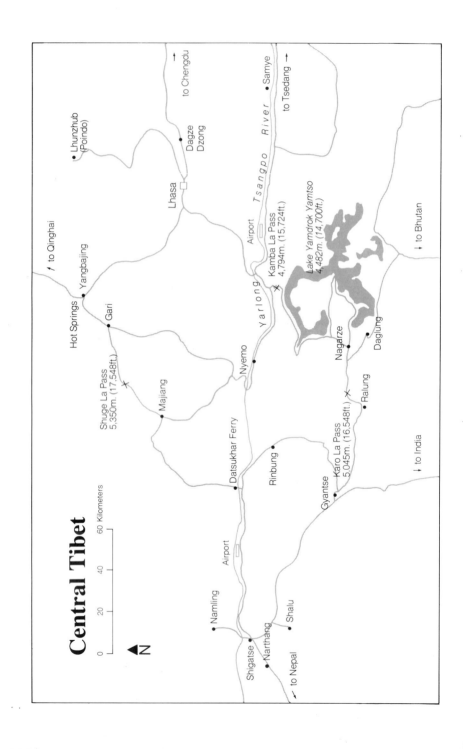

# Central Tibet

N

0    20    40    60 Kilometers

to Qinghai

Hot Springs
Yangbajing

Gari

Shuge La Pass
5,350m. (17,548ft.)

Majiang

Nyemo

Datsukhar Ferry

Rinbung

Namling

Airport

Shalu

Narthang

Shigatse

to Nepal

Gyantse

Karo La Pass
5,045m. (16,548ft.)

Ralung

to India

Daglung

Nagarze

Lake Yamdrok Yamtso
4,482m. (14,700ft.)

Kamba La Pass
4,794m. (15,724ft.)

to Bhutan

Yarlong

Airport

Tsangpo River

Samye

to Tsedang

Lhasa

Dagze
Dzong

to Chengdu

Lhunzhub
(Poindo)

into India, leaving Tibet essentially under Chinese military-backed control. Over the following years several thousand monasteries were disbanded and monks, nuns and lamas were encouraged by their Chinese protectors to embark on productive jobs. New roads and airfields were constructed making Tibet more easily accessible from China. The 14th Dalai Lama has remained in exile, declining to return if he is allowed only to settle in Beijing.

In the 1980s the Chinese introduced a policy of economic autonomy and religious freedom and a programme of restoration for the monasteries was launched at great expense to the Chinese. At the same time more and more Han Chinese were migrating, with the result that Lhasa and Shigatse are now predominantly Chinese. Settlers are encouraged with guaranteed jobs and housing, special loans and wages higher than they would be able to earn elsewhere in the country.

The only clarity in the situation of today's Tibet is that the Chinese set a high value on its strategic importance. Tibet's borders have also been redrawn with whole Tibetan regions absorbed into the surrounding provinces of Sichuan and Qinghai. Yet despite Chinese rule and migrations of both Han Chinese and Hui Moslems into their communities, the Tibetans have retained their sense of cultural identity.

It is hardly surprising that in the bleak but majestic landscapes of Tibet's highlands, the world of the spirit seems more real than the world of men. The silent landscapes of snow and ice, mountains, lakes and meadows have an unearthly beauty, inspiring veneration not only in the Tibetans for whom this beauty is a part of their everyday life, but in all those who experience it.

## LHASA

Because of Lhasa's altitude, 3,500 metres (12,000 feet) above sea level, most visitors need to take it easy the first few days in order to become acclimatized to the thin air. The best way to do this is to start your itinerary with a few short outings, taking rests in between. Strolls around the city and out along the banks of the **Lhasa River** are an excellent and not too taxing introduction to life in Tibet.

Chinese influence is apparent in the sharp contrast between the old Tibetan part of Lhasa and the newer section of the city constructed since the 1960s. Clustering round the Jokhang Temple, the old district contains a web of narrow lanes and houses of rough-hewn stone, brightened with whitewashed walls and painted woodwork. The new section of the city is drabber, and is dominated by wide boulevards with housing and office blocks set well back from the road behind high compound walls.

The Tibetans still dress in their traditional costumes—mainly because the clothes are so well adapted to the rigours of the climate. A garment common to both men and women is the *chuba*, a thick belted coat made from sheepskin. In winter the men wear felt or fur hats. The women wear their hair in braids or tucked under coloured scarves, and—on special occasions—elaborate headdresses. Their long dresses are usually black, brown or blue in colour, but the working pinafores of woven stripes (only worn by the married women of Central Tibet) are brightly coloured.

The two great sights of Lhasa are the Jokhang Temple and the Potala Palace. The **Jokhang Temple** is the home of the most precious Buddha image the country possesses—the Sakyamuni Buddha, brought from China by the Tang-dynasty princess Wen Cheng, who was married to the great King Songsten Gampo. In the main hall of the temple is a set of murals showing the arrival of Princess Wen Cheng in Tibet. The Jokhang is the most important site of pilgrimage in Tibet, and worshippers throng its halls and shrines. It is customary for them to circumambulate, in a clockwise direction, round the Holy of Holies, which contains the gilded and bejewelled statue of Sakyamuni. The roof of the Jokhang can also be visited.

Built on a hill overlooking the city, the **Potala Palace** is Tibet's best-known landmark. Once the spiritual and temporal palace of the Dalai Lama, it is now a museum with shrines and chapels maintained by monks. The Potala has two sections, known as the White and Red Palaces. The White Palace, built in 1653, rises in terraces to the central Red Palace, built in 1693, which is crowned with an ornate gilded copper roof. Inside the Potala, most of which is off-limits to visitors, there are open chapels and galleries which have fascinating wall paintings. The apartments of the 13th and 14th Dalai Lamas are open to visitors. The innermost room of the 14th Dalai Lama's apartment is left exactly as it was on the day of his flight to India in 1959. Visitors may also see the tomb of the 13th Dalai Lama, which consists of a huge stupa. For security reasons, it must be visited with a guide or a monk, because the interior has treasures of gold and precious gems.

A walk around the old section of Lhasa is full of discoveries: small temples being restored and lovingly decorated, street stalls selling anything from snacks to daggers, prayer flags fluttering above walls, and glimpses into the courtyards of Tibetan homes. At the heart of this section is the **Barkhor pilgrim path**, the street encircling the Jokhang Temple. As pilgrims are constantly walking around it in a clockwise direction (this is true of all Buddhist sites in Tibet), it is wise to follow suit in order not to offend or collide into them. On the Barkhor, devout pilgrims often make the circuit in a series of full-length body prostrations.

Southeast of the Barkhor Pilgrim Path is the **Moslem Quarter** of Lhasa, which has a mosque and *halal* restaurants.The **Tibetan Hospital of Traditional Medicine** makes a fascinating visit for those interested in herbal remedies and their history. Traditional medicine was once taught in the monasteries, the most famous of which was the old medical college on the summit of Chokpori Hill in Lhasa. It was reduced to

*Tibet's holiest statue of the Buddha, inside the Jokhang Temple, Lhasa*

rubble by the Chinese army in 1959, and a steel antenna was erected on the site. Religious pilgrims still walk the slopes of the hill.

Tibetan carpets, with their Buddhist motifs, are extremely attractive, and one can watch them being made at the **Lhasa Carpet Factory**. Tibetan performing arts are being revived, and the **School of Tibetan Performing Arts**, founded in 1980 as a gesture of Chinese tolerance, allows foreign visitors to attend music and opera rehearsals.

After years of closure, small city temples are being restored for worship. The **Ramoche Temple** in the north of the city, and the cave temple of **Palalubu** at the foot of Chokpori, are open to foreign visitors. Less frequently visited are the monasteries of **Chomoling**, **Muru Ningba**, **Tengyeling** and **Ani Gompa**. The last is Lhasa's only nunnery and worth a visit.

Travellers exploring the city should make time for an outing to **Gumolingka Island** in the Lhasa River—a favourite summer picnic place for Tibetans. Tibetans are generally friendly and welcoming and, in their love of open-air picnics, can show zealous hospitality. Foreign travellers have been known to reel back to their hotels in a stupor after generous (and unrefusable) refills of local liquor.

You can also visit the old summer palace of the Dalai Lama, the **Norbulingka**. The palace is about a 15-minute walk southwest from the Holiday Inn Lhasa in the west of the city. It was built by the seventh Dalai Lama as a summer retreat, and today it houses a small zoo which has rare Himalayan bears and snow lynxes.

Set against the bare hillside of Mount Gyengbuwudze, on the western outskirts of Lhasa, the **Drepung Monastery** was once the largest and the wealthiest in Tibet. A Yellow Hat foundation, the monastery was served by senior monks who were instrumental in the training of Dalai Lamas and who specialized in esoteric psychic practices. It was also the home of the Nechung, the State Oracle who, in trance, advised the Dalai Lama on important decisions. The Drepung was divided into four Tantric Colleges, each of which had its own special field of learning. In the chanting hall of the **Nuosenle College**, there is a model doll of the State Oracle in the regalia worn for prophecy. The chanting hall of the **Ngapa College** is also worth a visit—on its red doors are beautiful gold drawings depicting the history of the Dalai and Panchen Lamas. If there is chanting going on, visitors are usually still allowed to stay as long as they walk round the edge clockwise and refrain from making a noise.

On the northern outskirts of Lhasa lies **Sera Monastery**, a Yellow Hat Sect monastery which was once rival to the Drepung. Set against Tatipu Hill, Sera had three Tantric Colleges which were famous for their Bon tradition of occult teaching. Monks have returned to Sera and can be seen at prayer in their deep red robes and distinctive yellow hats which sweep upwards like a curved shell over their forehead. Worth looking for is the image of the horse-headed god in the **Gyetazang College** chanting hall. The treasure of the monastery is the gilded Chenrezi image, the Bodhisattva of Compassion, of whom all Dalai Lamas are said to be incarnations. The Chenrezi image is in the **Tsug-gyeng College** chanting hall.

The **Droma Lhakang Temple** lies 27 kilometres (17 miles) south of Lhasa. It is dedicated to the Indian Tantric master, Atisha, who came to Tibet in the 11th century. Atisha settled in Tibet to teach, and he was instrumental in the revival of Buddhism after two centuries of fighting and destruction which followed the overthrow of the royal family in the ninth century. The temple has many images of the Tibetan goddess, Tara, who was the guardian deity of Atisha. Tara is said to have been a princess who, when challenged by monks saying that a woman could never achieve enlightenment, set out to prove them wrong. When Tara did achieve enlightenment, she was deified. It is easy to identify her image, since it is usually depicted in white or green.

To the east of Lhasa, 70 kilometres (45 miles) distant, is the Yellow Hat Sect monastery, **Ganden**. Once Tibet's third largest religious community after Drepung and Sera, it was destroyed by the Chinese army in 1959 but was later rebuilt and is now in active use.

## GYANTSE

The traveller in Tibet often visits Gyantse on the way to Shigatse. Gyantse gives the impression today of being a small and inconsequential city, but that was not always so. Commanding the junction of two major caravan routes, one to India and the other to Nepal, the fortified city was of strategic and military importance and of great wealth. Until the early part of this century, Gyantse was Tibet's third city and a major gathering-point for nomads, who would come to sell their wool for export.

The wealth of the city was manifested in the foundation of **Palkhor Monastery**, built in the 14th century. The monastery has been badly damaged, but on no account should it be passed by. Its Nepalese-style stupa with painted eyes is of great interest. Known as the **Kumbum**, meaning 'Place of a Thousand Images', the stupa has a gilded tower topped by a parasol wrought in filigreed metal. The monastery itself has a vast wall, on which large *tankas*—Buddhist paintings on silk—are hung in the open air during the summer months.

Gyantse's fortress, the **Dzong**, was damaged by British artillery in 1904, during the Younghusband Expedition. The fortress was further damaged by Chinese troops in the 1960s. For those with time for a detour, a visit to the town of **Yadong**, just over 200 kilometres (125 miles) south of Gyantse, is recommended. Yadong has a wonderful prospect over the forests and peaks of the Himalayas. Close to the town is an old wooden monastery, built in Sikkimese style.

## SHIGATSE

Shigatse is set in the valley of the country's major river, the **Yarlong Tsangpo**. This river is better known by its Indian name, the Brahmaputra, for it flows from the western mountains of Tibet down through India to the Bay of Bengal. Near Shigatse, the Yarlong Tsangpo is a fast-flowing river of snowmelt which waters the farm fields around the city.

The journey to Shigatse from Lhasa is usually made by the southern route, past **Yamdrok Yamtso Lake** and via Gyantse. However, there is a longer but equally interesting northern route, which gives a contrasting picture of the Tibetan landscape. Many travellers visit Shigatse by one route and return to Lhasa by the other.

Shigatse once rivalled Lhasa for the political and spiritual control of Tibet. It was a centre of monastic learning, and had its own noble families, who used their wealth to found monasteries and thus create power bases. The city was dominated by the Red Hat Sect until the time of the fifth Dalai Lama who, with the backing of a Mongolian warlord, managed to subdue rival sects and unite the country under the leadership of the Yellow Hat Sect. The Panchen Lama, the abbot of the **Tashilhunpo Monastery**, reinforced the rule of the Dalai Lama from Lhasa.

Perhaps because the Panchen Lama at the time—the tenth—became the 'guest' of the Chinese in Beijing in the 1960s, Tashilhunpo was spared the worst of the excesses of the Cultural Revolution. It has now emerged once more as an active centre of worship and teaching. A Yellow Hat order, Tashilhunpo was founded in the 15th century, but it came to pre-eminence in the 17th century with the naming of its abbot as the first Panchen Lama. The sixth Panchen Lama is considered to be the greatest.

Tashilhunpo is a beautiful monastery, for it rises in stately terraces to a central gilded roof with decorated eaves and finials. Its distinctive rose-coloured walls are inset with dark wooden windows that are brightened with whitewashed borders. The monastery still practises the art of making m*andalas* (abstract meditation pictures) of coloured sands. Its courtyard has a high *tanka* wall, on which the huge coloured pictures are unfurled in the sun during festivals.

Visitors can view the **Panchen Lama's Palace**, which remains uninhabited. In the palace is a temple containing the tomb of the fourth Panchen Lama; it has a stupa wrought in gold and precious stones. On the upper level of the temple hang embroidered *tankas* made for the monastery in Hangzhou in the 1920s. Of special interest are the Panchen Lama's throne displayed in the main chanting hall, the sutra hall where the Buddhist canon (scriptures) is kept, the 20th-century statues of the Maitreya Buddha made in gold, copper and brass, and the roof with its chapels.

Travellers can join worshippers on a walk back to Shigatse from the monastery on a pilgrim path (again, the walk has to be done in this direction, since the route is

*Tashilhunpo Monastery, Shigatse*

clockwise). Also close to the Tashilhunpo is the Panchen Lama's **Summer Palace**. It is not open to the public.

Twenty-two kilometres (14 miles) south of the city is the **Shalu Monastery**, a Red Hat Sect monastery founded in the 11th century. The original buildings were demolished by an earthquake, and the present structure dates from the 14th century, when it was rebuilt in Mongolian style. Its most famous abbot was Buston, who was a clever administrator and an accomplished historian of Buddhism. The monastery was celebrated for its occult training. The influence of Bon, the ancient animistic religion of Tibet, was maintained in its teachings. You may notice the counter-clockwise swastikas (Buddhist swastikas are clockwise), which are Bon symbols. Like Tashilhunpo, the monastery has a collection of 20th-century embroidered *tankas* from Hangzhou, and a tradition of making coloured-sand *mandalas*.

## FROM SHIGATSE TO NEPAL

From Shigatse, there is a route to Nepal which is highly recommended for adventure travel. Despite the lack of comfort on the journey, this route is popular because of the breathtaking contrasts of scenery visible from the road. The traveller passes through upland river meadows and dun-coloured deserts, crosses passes offering spectacular vistas of the Himalayan peaks, and drops down into the warmer forest glades of Tibet's border with Nepal. The trip also offers a chance to see more off-the-beaten-track monasteries and villages. There are places for food and lodgings on the way.

A one-month visa for Nepal can be obtained in one working day from the Nepalese consulate in Lhasa. The consulate is also able to give up-to-date information on the condition of the road to Nepal. Now that tours are conducted on this route, independent travellers are advised to organize their transport well in advance since it may not be easy to find at short notice. It is possible to hire a jeep with driver from Shigatse to the border. Two days after setting out from Shigatse the traveller can expect to reach Zhangmu, where the border crossing may be made. Once over the border, a variety of onward transportation to Kathmandu will be waiting for the traveller. Depending on the state of the roads, the final lap of the journey to Kathmandu can be done in about eight hours. In August and September, the rainy season, the roads can be treacherous and certainly time-consuming to travel on. Those who have experienced it say that travelling from Lhasa to Nepal is less strenuous than vice versa, since the rapid change in altitude on the ascent can cause great fatigue and dizziness. Those already acclimatized to Lhasa's altitude will find the descent more comfortable.

West of Shigatse stand the almost unearthly walls of the **Sakya Monastery**. Its name means 'tawny soil', and its massive windowless walls rise from the earth like an enormous abstract painting of grey and maroon, with a single white-and-yellow stripe breaking the colour change. It was once the leading Red Hat Sect monastery of the region and enjoyed Mongolian patronage during the Yuan dynasty, when one of its abbots went to the court of Kublai Khan to convert the emperor. Kublai Khan made the monastery the centre of power in Tibet during his reign. The monastery has suffered damage, but sections of the 13th-century building can still be seen.

On the road to Nepal, the peak of Mount Everest, the highest mountain in the world, towers above the horizon in its lofty splendour. A detour can take the traveller to the base camp of the mountain at **Rongbuk**. If you decide to trek here, you must do so only after careful preparation, with enough food for ten days and adequate sleeping and cooking equipment.

North of **Nyalam**, on the road to Nepal, is a cave where the eccentric Buddhist saint and poet, Milarepa, spent much of his life. He is famous for his severe asceticism, acts of compassion and wild songs of poetry. The cave is close to a monastery dedicated to Milarepa, which was destroyed in the Cultural Revolution, but now restored by craftsmen and artists brought in from Nepal to help.

The last Tibetan town before crossing the border is **Zhangmu**. A sleepy town which appears to tumble steeply down a hillside, it has a beautiful setting of pine forests, deep river gorges and cascading waterfalls.

## When to Visit Tibet

Travellers should think seriously before travelling in the colder months. By late February and early March it starts to get warm during the day, and the Tibetan spring can be quite lovely. The summer is the most popular tourist season, when visitors often have a chance to observe Tibetan festivals and celebrations—of either a religious or sporting kind. Keep an ear to the ground for news of Tibetan horse races, wrestling matches and drinking sessions, which take place throughout the warmer months. Rain falls intermittently through June to September in southern Tibet. The Tibetan lunar New Year falls in January or February. Although it is cold then, it does provide a wonderful opportunity to enjoy a week of archery contests, religious dances and other ceremonies. The last day of the old year sees a dance by lamas in masks, known to foreigners as the 'Devils' Dance'. This is when evil influences are driven out to usher in an auspicious New Year.

# Sichuan

The vast inland province of Sichuan in southwest China is shaped like a deep dish, with a lowland river plain wedged within a serrated rim of towering mountains. To the west the foothills of the Himalayas jut skywards in snowy chains, and to the north the deep-brown folds of the Longmen range separate Sichuan from the

# Across a Crowded Room

At last Fourth Sister, urged by significant gestures from the others, brought forth—"We are going with Seventh Aunt to the cinema tomorrow and she wishes you to come also." Seventh Aunt was the daughter of Third Grandfather by his second marriage, a girl of my own age, unmarried, rather quiet and lacking in lustre. Though I had met her when I called upon the household I had little impression of her. Still, it was kind of her to invite me; I thanked Ninth Aunt, her sister, and accepted. Suddenly they were all talking at once.

"We are so glad you will come! For you are modern—you did not let anyone else choose a husband for you. Seventh Aunt asked especially for you. You see, it is because Third Grandfather is so out-of-date in his ideas! He thinks no modest and well-brought-up girl should presume to look at her fiancé before her marriage, but all should be arranged by the elders of the family. But where will you find educated young men these days who will agree to that? No cross-eyed or pockmarked brides for them—they insist on a pre-view. So there it stands, and how is Third Grandfather to find husbands for all his unmarried daughters? To be sure, there are cousins on the maternal side—two marriages already with them. But there is no boy cousin of an age suitable for Seventh Aunt."

I listened bewildered, unable to see any direction in this flood of information. "But the cinema?" I questioned.

"It is arranged for them to see each other at the cinema—oh, at a distance—Seventh Aunt and this brother of a friend. It is very daring and Third Grandfather would be furious if he knew. But Seventh Aunt has been looking about for herself, since she is past twenty-one and it is time she was married. And this school friend of hers has a brother who is thinking of marrying. So it is planned for Seventh Aunt to go with us to the cinema tomorrow, and this girl and her brother will be there. We shall know who he is, seeing him beside his sister. And she will point out Seventh Aunt to him. So they will have a chance to look, and if they are pleased with each other—who knows?"

Seventh Aunt called for us early; we were the first to arrive at the cinema. We sat alone in the empty building, a small group in the front row of the balcony. Seventh Aunt was pale with excitement; her eyes looked feverish. She was dressed plainly, but her hair on either side of her narrow white face was a mass of frizzy ringlets, stiff as wire, shining with oil. There is no regulation in the ancient prescribed observances of mourning concerning permanent waves. She was nervously vivacious, playing the hostess, passing pea-nuts and sweets, calling for tea, which was served us on the balcony rail, commenting on the people drifting in. The auditorium filled up. It was almost time for the picture. Seventh Aunt's sprightliness became a little distrait as she endeavoured to keep up the conversation and watch the people coming in. Suddenly she was silent, her hands clasped in her lap. Fourth Sister touched my arm— "There he is!"—and pointed to a couple walking down the aisle to seats well forward. The top of a shiny black head and the shoulders of a brown, Western-style coat were all we could see of this young man who might marry Seventh Aunt. He and his sister settled themselves, then turned about in their seats, craning upward—the lights went out.

At the interval, when the lights came on, Seventh Aunt's cheeks were blazing with patches of pink, a little unevenly applied by touch. She sat like an idol with eyes downcast, but under her eyelids she stole swift glances at the young man. At that distance, and to my unbiased view, he was merely a somewhat chinless face with glasses. At the close of the picture we were stumbling toward the stairs before the last ficker of the film, to reach the lobby before he came out. He might—it was possible— he might ask for an introduction. . . . Past bobbing heads we had a closer glimpse of him, a side view as he passed, confirming my impression that he was chinless and quite undistinguished. He did not pause or look about. Seventh Aunt blinked rapidly. "The lights hurt one's eyes after the darkness in there. . . ." We all began to talk about the picture.

After two or three days the young man's sister called. She talked of many things, but did not mention her brother. No one asked. Everybody understood. The look had been unfavourable. He was not interested further.

Han Suyin, Destination Chungking

neighbouring province of Shaanxi. To the east, the turbulent Yangzi and its tributaries flow between the deep cuts of mountain ranges which sweep from north to south.

Sichuan, which means 'four rivers', is named after the four tributaries of the Yangzi: the Jialing, Minjiang, Tuojiang and Wujiang. The rivers run in deep gorges through sparsely inhabited upland regions, before they reach the rich soils of the alluvial plains at the centre of the province.

The fertile river plains of Sichuan are the granary of China, producing enough rice and wheat to export surpluses to other parts of the country. With 11 frost-free months, fertile soil and an abundance of rainfall, double cropping and three rice harvests a year are possible. The villages of the lowland regions of Sichuan are prosperous and attractive, tucked into bamboo thickets amidst glittering fields of wet paddies and neat terraces of vegetable fields and orchards. The agrarian reforms which were implemented throughout China in the past decade were pioneered here by Premier Zhao Ziyang in the late 1970s. At that time he was head of the provincial party committee in Sichuan. He was so successful in restoring Sichuan's agricultural economy that the Sichuanese coined a rhyme: *Yao chi fan, Zhao Ziyang*. Translated, it means, 'If you want to eat, find Ziyang', thus making a pun on *zhao*, which means 'find', as well as sounding the same as his surname.

The most remote mountainous regions of Sichuan are populated by minority peoples. In the far west of the province, for example, there are large communities of Tibetans, and in the south, the Yi congregate around Liangshan. Perhaps these are the most attractive regions for the foreign visitor to explore. But there are more accessible and equally attractive destinations in Sichuan, such as the Buddhist caves of Dazu, the holy mountain of Emeishan, and the ethereally beautiful highland reserves of Jiuzhaigou and Huanglong. Of the province's major cities, visitors are most likely to visit Chengdu, the capital, and Chongqing, which in fact became independent from Sichuan when it was created a municapality in March 1997, before steaming east down the Yangzi.

For details of the Yangzi port cities, including Chongqing, *see* page 225. For the Buddhist mountain of Emeishan in western Sichuan, *see* page 259.

## CHENGDU

Chengdu may be a large, modern city, but its ways are more those of the countryside than the town. Life is taken at an easy pace, teahouses are always full, and market stalls overflow with an abundance of farm produce brought in from the surrounding villages. The city centre is softened by trees shading the pavements and wide boulevards. The old city hugs the Jin River in a tangled pattern of lanes overhung by two-storey frame houses painted a dusky red. Chengdu rose to prominence in the Three Kingdoms period (220–265) as the capital of the state of Shu (even today, Sichuan is referred to by the name of Shu). Chengdu is the provincial capital, although

Chongqing in the east of the province is the foremost industrial centre. The city was once among the most splendid in China, with its own grand city walls (pulled down in 1949) and Vice-Regal Palace, destroyed in the 1960s. The Sichuan Exhibition Centre, fronted by a white marble statue of Mao, 12.26 metres high to correspond with his birthday on December 26th, now occupies the site (*see* picture on page 69).

In the rural western suburbs of Chengdu stands **Du Fu's Thatched Cottage**. Du Fu (712–770) was a Tang poet who lived in Chengdu for a brief but productive period during which he wrote more than 200 poems. During the later Song Dynasty, a thatched cottage shrine was built in memory of the original cottage, which he described in the poem 'My thatched cottage is wrecked by the autumn wind'. The present buildings date from 1500 and 1811, when major restorations were undertaken. In the front hall are two wooden screens, one of which has a biography of the poet carved out in Chinese characters. In the shrine itself stand clay figurines of Du Fu, which date from the Ming and Qing dynasties. The garden walks around the shrine are lovely, and many different types of bamboo have been planted to shade the paths. There is a lively teahouse in the grounds.

Set in the southern suburbs of the city are a series of halls called the **Zhuge Liang Memorial Halls**. They commemorate the great military strategist Zhuge Liang, who was adviser to the King of Shu in the Warring States period (475–221 BC). The halls were first built in the fourth century, but the present buildings date from 1672. On display are three bronze drums, believed to have been used by the armies of Shu under Zhuge Liang.

**Wenshu Yuan**, also known as the Manjusri Temple, is located south of the railway station. The temple is dedicated to the God of Wisdom or by his Sanskrit name Manjusri. On the way to the entrance, you will walk down a narrow lane flanked by stalls selling all that is necessary for worshipping in the temple—'hell money' for burnt offerings, candles, firecrackers and so on. Wenshu Yuan is the headquarters of the Chan (Zen) Buddhist sect in Sichuan.

Finally, the **Precious Light Monastery** (Baoguang Si) is worth a visit. It was founded in the Han dynasty and houses a fine collection of Buddhist treasures as well as modern paintings. Its 1,000-year-old Sheli Pagoda is a beautiful structure which is Chengdu's own version of a leaning tower—its top eight storeys tilt slightly to one side. A craft market held outside the monastery walls is popular with both local and foreign visitors.

## OUTINGS FROM CHENGDU

One of the world's first irrigation systems can be found outside Chengdu. This hydraulic system at **Du River Dyke**, was created in the third century BC by Li Bing, a minister in the ancient state of Shu. Its scale and sophistication are a tribute to the

*Women from China's minority nationalities at a festival gathering*

scientific genius of ancient China. The network of dykes and canals not only controlled flood levels on the Minjiang, a major river in Sichuan, but also created an irrigation system vital to the agricultural development of the region. Close to the dyke are several old temples, one of which—the **Two Princes Temple**—is dedicated to Li Bing and his son.

One of the most splendid sights Sichuan has to offer is the great statue of the Maitreya Buddha carved on a river cliff at **Leshan**. The statue overlooks the confluence of the Min, Qingyi and Dadu rivers to the south of Chengdu. Carved in the eighth century, the seated Buddha is 71 metres (220 feet) high, and is the largest Buddha image carved in China. It has an extraordinarily gentle and serene face, which is now overhung with trees growing in the gardens at the cliff top. It is also out of proportion and slightly grotesque. The best way to see the statue is to take a boat along the river. On either side of the statue stand carved warriors who, though they are imposing, are dwarfed by the size of the Buddha.

Opened to tourists in 1982, the **Buddhist Caves of Dazu**, to the southeast of Chengdu, are reason enough to visit Sichuan. The caves are scattered over 40 different locations and contain more than 50,000 carvings dating from the Tang and Song dynasties. Because the carvings are in Sichuan, an area historically isolated from the strongholds of power either in the north or around the lower Yangzi valley, they have escaped much of the destruction suffered by Buddhist centres elsewhere. The two most visited cave complexes are **Beishan** and **Baodingshan**. However, adventurous visitors can easily reach the more remote cave centres with the help of local guides.

The sculptures of Beishan date from the late Tang Dynasty and are best seen at a the site known as Fowan, a crescent-shaped cliff within walking distance of Dazu town. Look for the carvings of grottoes number 136 (known as the 'Wheel of the Universe') and number 245, which illustrates the 'Western Paradise' and consists of more than 500 figures. The sculptures of Baodingshan date from the Southern Song Dynasty and are found at 13 different locations. The monk, Zhao Zhifeng, made the master plan for these Buddhist carvings, and a miniature of that master plan survives to this day. The rock sculptures are concentrated at Dafowan, where you will find a series of narratives based on the Buddhist scriptures. But what is special about them is the inclusion of everyday scenes of rural life.

The highway from Chengdu to the border with Shaanxi Province is known as the 'Ancient Road to Shu', famous in Chinese history as one fraught with danger and obstacles. Today, the traveller can make the journey by hiring a jeep or by local bus. The only link between the remote region of Sichuan and the northern provinces of China, the route—with its high mountain passes—was of great strategic importance, especially in times of war. Many of the stories associated with this route relate to the Three Kingdoms period, when the state of Shu was at war with its northern rival, the

Wei. On the way north there are five famous passes—Seven Bends (Qipan), Skyward (Chaotian), Flying Immortals (Feixian), Heavenly Might (Tianxiong) and Sword Gate (Jianmen).

The small town of **Jiange** is remarkable for its ancient wooden buildings, which have survived from the Ming Dynasty. North of Jiange is **Guangyuan**, the last city before Sichuan ends and Shaanxi begins. The city is notable for being the birthplace of Wu Zetian (625–705), the only woman sovereign in Chinese history.

Northern Sichuan encompasses areas of great natural beauty. Two of these are the nature reserves of **Jiuzhaigou** and **Huanglong**. Getting to them involves a 480-kilometre (300-mile) drive by jeep or bus from Chengdu along a far from well-maintained road. On the other hand, because you are travelling towards a mountainous area, you also pass through some of the most stunning landscapes in China. Jiuzhaigou, a valley more than 2,000 metres (6,500 feet) above sea level, is named after the nine Tibetan settlements in the area. It is studded with crystalline lakes, rimmed by snow-capped mountains and splashed by waterfalls. Huanglong is also a highland valley, but here the terrain has been marked by the steady depositing of calcium carbonate over aeons of time, so that strange-looking limestone formations crop up here and there, washed by icy snowmelt and broken by shallow pools of mineral-laden water. The cool highlands are the natural haunt of the Giant Panda, but the number of these shy creatures has been much depleted, and they are rarely seen in the wild nowadays.

## The Road to Tibet

Public Security Bureau regulations concerning the openness of the the the road to foreigners notwithstanding, the overland route to Tibet passes through hostile terrain making it a most difficult journey. At the time of writing, summer 1997, it is forbidden to travel overland between Chengdu and Lhasa, however the route west as far as Kangding is open to tourists. Even going only that far may involve many a roadside delay: mudslides and rockfalls are commonplace and therefore the excursion should only be considered by those with time on their hands.

On the first day's travel west escaping from the masses and humidity of the Sichuan Basin, buses reach **Ya'an**. The country to the west is wild and steeped with the history of the Central Red Army's passage through the region in summer, 1935 on their Long March. Nationalist leader Chiang Kai-shek came to Ya'an thinking he was finally going to wipe out Mao's Central Red Army. At the very least he expected to prevent them crossing the torrent of the Dadu River, a tributary of the upper Yangzi, an action which might have forced them to perish in remote western parts. The two leaders were just 80 kilometres apart. Between them was Erlang Shan, a 3,437 metre pass (the road across it has just been rebuilt by the People's Liberation Army).

Miraculously, Mao's forces captured 'the Fixed Bridge of Lu', named after the engineer who built it in 1701 for the Kangxi Emperor. Nationalists defending **Luding Bridge** had removed its wooden planks, leaving only bare chains, but miraculous heroism won the day. Mao's forces escaped through northern Sichuan, evading the Nationalists completely by crossing high mountains and an uninhabited plateaued grasslands, before making their way for northern Shaanxi to establish a new revolutionary base area.

**Kangding**, in the the Ganzi Tibetan Autonomous Prefecture, is the next town west of Luding. These small mountain towns have remained Tibetan in character, despite recent influxes of Chinese settlers. Kangding is famous for its horse racing, the big races being held every year on Buddha's Bathing Day (the eighth day of the fourth lunar month, in early summer).

At **Xinduqiao**, the highway divides into two sections. The northern part goes through Ganzi, Maniganggo and the Chola Mountains, to Dege and Qamdo. The southern section goes via Batang. Both roads offer views from the high passes over the folded mountain mass of the Qinghai-Tibetan plateau. Dege, on the northern run, is well worth a visit, since it has a traditional Buddhist printing press, where sutras are printed by hand from wood blocks. Also on the northern route is Qamdo, the largest town in eastern Tibet. The men of Qamdo have a reputation for being fierce warriors and hunters, who in earlier times made their living from banditry.

## MINORITIES

Fourteen different minority groups live in Sichuan: the Tibetans, Yi, Miao, Qiang, Hui, Tujia, Bouyei, Naxi, Bai, Zhuang, Dai, Mongolian, Manchu and Lisu. Their communities are predominantly in the remote mountainous regions of the north, west and southwest of Sichuan, although several of these minorities can be found in other Chinese provinces as well. Many of their districts are being opened up by local authorities in order to attract foreign travellers and bring greater prosperity to the minorities. Of special interest are the Qiang people, who live in **Maowen County**, north of Chengdu. The Qiang are known for their small castle-like dwellings, which were built on hilltops. The castles are no longer inhabited, but they were made with such fine craftsmanship that they are still standing after 700 years. Their women are skilled needlewomen. To this day, they retain their distinctive dress of brilliant-coloured robes and cloth turbans decorated with tassels.

# Yunnan

Yunnan Province is in the far southwest of China. It is of special interest to many travellers because of its large and diverse population of minority peoples. Twenty-four different ethnic minorities live in this province which borders Burma, Laos, Vietnam and Tibet. Many of these peoples have lifestyles, religious customs and costumes more in common with their Tibetan and Southeast Asian neighbours than with the Han Chinese.

The presence of these peoples endows Yunnan with a different atmosphere to China's northern provinces. Until quite late in its history, the region was not directly under Chinese control. Its earliest inhabitants were the Dian people, the same name that is given to Kunming's lake, and they were known to have lived around Kunming in the first millennium BC. Wonderful bronze implements from their culture have been found in excavations outside the city (these are now on display in the Yunnan Provincial Museum in Kunming itself). During the Tang Dynasty, the Nanzhao Kingdom held sway over Yunnan, later to be replaced by the Dali in the 12th century. In the next century, the Mongol conquerors of China brought Yunnan under the aegis of their Yuan Dynasty. As a means of controlling their new territory, the Mongols brought in Muslims to settle in the area and act as their political agents. Yunnan's Muslim population has grown and thrives to this day. Yet even as late as the Ming and Qing dynasties, the imperial court saw Yunnan as a distant and unattractive outpost, using it in much the same way as the British used Australia in the 18th century—as a place for dumping unwanted persons.

Yunnan is also the original home of many of the plants and trees which were introduced to the West from China. Camellias, rhododendrons and tea, to name but three, all trace their origins to the high plateau in China's southwest which is Yunnan. The plateau rises steeply towards the northwest and the Himalayan mountain chains, while the lower-lying regions are in the south, on the borders of Burma, Laos and Vietnam. Its average elevation is about 2,000 metres (5,000 feet). The high altitude of the plateau and the tropical location of the province give it a mild and warm climate throughout the year—ideal for travellers, even in the winter months. The province has long been known as the Land of Eternal Spring. Three great rivers flow south through Yunnan from the northern border with Tibet: the Salween, Mekong and Yangzi. The Salween and Mekong continue on into Burma and Laos, but the Yangzi turns in an enormous loop to flow north into neighbouring Sichuan Province.

There are three great adventure destinations in Yunnan: Dali, Lijiang and Xishuangbanna. Though they have become very popular with China travellers, they are still unspoilt. All three regions are renowned for their natural beauty of setting, historic sites and, of course, their minority peoples. Dali and Lijiang lie to the northwest of Kunming, the provincial capital, in the high plateau region of Yunnan. Xishuangbanna is in the south of the province, where the tropical jungles and riverside villages make the region a natural geographical and cultural extension of Southeast Asia.

The popularity of these three destinations should neither deter the independent traveller from including them on an itinerary, nor detract from the exploration of other, less well-documented regions. Yunnan, perhaps more than any other region except Tibet, appeals to the traveller for whom the journey itself is the adventure.

## KUNMING

Kunming's Lake Dianchi is like a blue-glazed dish edged with a painted trim of green. The lake's great beauty and Yunnan's gentle climate make Kunming—the capital of the province—appealing even in the winter months when much of the rest of China is too cold to attract many visitors. But it is the variety of peoples in the region which usually draws travellers to Yunnan, and for many travellers, Kunming is a staging post for journeys to the towns and villages of these peoples, rather than a destination in itself. But even if time does not allow a journey far beyond Kunming, there are many opportunities to learn about the minorities and to see their handicrafts in the museums and shops of the city. And the city itself has its own pleasures—wonderful gardens and parks, teashops and markets, excellent street snacks including the local speciality 'Crossing the Bridge Noodles', and many old temples and pavilions.

## CITY SIGHTS

A good starting place for a visit to Kunming is the **Yunnan Provincial Museum**. It has an excellent section on the minorities, which acts as an introduction to the peoples of Yunnan and their varied lifestyles. You will note that the Dai women, whose villages lie close to the borders of Laos and Burma, wear the sarong that is seen all over Southeast Asia. It is here that you will also see the fine bronzes of the Dian Kingdom, which has been dated back to 1200 BC. These bronzes deserve careful scrutiny, since they show detailed scenes of daily life. The animal bronzes are especially noteworthy.

Close to the zoo in the north of the city is the Buddhist **Yuantong Temple** and its adjacent park. The park is famed for its flowering shrubs and trees: cherry in spring, rhododendrons in summer, chrysanthemums in autumn and camellia or magnolia in winter. The temple itself dates back a thousand years or so, and has been attractively restored.

Just south of Jinbi Lu are two ancient pagodas dating from the ninth century— **East** and **West Temple Pagodas**. The former can be visited and is notable for its four golden (copper) roosters on the summit. The latter is visible from the street but cannot be visited at the moment.

Yunnan's large Moslem community dates back to the Yuan Dynasty. Five mosques are open in Kunming, and can be visited if proper attire is worn and cameras are used with discretion. The largest mosque is on Shuncheng Jie, in an Islamic neighbourhood which is also worth exploring for its small shops and *halal* (Moslem) restaurants.

## OUTINGS FROM KUNMING

In a woodland setting about 12 kilometres (seven and a half miles) northwest of Kunming lies the **Bamboo Temple**. A legend tells of the temple's foundation in the Tang, when two princes chased a rhinoceros to a spot where monks appeared holding staves of bamboo, which then miraculously turned into groves of bamboo. The temple is noted for its 500 luohan, or bodhisattvas, carved in the 19th century.

In the northeast of the city, 11 kilometres (seven miles) away, the **Copper Temple** or Golden Temple (Jindian) can be reached after a dramatic climb through pine woods. The attractive temple with its wrought-copper roof stands on a marble terrace and is dedicated to the Taoist deity, Zishi.

Most travellers to Kunming will want to take one of the numerous ferries which traverse **Dianchi Lake** at various points. The western shores of the lake rise steeply towards **Western Hill**, a range of four mountains famous for its temples and magnificent views. The **Huating Temple**, Kunming's largest Buddhist monastery, has an imposing garden with an ornamental lake, the enclosing decorative wall of which is intersected by stupas. Higher up the mountain is the **Taihua Temple**, which also has a garden setting of great charm. The back of the temple has a hall dedicated to the Guanyin, Goddess of Mercy. In her Indian incarnation, she was depicted as a male. However, the Chinese have endowed her with the grace and compassion of a Buddhist Virgin Mary. In this temple she is even portrayed holding a male child.

Beyond the Huating Temple rises the **Sanqing Temple**, a Taoist shrine. There is little left of the original interiors, but a rest at the temple teahouse is recommended before a walk to **Dragon Gate**, where the view of the lake below is unsurpassable.

**Daguan Park**, on the north shore of the lake, contains a pavilion which houses a cultural treasure in the form of a poem inscribed on its facade. Written by a Qing-dynasty scholar, it extols the beauty of the scenery of Kunming. The park itself is attractive, with a landscape of lakes and willow-edged causeways.

On the eastern and southern shores of the Lake Dianchi, fields and villages stretch down to the water. A bus or taxi journey to some of the smaller villages and towns will show rural life just beyond the city. A visit to the small town of **Jinning** is recommended for its museum honouring the birthplace of Zheng He, the great Ming-dynasty eunuch admiral. His expeditions beginning in 1405 took him as far as Arabia and Africa, well in advance of the journeys of the Portuguese and Spanish explorers

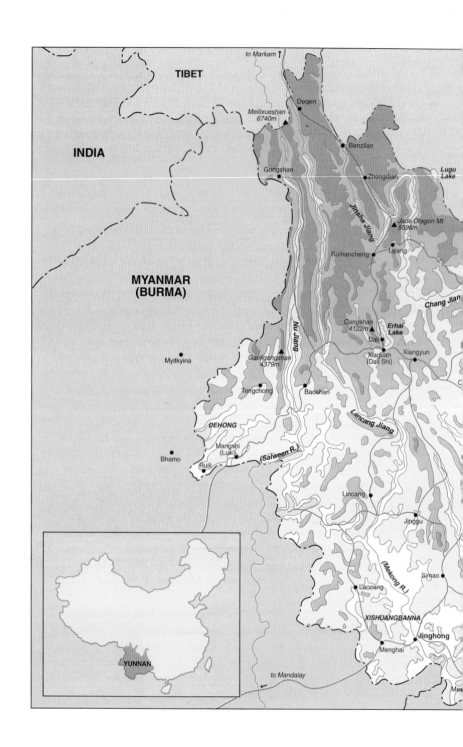

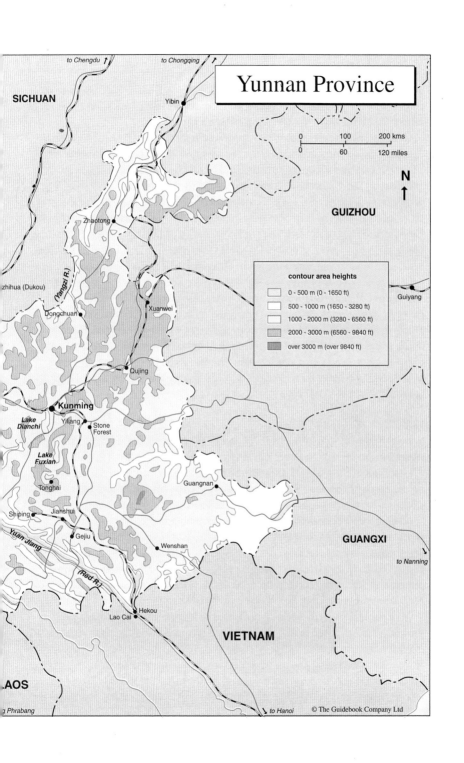

in the 15th century. These expeditions did not result in China establishing a trading empire, however. The museum shows the extent of his seven great voyages, which he achieved with the aid of the Chinese-invented compass.

Seventeen kilometres (ten miles) northwest of the city lies the **Kunming Botanical Garden**. Travellers interested in gardening should make a point of visiting here. The mountains and valleys of Yunnan harbour over half of China's indigenous trees and flowers. Many flowering shrubs, such as the rhododendron and camellia, which people from the West now see as a natural part of their own landscape, were first collected in Yunnan by European plant-hunters. Close to the garden is the colourful Taoist temple known as **Black Dragon Pool**. As with many dragon legends, the dragons of this story were destructive, only being mastered by a Taoist scholar who banished nine of them and tamed the tenth. This one is said to live in the pool.

The most popular one- or two-day outing from Kunming is the **Stone Forest**, 126 kilometres (79 miles) southeast of the city. This can be reached by coach tours or, for the more adventurous, by train to **Yiliang** and from there by bus. The Stone Forest is a strange place, with limestone pinnacles and rocks standing like petrified trees. The outcrops are not a fossil forest but the result of water erosion—just like the mountains of Guilin, except on a smaller scale. The area is the home of the Sani people, who delight in offering their handicrafts to visitors and often give song and dance performances in the local hotel.

## DALI

West of Kunming, 400 kilometres (250 miles) along the old Burma Road, stand the **Azure Mountains**, whose slopes rise in soft furrows above the lakeside plain of Dali. The richness of the plain's black soils, the marble deposits buried in the mountains, the waters of **Erhai Lake** (Ear Lake) teeming with fish, and the ribbons of small streams which water the fields, all help to make Dali a prosperous region.

Dali is the name of the region and of the region's principal town. It was once the capital of the Nanzhao Kingdom, when Yunnan was ruled by its own tribal people and had little interference from the Chinese empire. At the height of its power in the eighth and ninth centuries, the Nanzhao Kingdom sent armies to conquer parts of present-day Burma and Laos. In the tenth century, the kingdom was renamed Dali, but it was only brought under Chinese rule in the Yuan Dynasty.

The predominant ethnic group in Dali is the Bai, whose young women adorn themselves in bright red tunics, multicoloured aprons and intricate hats with tassels, braided ribbons and woven fabric. Getting to Dali involves going first to **Xiaguan**, the largest city in the region and the transportation hub of western Yunnan. At present it can be reached only by road, since there are no flights and no railway. Xiaguan has a lakeside park with a botanical garden famous for its camellias, azaleas and magnolia.

Also in Xiaguan is a **Tea Factory**, where Yunnanese tea is processed into 'bricks' for export to Tibet and the rest of the world. Otherwise there is little to see in the city.

The more attractive stone-built town of Dali itself, with its whitewashed walls and grey tiled roofs, invites exploration. In the north of the city stand the **Three Pagodas**, the largest of which is striking in its unadorned simplicity of form. These pagodas were once part of a great temple complex. Close to the Three Pagodas is the **Marble Factory**, where the stone is cut and polished to reveal natural patterns resembling clouds and mountains. Supplies come from the Azure Mountains and have been quarried for 1,200 years. This famous local industry is invoked every time the Chinese word for marble is used—*dalishi* (Dali stone). For those who love legends and a good walk, a visit to **Butterfly Spring** is recommended. However, it is unlikely that you will see any butterflies now.

The perfect way to enjoy the local sights is by boat on Erhai Lake. CITS arranges boat trips or, with a little bargaining, you can hire boats on the waterfront. The western shore of the lake is flat, with cultivated fields, and the rocky eastern shore is interesting for its small, dry-stone-walled villages, with their moored fleets of boats. The lake's islands are worth exploring: **Golden Shuttle Island** for its Buddhist temple and pavilion, and **Xiaoputuo Island** for its picturesque temple dedicated to the Goddess of Mercy, Guanyin.

## Outings from Dali

To the northeast of Dali rises **Chicken Foot Mountain** (Jizushan), so named because of its striated ridges which resemble a chicken's foot. Formerly this mountain drew Buddhist and Taoist pilgrims from far and wide, and its slopes were studded with temples and monasteries. Sadly, all the most important religious sites were very badly damaged during the Cultural Revolution, and little remains of Jizushan's former glories. However, a seventh-century pagoda has survived, as have small sections of the old walnut forests which once supplied timber to the people of the plain.

For those with time to spare, a visit from Dali to the renowned Buddhist caves of **Stone Bell Mountain** is highly recommended. The caves are in a remote area north of Dali, 130 kilometres (81 miles) away, but they reward the traveller with carvings dating back to the Nanzhao Kingdom. Of special interest is a cave full of depictions of female genitalia. With special permission from CITS, visitors may plan a trip to the early iron suspension bridge called **Rainbow Bridge** (Jihongqiao). The Chinese people were the first in the world to build iron suspension bridges. This one is a reconstruction dating from 1475, but a similar bridge is known to have existed at this site for a thousand years or so. Inscriptions carved on nearby cliffs attest to the role played by the Rainbow Bridge in linking the area with India, Burma and Siam.

# CHINESE PAINTING

Chinese painting has a long and eminent history, being considered the ultimate accomplishment of the Chinese scholar. There are, however, two traditions of Chinese painting—the scholar and the professional/artisan. Both these traditions have overlapped and influenced each other, but in general the scholar tradition has retained the greatest prestige.

The development of the scholar tradition becomes clear with the advent of the Tang Dynasty, even though few of the surviving Tang paintings are original. They are mainly copies made in later centuries. Indeed, copying was considered an important part of the practical study of painting, and there is a long tradition in Chinese painting— as in the other arts—of learning from past masters.

By the Song Dynasty—considered by many to be the apogee of Chinese landscape painting—there was an established tradition of painting styles and repertoires as well as a rich vocabulary of symbols and emblems used as an inner language in the paintings. The main categories of subject matter evolved into four classes—landscape, people and objects, birds and flowers, grass and insects. Of the four, the most esteemed was that of landscape. In the Northern Song Dynasty, masters such as Li Cheng, Fan Kuan, Guo Xi and Xu Daoning created magical, monumental landscapes and mists in which, if humans had a place at all, it was a minor one.

It is in these classic landscapes that the fundamental difference between Western and Chinese painting can be identified: perspective. After Giotto's work in 13th-century Italy, Western painting developed with a single fixed perspective. However, Chinese painters, although they were aware of perspective, rejected the device of a single disappearing point, creating instead landscapes in which the viewer *becomes* the traveller within the painting. The problems which such a technique creates are solved by the inventive use of space and by giving the picture shifting layers of perspective. Expanses of mist and water convey subtle shifts of vision. As you view a hanging scroll,

*continues*

*Landscape, ink and colour on paper, Li Hua Shen*

your eye moves upwards to the summit of the mountains in a series of scene-changes. With a horizontal scroll—traditionally viewed an arm's length at a time—the same effect is achieved from right to left.

The second major difference between Western and Chinese art lies in the medium itself. Most Western masterpieces are worked in oil. Chinese paintings are worked in black ink on silk or absorbent paper, sometimes using mineral colours—and those sparingly. The two traditional colours of Chinese painting are blue and green. Since the artist chose to capture the spirit or essence of his subject, rather than recreate it in loving detail, the use of black ink in a variety of tones and strokes has always been much more evocative than definitive in intention. Using brush and ink leaves no room for error. Once the brush is on the paper, it must be moved with strength and fluency if the painting is not to be rendered lifeless. Unlike the artist in oils, the Chinese painter has no chance to change or paint over his initial strokes. The importance of the brushstroke meant, in turn, that the development of the Chinese artist was intimately linked to that of the calligrapher. The scholar painter aimed to achieve an easy, inspired fluency of style which was unerring. To some extent, this explains why the noted poet and calligrapher of the Song Dynasty, Su Dongpo, saw the arts of poetry, painting and calligraphy as indivisible. In Chinese art, part of the beauty of the painting lies in the poem which the artist selects to write at the side of his work, as well as the style in which he decides to write it. Manuals on brushwork were compiled so that young artists could admire and copy the past masters, learning for example how they painted trees in winter or spring and precisely which brushstrokes they used.

Nature was the major preoccupation of the Chinese scholar artist. He made choices of subject in harmony with his own mood and the season of the year. Indeed, he believed that nothing could be painted without an understanding of the essential character of nature. Thus, landscape painting for him was less a celebration of the individuality of a particular place than an evocation of the spirit of *all* landscapes, captured in one particular scene at one particular season.

In his treatment of birds, animals and flowers, the Chinese painter also had little in common with his Western counterparts. The *nature morte* (still-life) of European painting would have been distasteful to him. The Chinese tradition is to show animals and flowers alive in their natural setting. Much attention is paid to detail here, and the artist is expected to depict how the plant or tree changes with the seasons, how an animal or bird moves and stands. This does not mean that Chinese renderings of flora and fauna are realistic. Rather, they are 'true' to the nature of the subject.

This also applies to the inner vocabulary of the Chinese painting. These emblems and symbols are an important part of the artist's intent. The four favourite subjects of the scholar painter are bamboo, plum, chrysanthemum and orchid, all of which reflect the qualities which the scholar strives to achieve in his own conduct. The bamboo bends but is not broken. The plum blossoms in winter, rising above adverse conditions, as does the chrysanthemum, while the orchid represents fragrance and elegance of form. The scholars of the Ming and Qing dynasties turned these four subjects into a veritable fashion.

## LIJIANG

Part of the delight in going to Lijiang lies in the journey itself. From Dali you have no choice but to go the 196-kilometre (122-mile) distance by road. As it climbs upwards into the mountainous region of northwest Yunnan, the road passes through forest glades of rhododendrons and azaleas, while ahead rise the stark, snow-tipped peaks of the **Jade Dragon Snow Range**.

Lijiang is the home of the Naxi people, who speak a language of the Tibeto-Burman group, and dress in black or deep blue. Other smaller minority groups live around Lijiang, including the Lisu, Pumi and Nuosu Yi. The Pumi are more brightly clad than the Naxi people, and the Lisu can only be seen by visiting the more remote districts close to the Nujiang (the Chinese name for the Salween River).

The Naxi were traditionally a matriarchal tribe, whose property was passed through the youngest female child; the men were in charge of gardening, music-making and child-rearing. In the present more liberal climate in China, the traditional Naxi orchestras are being revived. The Naxi are also notable for their shamanist traditions. Shamans (spirit mediums) were common in ancient China, and they still survive amongst the remote Siberian tribes, in Korea, and in Tibetan communities. The shamans, or *dongbas*, of the Naxi were responsible for transmitting the learning

*Moon-Embracing Pavilion at Black Dragon Pond in Lijiang, with Jade Dragon Snow Mountain (Yulongxue Shan) in the background*

of the tribe into their own pictographic script—now being translated into Chinese in a major attempt to preserve the Naxi heritage.

Lijiang itself falls into clear parts: old and new. The old part is infinitely more interesting, with its pebbled paths, potted mountain plants and small restaurants serving *baba*—deep-fried wheat cake, offered with a variety of fillings. The park known as **Black Dragon Pool** is the principal attraction of the town, with its **Moon Embracing Pavilion** (a modern reconstruction, since the Ming pavilion was burnt down in 1950 by a drunken cadre and his mistress in a fit of suicidal romanticism— or vandalism). One of the adjacent buildings is used to house the **Dongba Cultural Research Institute**, and another, the **Dragon God Temple**, is a setting for flower and art shows. The **Five Phoenix Hall**, a piece of whimsical architectural bravura, was once part of the Fuguo Temple which no longer exists. The hall is one of two buildings from the temple which were transferred intact to the Black Dragon Pool park in recent years.

Fuguo was one of the Five Famous Temples of Lijiang, the remaining four of which are scattered around the town at different sites. These temples were founded under the patronage of Mu Tian Wang, the 17th-century Naxi king. He was a religious man, instrumental in the growth of the Red Hat Sect of Buddhism in his domain. The **Jade Summit Temple** is famous for its setting in a pine forest, and for a camellia tree which in late February or early March flowers in such profusion that locals claim it has 20,000 blossoms. A trip to the **Temple of Universal Benefaction** includes a pleasant walk up a mountain trail. In the temple, Tibetan *tankas* have survived destruction, as have a few Buddha images. A few miles south of the town, the **Peak of Culture Temple** was famous in its time as a meditation centre. Above the temple is a hole in the earth, near a sacred spring where monks would stay for over three years to engage in intense meditation. The fourth temple to survive, the **Zhiyun Si**, in the nearby town of Lashiba, is now a school.

## Outings from Lijiang

The mighty Yangzi River sweeps through the northern part of Yunnan, and can be seen at the dramatic **Tiger Leaping Gorge** as it roars through sheer walls, 4,000 metres (10,000 feet) below. According to legend, a hunted tiger was able to make its escape from one side of the narrow gorge to the other in one single bound. At the point where the Yangzi makes its great turn northwards lies Shigu (Stone Drum) village, so named because of a memorial stone drum commemorating a victory by Chinese and Naxi troops over a Tibetan force in 1548. **Shigu** is known in modern Chinese history as a crossing-point of the Red Army on its Long March. In 1936, the survivors of the communist army reached Shigu, where the local citizens helped ferry them across the river to escape the Nationalist troops in pursuit.

The village of **Nguluko** is interesting for two reasons: it is typical of the smaller Naxi villages in its setting, and in the 1920s it was the home of the Austro-American explorer and botanist, Joseph Rock, who pioneered research on Yunnan's flora and Naxi ethnology. This Austro-American botanist and explorer came to Lijiang in 1922 and more or less remained here for the next 29 years. His house can still be visited. It was here that Joseph Rock did his research into Yunnan plant-life and recorded the results of his discoveries. The ancient town of **Baoshan**, to the north of Lijiang, is a rare sight because it is one of China's few remaining walled towns.

## XISHUANGBANNA

Located in the south of Yunnan Province and bordering Burma and Laos is the Xishuangbanna Dai Autonomous Prefecture. The Dai people are one of Yunnan's largest minority groups. About a third of the total population live in Xishuangbanna along with 12 other minority groups and a few Han Chinese.

Scarcely anything is known about the early history of the Dai. Their language and culture suggest that the Dai share a common ancestry with the Thais. What *is* recorded is that in the second century BC Dai chieftains sent tributary missions to the Han emperors. Between the eighth and 12th centuries Xishuangbanna was incorporated into the Nanzhao and Dali kingdoms. From the 14th to the 19th century a policy of pacification was practised by the Chinese imperial administration to keep control of the border areas. But it did not deter first the French—with their base in Indochina— and then the British from encroaching into this southwestern outpost. The incursions were short-lived, however. During the first half of the 20th century, Yunnan, in common with many other areas in China that were far from the seat of government, was controlled by a warlord. The area was taken over by the communists in 1950 and— except for the tragic decade of the Cultural Revolution, when minority peoples were treated atrociously—Xishuangbanna has enjoyed relative autonomy in local administration.

The Dai go their own way in religion as well, sharing their Buddhist practices and festivals with their Burmese and Laotian neighbours. Their temple and stupas closely resemble such architecture found in Southeast Asia, and their famous water splashing festival is similar to Thailand's Songkran celebration. The water splashing festival takes place over three days in the middle of April, and marks a legendary triumph of the forces of good over a destructive demon. It is also a symbolic occasion for the washing away of sins. During the three days of celebration, the Dai go around splashing each other—and any passerby—with water. It is difficult to visit the town during the festival because of a shortage of transportation and lodgings.

Xishuangbanna is tropical, with a rainy season lasting from June to October. The capital is **Jinghong**, which now has an airport to receive flights from Kunming. The

*The village of Meirendao in the Three Gorges—its populations is being relocated by the government due to the new dam project*

alternative is a two-day bus journey which passes through stunning scenery of steeply terraced rice paddies and lush jungles. Jinghong is an unassuming city which comes to life only on market days. The **Tropical Crops Research Institute** in the western district of the city is often visited. Beyond Jinghong and close to the Mekong River are many interesting Dai villages built on stilts. Stilt houses are common throughout Southeast Asia as an answer to the problem of river flooding. The roofs of the Dai houses are similar to the double-eaved Malay and Thai houses, designed for maximum ventilation and to protect against the heavy tropical rains. There are also markets where Dai, Hani and Jinuo women in colourful embroidered clothing sell jewellery and handicrafts.

An early morning one-hour boat ride downstream on the Mekong will take you to **Menghan**, a small Dai village with a few dusty roads and an excellent market. The village stands on **Olive Plain** (Ganlanba), covered with large plantations of rubber and fruit.

At the town of **Menghai**, west of Jinghong, tea growing and processing is the main industry. The tea grown is the famous Pu Er variety. At nearby **Mengzhe**, also an area of tea plantations, is the **Manlei Great Buddha Pagoda**.

Another fine expedition is to follow the road from Jinghong to the Burmese border. **Damenglong**, 70 kilometres (43 miles) southwest of Jinghong, is just eight

*(opposite page) Upper Yangzi River near Lijiang in Yunnan Province, just below Tiger Leaping Gorge. The only access to this valley is via the narrow tracker's path cut into the cliff face on the right*

kilometres (under five miles) from Burma. Burmese traders cross the border on Japanese motorbikes and tractors to bring Burmese cosmetics, jade and farm produce to exchange for China-made household goods and motor parts. Close to Damenglong is the **White Pagoda**, a 13th-century structure with eight small stupas surrounding a taller, central spire. Devout Buddhists leave offerings of money, flowers, fruit and embroidered cloth at the 'footprints of the Buddha' in the shrine inside the base of the pagoda. Around the town are paddy fields and lush vegetation, and there are some beautiful hikes in the hills nearby, even up to the Burmese border.

# The Yangzi River

The Yangzi River (Changjiang to the Chinese) offers travellers many kinds of expeditions. The river can be travelled by scheduled steamers or luxury cruise ships for the 2,500 kilometres (1,500 miles) between Chongqing and Shanghai. There are also side-trips to small riverside towns and a boat ride up the Daning River. But for those keen to see the remote upper reaches of the Yangzi—impossible to navigate due to its turbulent course through mountain meadows and narrow gorges— overland expeditions to northern Yunnan, Tibet, and even as far as the river's source in Qinghai, are possible.

The Yangzi is a great waterway, although navigation on it was fraught with difficulty until the later half of this century. Since 1949 the government has undertaken major hydraulic schemes to keep the waters in check. Although the rapids of the Three Gorges are still an unpredictable force, they are no longer so threatening since Chinese troops dynamited most of the worst obstacles in the 1950s. At Yichang, the Gezhouba Dam has already broken the river's flow, while the Three Gorges Project—China's largest construction project since the Great Wall and Grand Canal—will eventually raise water levels in the gorges and necessitate the relocation of one million people and scores of historical sites.

All this is changing the face of the river. Yet the 'taming' of the Yangzi has not taken away the sense of adventure. With the lifting of more and more restrictions on travel to small towns along the river's course, a voyage up or down the Yangzi now offers a glimpse of river communities previously unknown to the foreign traveller.

However, for all its side-trips and diversions, the river itself is the heart of the Yangzi expedition. Few travellers can fail to be impressed by the dawn voyage through the towering walls of the Three Gorges, or the excitement of turning out of the mouth of the river into the hectic waterway of Shanghai's Huangpu Creek. But the river also has its quieter moments and sights: the evening flight homeward of geese across the bows of the ship, a glimpse of a riverside pagoda, the passing of small craft with their lamps lit at night, or the thick flow of the river as it pushes past the shoreside fields of young rice.

With a little imagination, the history of the river can be brought to life, too—the epic battles of the Three Kingdoms, Kublai Khan crossing the river with his navy on his way to conquer the Song empire of the south, and more recently, the tea clippers of the 19th century which raced from Hankou to London with the first of the season's tea.

## THE RIVER JOURNEY

Yangzi travellers can choose the slower journey upstream, embarking at Shanghai or Wuhan, or the downstream trip embarking at Chongqing. Most tour groups are taken along the Yangzi in the dozen or so cruisers which make several stops *en route* for passengers to visit riverside towns. However, independent travellers usually take the regular steamer line, with a change of boat at Wuhan. The steamers do not always stop long enough for the traveller to disembark and take a walk round the smaller places along the way, so an organized tour is—at the moment—the best way to see the river.

Chongqing is the usual embarkation point for the journey downstream. The new municipality is the main industrial centre of southwest China, and the city served as the country's capital during the Sino-Japanese War. During this period, the city's notorious foggy weather saved it from being destroyed by Japanese bombers. Chongqing's history stretches back to the fourth century BC, when it was known as Yuzhou. Built at the confluence of the Yangzi and Jialing rivers, it was a settlement of strategic importance, serving as the capital of the ancient state of Ba during the Zhou Dynasty. Little is known about the men of Ba, except that they buried their dead in boat-shaped coffins which were then placed on cliff ledges above the river. Some of these strange coffins can be seen in the Chongqing Museum.

The modern name of Chongqing, which means 'Double Celebration', was adopted by a Song-dynasty prince from Yuzhou when he became emperor.

Set on a promontory on the north bank of the Yangzi, the city has outgrown its original site and spilled over to the adjacent banks of both the Yangzi and Jialing. Cable cars and bridges connect the newer districts of Chongqing with the older cliff-side city centre. Most visitors are taken to Pipa Hill at dusk to view the city. It is an attractive sight of steep lamplit streets sweeping down to the dark waters of the river below. Tour itineraries sometimes include visits to the Red Rock Village (Hongyan Cun) and the Cassia Garden (Guiyuan), which were communist headquarters during the 1930s and 1940s, but these are somewhat drab sights. Instead, walk down to the Chaotianmen docks to see the harbour and all the craft on the river (you do not necessarily embark here if you are joining a tourist ship).

The nearby town of Fengdu was traditionally known by its nickname of 'Ghost

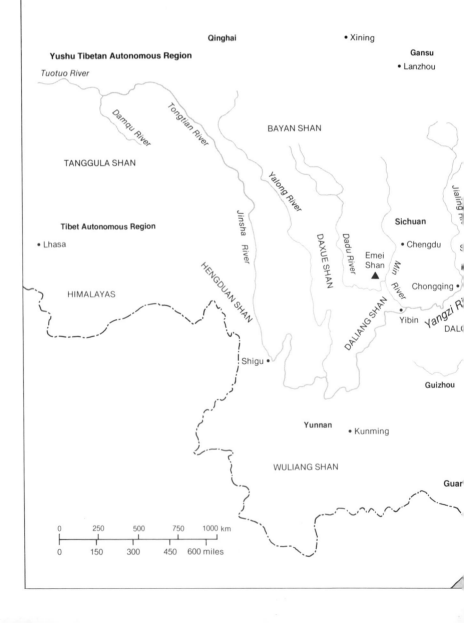

# The Course of the Yangzi

City' and it has a temple dedicated to the King of the Underworld. This strange association dates back to the Han Dynasty, when two scholar-recluses who lived in the town were believed to have achieved immortality. The combination of their names results in the title 'King of the Underworld'!

**Fuling** was the site of the royal tombs of the fourth-century state of Ba (it was from here that many of the boat-shaped coffins, now in the Chongqing Museum, were excavated). The most important archaeological treasure in Fuling is a set of carvings along the rocky shore of the Yangzi, which are only exposed when the river drops to a very low level. These carvings consist of 14 fish and stone inscriptions, giving information on ancient hydrology and cosmology.

The name of **Shibaozhai** means 'Precious Stone Fortress'; the precious stone in question is a 30-metre-high (100-foot) rock which juts into the air. This rock is said to resemble a stone seal. (Seals in traditional China were carved at the base and used as a form of official signature.) In the Qing dynasty, a temple was built on top of the rock. Originally, the temple could only be visited by climbing up an iron chain, but in the late 19th century a nine-storey wooden pagoda was built next to the rock so that the ascent could be made by staircase. An extra three storeys were added this century, and now the 12-storey red pagoda rises alongside the rock to the base of the temple. A local legend tells of a hole in the rock through which flowed a ceaseless supply of rice for the monks of the temple. A greedy monk thought that he could make his fortune by enlarging the hole to get more rice, but he was punished when the miracle of the rice flow ceased the moment the hole was made bigger.

**Wanxian** is the overnight stop for the scheduled steamers before they negotiate the Three Gorges by morning light. The city is an ancient river port and once had a thriving junk-building industry. Passengers usually enjoy the stopover here because of the city's night market, which sells delicious, locally grown citrus fruits and a wide selection of bamboo and rattan handicrafts. On the outskirts of the town is **Taibai Rock**, where the Tang-dynasty poet, Li Bai (Li Po) is said to have stayed. The rock-face around the memorial pavilion to the poet is covered with stone inscriptions.

Facing south over the river, the town of **Yunyang** is famous in stories from the Three Kingdoms period (220–265). This period in Chinese history has much of the romance which the English associate with the tales of King Arthur, except that there is a firmer historical background for the Chinese tales. In Yunyang it is said that General Zhang Fei of the Kingdom of Shu (the kingdom which covered most of present-day Sichuan) was assassinated. In his honour, the **Zhang Fei Temple** was built, which still stands today. Stone carvings from the fifth and sixth centuries have been housed in the temple, which has a tranquil setting amidst gardens and rock pools.

**Fengjie**, guarding the western entrance of the Three Gorges, is also associated with the Three Kingdoms period. It was here that Liu Bei, the King of Shu, died in despair after his armies were routed by the forces of Wu. The famous general of the state of Shu, Zhuge Liang, trained his troops in military strategy in the fields around Fengjie. The town has an attractive setting, and parts of its Ming-dynasty ramparts as well as one city gate are still intact. It has open-air markets, where the varied produce of the local countryside is sold.

Baidicheng—or White Emperor City—is reached by ferry from Fengjie. It offers splendid views into the mouth of the Qutang Gorge, and has a temple which was originally dedicated to the mythical White Emperor. In the Ming dynasty, the temple was re-dedicated to General Zhuge Liang. One of its halls contains a 'Forest of Steles', a collection of tablets which includes several rare stone carvings. The Bamboo Leaf Poem Tablet, on which the characters of a poem are engraved in the form of three bamboo branches, is one of only three of its kind in China.

## THE THREE GORGES

The Three Gorges of the Yangzi extend for 200 kilometres (125 miles) of the river's course, and span the boundary of Chongqing Municipality and Hubei Province. The first gorge on the downstream voyage is the Qutang. It is the shortest gorge, but visually the most dramatic. The second, the Wu (Sorceress) Gorge, is flanked by enchanting scenery of forest-clad slopes rising into strangely formed mountain peaks. The final gorge, the Xiling, is the longest of the three, enclosing banks of shoals and rapids which turn the muddy river to a coffee-coloured froth.

The gorges push the river into a funnel of furious water, which in places has a velocity of 80,000 cubic metres (105,000 cubic yards) a second. At some points, the river is squeezed to a width of less than 100 metres (330 feet), and the water flow can reach 25 kilometres (15 miles) an hour. After the year 2000, the Three Gorges will remain, but with altered geography due to the new dam project. Water levels will rise by up to 100 metres, making both the river's flow slower and water in its gorges deeper and wider. Doubtless, ships' captains will welcome the easier navigation.

The most spectacular of the gorges, the **Qutang Gorge**, was known to foreigners in the last century as 'The Windbox'. The name seems inappropriate on a fine day with a light mist hanging between towering cliffs, which themselves soar in deep shadow to over 1,200 metres (4,000 feet) either side of the river. Yet in a storm, with a high water level, the gorge was impossible to navigate, and many lost their lives while travelling through the Qutang. Look out for the Meng Liang stairway, a series of holes on the rock-face which stops half-way up the river cliff. High on the slopes of the rock-face were found some of the 2,000-year-old coffins from the state of Ba, now on exhibit in the Chongqing Museum.

Passengers on the cruise ships can disembark at **Wushan** and transfer to small motorboats for a river journey through the Three Lesser Gorges of the **Daning River**.

The Daning is a tributary which rises in Shaanxi Province and flows south into the Yangzi. Its mini Three Gorges are known as the Dragon Gate Gorge, the Misty Gorge and the Vivid Green Gorge. During the river trip, the boats motor upstream for 50 kilometres (30 miles) through the tranquil scenery of verdant river cliffs and terraced fields, before turning back to course downstream with the current. In the quieter reaches of the gorges, golden-haired monkeys still roam in chattering bands. The region is famous for rare medicinal herbs.

The twelve peaks of **Wu Gorge** all have poetic names. They include Fir Tree Cone Peak, the Gathered Immortals Peak, and the Assembled Cranes Peak. As the Chinese have a great love of weaving legends around strange natural phenomena, these gorges and mountains are therefore among their best-loved landscapes. The most renowned peak in this sense is **Goddess Peak** (Shennu Feng), which is said to resemble the figure of a maiden kneeling in front of a pillar. Legend has it that the young goddess was the daughter of the Queen Mother of the West, who fell in love with this lonely spot and made her home here. At the foot of the Gathered Immortals Peak is another relic associated with Zhuge Liang. It is known as the **Kong Ming Tablet**, and has carved inscriptions in the calligraphy of the general and military strategist. The characters are large enough to be seen from the boat as it moves on to the small town of **Peishi**, which marks the border between the provinces of Sichuan and Hubei.

**Xiling Gorge**, the next on the river, runs for 75 kilometres (45 miles) through slopes planted with orange groves. The gorge is divided into seven smaller gorges, the most famous of which are the Gorge of the Sword and the Book on the Art of War, the Gorge of the Ox's Liver and Horse's Lung, the Gorge of the Yellow Ox, and the Gorge of Shadow Play. The shoals and rapids within Xiling were the most treach- erous of all obstacles in the Three Gorges. Until the 1950s, boats were hauled over them by trackers, whose backbreaking job would guarantee them an exceedingly short lifespan. A folk song about one of the most dangerous shoals has the following words: 'May the gods protect us as we sail through the Blue Shoal. If the Dragon King gets angry, then both men and boats are finished!' The Blue Shoal, like all other river obstacles, was dynamited in the 1950s to make the Yangzi safer for navigation.

Just beyond the Three Gorges, the flow of the river is broken by the 70-metre- high (230-foot) barrier of the Gezhouba Dam. The dam harnesses the energy of the Yangzi's current, and the projected annual output of the dam is 138 billion Kwh. Boats have to pass through one of the three shiplocks on either side of the dam.

**Yichang** marks the end of the upper reaches of the Yangzi and the beginning of the broader, middle reaches of the river. The city was an important river port, where goods were unloaded from the larger ships used further downstream, or from the smaller ships which travelled upstream through the gorges. West of the city there is a small cave, which is famous for its Tang and Song inscriptions of poetry. It is known as the **Three Travellers Cave**, after three Tang-dynasty poets who first met there. The hill above the cave is an excellent place to go to enjoy a view of the eastern entrance of the Xiling Gorge. Yichang also marks the site of the legendary Yiling Battle between the states of Shu and Wu in the third century. The Wu army was smaller and weaker, but it used fire to destroy the camps of the Shu army. The King of Shu, Liu Bei, was bitterly disappointed after this battle and died soon afterwards in Fengjie. Further downstream on the north bank is the town of **Shashi**, with its riverside **Pagoda of Longevity**, built in the reign of Emperor Qianlong in the Qing dynasty.

**Dongting Lake**, below Shashi, was once China's largest freshwater lake. However, silting and land reclamation have reduced its size, and now it ranks second. Legends about Dongting abound. One Tang-dynasty story has the lake as the home of the King of the Dragons. The lake was part of the intricate waterway system which allowed goods from the very south—as far as Guangzhou—to be brought by way of the Xiang River (a tributary), through the lake, along the Yangzi down to Yangzhou, and then up the Grand Canal to the imperial capitals in the north.

## The Lower River

The triple city of **Wuhan**, which spans the confluence of the rivers Han and Yangzi, is for many travellers the end or the beginning of their river cruise. Wuhan has always been the Yangzi's major inland river port, since it marked the furthest point to which seagoing vessels could sail. In the last century, the city became a Treaty Port and grew rich on the tea trade which was centred on **Hankou** (one of the three connected cities).

Hankou was the city with the foreign concessions, and to this day has remained the commercial centre of Wuhan. As for the two other cities, **Hanyang** is on the same side of the river, to the south of Hankou, while **Wuchang** sprawls along the opposite bank. In Hanyang there are two famous sights—the **Lute Pavilion** and the Buddhist **Guiyuan Monastery**. The Lute Pavilion comprises a series of terraces and pavilions set amidst attractive gardens. It lives up to its musical name, since it is now a popular place with elderly music lovers who gather here for open-air performances. The Guiyuan Monastery was founded in the Qing dynasty and became an important centre for Chan (Zen) Buddhist scholarship. It has a collection of 500 carved and gilded *luohans* (Buddhist disciples), which are considered works of great craftsmanship. Attached to the monastery is a vegetarian restaurant.

Wuchang is linked to an important event in Chinese revolutionary history, for it was here that the military uprising started, which was ultimately to topple the Qing Dynasty and bring about the founding of the Chinese Republic. Visitors can see the **Headquarters of the 1911 Revolution**, which is known locally as the Red House.

*The Hankow flood, 1931*

A statue of Dr Sun Yat-sen stands outside the building. Another place of special interest in Wuchang is the **Hubei Provincial Museum**, which houses artifacts excavated from the Warring States period tomb of the Marquis of Zeng. An impressive collection of 65 bronze chime bells forms part of the tomb's treasures.

Leaving Hubei Province, the next port of call is **Jiujiang**. Once an important river port for the tea trade, Jiujiang now thrives on its cotton industry. The city lies just west of **Poyang Lake**, one of China's best-known nature reserves, a wintering ground for rare white- and red-crested cranes, as well as storks and wildfowl. Jiujiang is the stopping-off point for visits to the mountain resort of **Lushan**. Lushan is attractive in spring, when the azaleas are in flower, but it receives a heavy swell of visitors in the summer months, when the mountains offer a cool retreat from the baking temperatures of the Yangzi plain. Close to Jiujiang is **Stone Bell Hill**, which overlooks the spot where Poyang Lake meets the Yangzi. The hill is chiefly of interest for its unsolved mystery—nobody can quite give an explanation for a strange bell-like sound that can be heard on the hill, though some people believe is caused by flowing water. In the Song dynasty, the poet Su Dongpo was so intrigued by the hill that he came here three times.

**Xiaogushan**, below the mouth of the Poyang, is a small riverine island which, through silting, has now become part of the north bank of the river. Legend tells of a maiden, Xiaogu Niang Niang, who when eloping with her lover on a flying umbrella, dropped her slipper into the river. The slipper miraculously turned into an island.

The girl and her lover fell from the sky and became mountains divided by the river. There is a temple on the island dedicated to Xiaogu Niang Niang, which is visited by infertile women who come in the hope of bearing a child. Downstream, again on the north bank, is the octagonal Ming **Zhenfeng Pagoda** of Anqing. By now the Yangzi is in Anhui Province. Anhui's two great scenic sites are the mountains of Huangshan and Jiuhuashan. To get there, travellers on the river use **Wuhu** as the stopping-off point. Wuhu is situated at the confluence of the Qingyi and Yangzi rivers. As this was a danger spot for navigation, a pagoda was built to act as a lighthouse. It was named **Zhongjiang**, or 'Mid-River', **Pagoda**, and does indeed mark the mid-point of the lower Yangzi, from the mouth of Poyang Lake to the estuary above Shanghai.

For **Nanjing**, *see* pages 91-98.

**Zhenjiang** was a city of great strategic importance in the Three Kingdoms period and it served as the capital of the state of Wu. It is here that the Grand Canal intersects the Yangzi, thus making Zhenjiang an important trading centre. The hills around the city were the source of inspiration for many painters of the Southern Song school. In the middle of the river at Zhenjiang rises **Jiao Hill**, where the Song-dynasty painter Mi Fei, and the poet Lu You, had stone inscriptions carved in their own calligraphy. The nearby **Jin Shan** was once a riverine island, but silting has joined it to the southern bank of the river. The monastery of Jin Shan is still an important place of Buddhist pilgrimage. To the northeast of the city lies **Beigu Hill**, considered to be the most beautiful of Zhenjiang's hills. It appears in many of the stories in the *Romance of the Three Kingdoms* (*see* Recommended Reading, page 332).

To the north of the Yangzi, on the Grand Canal itself, lies the city of **Yangzhou**, once one of the wealthiest of Chinese cities. During the Tang dynasty, its merchants thrived on the salt trade (which was an imperial monopoly) and gave their patronage to the many artists who flocked here. Today, Yangzhou has retained its traditional charms. One of the most delightful ways to pass your time here is to stroll through the lanes which thread between the city's canals. The buildings around the **Slender West Lake** are some of the finest, with their simple whitewashed walls and contrasting dark-grey tiled roofs, which sweep up into flying eaves. A large community of Arab traders resided in the city in the Yuan dynasty, and the city mosque, the **Xianhe Si**, dates from the 13th century. Puhaddin, who was the 16th-generation descendant of Mohammed, came to China in the mid-13th century and was buried in Yangzhou. In the **Museum** there is a good collection of the works of the Eight Eccentric Painters of Yangzhou, who lived in the 18th century. Unlike most scholar-painters of the time, who regarded painting as a purely academic pursuit, these painters were so unconventional as to make their living from the sale of their works to the wealthy merchants of Yangzhou.

For **Shanghai**, *see* pages 119-131.

# Fujian

The coastal province of Fujian in southeast China is one of the areas least explored by foreign visitors. Yet the province offers some of the best sightseeing, historic sites and local cuisine found anywhere in China, with the bonus of a warm, sub-tropical climate which makes winter visits an attractive option. The four main cities of Fujian are the capital Fuzhou, Xiamen (Amoy), Quanzhou and Zhangzhou. In the north of the province is the scenic area known as the Wuyi Mountains.

Fujian has a long indented coastline backed by steep and rugged mountains where much of the soil is too poor for rice farming. The Fujianese have traditionally earned their living from the sea, and by growing fruit, vegetables and tea. Poverty and the beckoning seaboard had encouraged emigration since the end of the Song Dynasty. In the 19th and early 20th centuries, the existing land tenure system forced many more poorer peasants to emigrate, and now the overseas Fujianese community is second only to that of the Cantonese. Most overseas Chinese from Fujian settled in Southeast Asia, with a large proportion in the Philippines. Taiwan, lying only 160 kilometres (100 miles) across from Fujian, has also had its share of Fujianese emigrants in the last three centuries. So many people on either side of the Taiwan Straits share common ancestors and speak the same dialect that the renewal of ties which has come with China's more liberal economic climate is hardly surprising. Although there is still no official direct diplomatic contact between the two governments, trade between Fujian and Taiwan has grown in leaps and bounds. Much of it is channelled through Hong Kong. Rare medicinal herbs and fungi collected in the mountains of Fujian, not to mention tea and other foodstuffs, have a ready market in Taiwan, while the People's Republic has a voracious appetite for made-in-Taiwan consumer goods (which can be anything from fashion clothes to telescopic umbrellas). Altogether, the role of the overseas Chinese (*huaqiao*) in Fujian's development is extremely significant. They have made substantial investments in the Xiamen Special Economic Zone, for example.

Fujian has a long history of trade with the outside world. In 1842—by the Treaty of Nanking—Fuzhou and Xiamen (then known as Amoy) were two of five Treaty Ports opened to foreign commerce and residence. The city of Quanzhou had a large foreign population during the Tang and Yuan dynasties, including many Arabs. Their descendants, and their converts' descendants, still live in distinct Moslem communities throughout the province. Many of the mountain people of Fujian are not Han Chinese. One of the most distinctive minority communities is the She people. Young people from the She villages can often be seen working in the cities in order to save enough money to get married. The girls wear headdresses of bright scarves over a

*Chinese jossmen, Fuzhou*

frame shaped like a coathanger without the hook. They are very shy and never seem to mix with the local Chinese or wish to be photographed.

There are some wonderful off-the-beaten-track places to visit in Fujian, if you are willing to take local buses and wander at will. If you are visiting in the warmer months, the coast has some lovely golden sand beaches.

Local cooking places emphasis on what is readily available—fresh vegetables and seafood—and is delicious. With the influx of overseas Chinese tourists, who come back to visit their ancestral villages, new hotels have proliferated and transportation is much improved. Direct bus services from Hong Kong have made Fujian as accessible by land as it always has been by sea.

## Fuzhou

The provincial capital of Fuzhou has a glorious setting on the banks of the Min River, against a backdrop of mountains. It has grown up around three hills—Yushan, Gushan and Wushan—which are areas of scenic interest, with numerous pavilions, temples and museums. The city is famous for its lacquerware and puppet troupe, but other reasons to visit the city are its excellent seafood restaurants, various craft factories, and excursions to the numerous old temples around the city.

**Yushan** lies in a striking location at the mouth of the Min River and, although small, it has three temples, several pavilions and the famous **White and Black Pagodas**, which are the landmarks of the city. These pagodas were first built in the tenth century and each has seven storeys. You will also find the **Fuzhou Antique Shop** on Yushan.

West of Yushan lies the small hill of **Wushan**. The hill was originally a place of Taoist retreat. It has many small pavilions sited to offer views over the countryside and river estuary. There are several stone carvings on the hillside, the most remarkable of which is an image of Buddha on the southeastern slope. Close to Fuzhou University, the **Xichan Temple** is a lively city temple, which has been restored by donations from overseas Chinese.

Just outside the city, the **Gold Mountain Temple** is situated on an island in the middle of the Wulong River, and is reached by raft. On the eastern outskirts of Fuzhou, on **Drum Mountain** (Gushan), one of the scenic resorts of the city, there is the **Bubbling Spring Temple**, which is approached by walking up a stone stairway lined with flowering shrubs. This temple is a major religious centre, with a community of several hundred monks. A visit to the **Snow Peak Temple** in the hills north of Fuzhou offers a chance to enjoy a drive through the countryside and walks in the hills. While there, it is worth looking for the **Withered Wood Temple**, a charming ninth-century structure found off the road in a rustic setting.

Visitors will not want to leave Fuzhou without some momento of its famous handicrafts. Stone carving, lacquerware and cork sculpting are the 'Three Handicraft Treasures of Fuzhou'. These can be found at the craft factories or on Wusi Lu, not far from the Overseas Chinese Hotel.

## QUANZHOU

South of Fuzhou, on the banks of the Jin River, lies the ancient port city of Quanzhou. Its quiet, prosperous air belies its distinguished history as China's first port in the Song and Yuan dynasties. Its harbour silted up in the Ming dynasty, and it is now of minor importance, but nonetheless it remains the commercial centre for the surrounding farmlands.

As a reminder of Quanzhou's maritime links, the Muslim community flourishes. From the Tang to the Yuan dynasties, Arab merchants traded and settled in Quanzhou, which they called 'Zaytun'—the Great Emporium. The **Grand Mosque** is a short walk from the Overseas Chinese Hotel. Built in the first years of the 11th century, it continues to be an active centre of worship. Just to the east of the city is **Lingshan** (Ling Hill), which is the burial site of two Muslim missionaries who came to the city in the Tang dynasty.

In the old quarter, to the northwest of the city, the **Kaiyuan Temple** is one of the most famous in the region. It was founded in the Tang dynasty and has some fine examples of Buddhist architecture and statuary dating from the Song dynasty. To the east is the **Ancient Boat Exhibition**, the remains of a Song-dynasty seagoing ship excavated downstream of the city and now housed in this hall. A dramatic new museum, with towers shaped like junk sails, has opened with exhibits related to the era when Quangzhou was the major port on the so called 'Maritime Silk Road'.

In the same direction, the road passes through **Hui'an County**, where the women traditionally dress rather differently from the majority, in vividly reds, greens and blues, with an intriguing headdress of floral scarf and bright yellow conical hat.

## ZHANGZHOU

Like Quanzhou, Zhangzhou was also a major port city, until it was eclipsed by the nearby port of Xiamen when its tidal creek silted up. Zhangzhou now serves as a market for the farmers of the rich, fertile plain of the Jiulong River. The area is famous for its tropical fruits, such as pineapples, bananas, lychees and *longyans* (Dragon's Eyes), as well as for the popular Chinese New Year flower, the narcissus, which is grown for special effect in water. The city is also renowned for its art galleries, craft factories and local opera troupes, which often give open-air performances.

# Politics in Command

*One afternoon when we were making dazibao, Little Mihu came running into the classroom waving a magazine and shouting, "Big discovery, big discovery!" We clustered around. Little Mihu was holding the May issue of China Youth. He jabbed his finger at the back cover, a scene of young people carrying bundles of wheat in baskets slung on shoulder poles. Behind them stretched a golden ocean of wheat.*

*"Look at the red flag in the background," Little Mihu said excitedly. "It's fluttering toward the right. On the map, right is east and left is west. So the wind must be blowing from the west. Chairman Mao says the east wind should prevail over the west, but here the west is prevailing over the east!"*

*That was not all. Little Mihu turned the back cover side-ways and traced his finger through the wheatfield, pointing out some light-colored steaks. "Here are four characters, do you see?" "Oh my!" somebody gasped. "Long live Kai-shek!" I saw it too, the veiled message in praise of Kuomintang leader Chiang Kai-shek.*

*The magazine passed from hand to hand. We were shocked that the enemies of socialism would be so bold as to issue a public challenge and amazed that they had figured out such a clever way to do it. Now we understood why the newspapers were warning us that counterrevolutionaries had wormed their way into the very heart of the Party's cultural apparatus. Nothing could be taken for granted anymore.*

*A few days later, Little Bawang pointed to Chairman Mao's portrait at the front of our classroom and exclaimed, "Look! Chairman Mao has only one ear!" Sure enough, the face was turned slightly to the right, showing only the left ear. A few students laughed. "What are you laughing about?" Little Bawang snarled. "This is a serious political problem. Every normal person has two ears, so why did this painter paint Chairman Mao with only one?" The class divided into two schools of thought. Yuling and I and a few others saw the missing ear as a question of artistic realism. But Little Bawang's view won over a majority. They began discussing whether to report the missing ear to the School Party Committee.*

The China Youth cover was the talk of Yizhong. Everyone was on the lookout for more incriminating evidence, and every day fresh dazibao reported the latest findings. One group of students claimed to have found a snake on the face of Lenin, whose portrait hung beside the portraits of Mao, Marx, and Stalin in the back of the school auditorium and several other meeting rooms. Others said the snake was no more than a shadow on one side of Lenin's nose. Another group found a sword hanging over Chairman Mao's head in a photograph that showed him standing on the rostrum in Beijing's Tiananmen Square. Others said the sword was a painted beam. There were a few more imaginative discoveries, but none was as convincing as that pernicious message on the back cover of China Youth.

The search spread. Nothing was immune from suspicion. Taking their cues from the newspapers, students found problems with short stories, novels, movies, and plays. The critiques that appeared on the walls each day became more and more intricate. The headline-style dazibao were joined by much longer xiaozibao, "small-character posters."

One poster criticized a literature textbook for spreading decadent bourgeois ideas because it included a poem about young people's minds turning to love in the spring. One chastised our geography teacher, Teacher Liu, for entrancing us with descriptions of the grasslands of Mongolia and the mountains of Xinjiang instead of inspiring us with Mao Zedong's revolutionary thought.

By now, layer upon layer of paper covered the school walls. The debate had expanded far beyond the bounds of the Three Family Village, although the Three Villagers' names still appeared here and there, usually covered with big red X's, the symbol used on court decrees to signify the death sentence.

*Gao Yuan*, Born Red

In the south of the city lies **Nanshan Temple**, an important Buddhist monastery which runs a vegetarian restaurant open to the public. One of the monastery's treasures is a milk-white jade Buddha, which was brought to China from Burma.

Further south, the **Hundred Flower Village** is a botanical garden which was started in the Ming dynasty. It is a wonderful place to come and enjoy flowers and a display of *pen jing* (miniature trees, usually known by the Japanese name of *bonsai*). In the summer, the Lychee season can be enjoyed with a visit to the Lychee orchards, which are a few kilometres east of the garden.

## XIAMEN

On the southern coast of Fujian, the thriving commercial city and port of Xiamen is one of the success stories of China's current economic reform programme. Because of its beautiful setting, on an island linked to the mainland by a narrow causeway, no heavy industry has been allowed in the city, and it has a pleasant pollution-free atmosphere. Its rocky shores face several offshore islands on the eastern side, one of which—**Gulangyu**—is the city's own resort, with old villas and car-free lanes. Another close-lying island, **Quemoy**, is held by Nationalist troops of the government of Taiwan.

The inevitably sensitive coastal defences meant that Xiamen was off-limits to foreign tourists until the early 1980s. The city is China's third Special Economic Zone, and it has a growing electronics industry as well as a port with good facilities for seagoing vessels. An extended runway at Xiamen Airport now allows Jumbo jets to land.

East of Xiamen's city centre, the Buddhist **Nanputuo Monastery** rises in terraces and courtyards against the slopes of Wulao Mountain. The monastery has one of China's few Buddhism schools, and runs a vegetarian restaurant in a side courtyard of the temple. Not far away is the **Overseas Chinese Museum**, built by Fujian's favourite son, Tan Kah Kee, who made a fortune in Singapore and returned to his birthplace to give generously of his time and money. In the museum the story of the Chinese diaspora is told through 6,000 exhibits.

The lovely island of Gulangyu has golden sand beaches for swimming in warmer months, narrow lanes full of hawker stalls, and the Lotus Flower Monastery, known locally as the **Sunlight Monastery**. It stands on the high point of the island called **Sunlight Rock**, which, climbed at dawn, gives an excellent view of the sunrise over the sea. The island has four churches, and every Christmas Eve a carol service is held on the island.

## WUYI MOUNTAINS

Finally, in the northwest of the province, is the marvellous resort area of the Wuyi Mountains, popular since the second century BC. A trip to these mountains takes you through scenery as evocative as the landscapes of Guilin. Most visitors enjoy a trip on the **Nine-Twist Stream** (Jiuqu Xi), punting past sheer cliffs, strange rock formations and flowery river banks. Many famous visitors have come here over the centuries, and the various stone inscriptions by the side of the river have been carved in the calligraphy of well-known painters, poets and scholars. Of special interest is the exhibition of 3,000-year-old boat-shaped coffins which were found on ledges high up on the river cliffs. Horticulture enthusiasts and bird-watchers will wish to make an expedition to the **Wuyi Nature Reserve**, filled with a sub-tropical virgin forest and a variety of flora which excited European botanists in the 19th century. In addition, tea is cultivated by the 3,000 villagers who live in the area. The reserve is also a migratory stopping-place for birds.

*Fujian Province, early 1900s*

*(following pages) The red sandstone peaks of Longhu Shan, near the town of Yingtan in Jiangxi Province. These oddly shaped peaks are an extension of the Wuyi mountain range of Fujian (see above)*

## CHINESE CALLIGRAPHY

Chinese people have a special reverence for the arts of calligraphy and painting. In traditional China, the scholar class considered the practice of calligraphy, painting and poetry to be the highest skills an educated man could acquire. Scholars who took the imperial examination were often judged by the quality of their handwriting, and even the best essay, if written in a poor hand, could result in failure for a candidate. How a man wielded his brush was believed to indicate his character and qualities. Even today, when most students use pens rather than brushes to write their university exam papers, a good hand is still admired.

Calligraphy is an art form in China because of the special nature of the Chinese language. Writing Chinese characters involves making a variety of strokes which need to exhibit emphasis, fluidity, lightness and balance, and the discipline lends itself to creative interpretation. The earliest Chinese characters were cut on the shells of tortoises or the bones of animals, and later they were inscribed on bronze vessels. Their shape was clearly influenced by the fact that a sharp implement was used to etch the words on a hard surface. In the earliest style of Chinese calligraphy, known as *Zhuan Shu* (Seal Script), the strokes of the characters are curved and pictorial in style, reflecting the representational quality of the early characters. To this day, calligraphers still practise the writing of Seal Script and—as its name suggests—it is most commonly used in the carving of seals.

During the Qin Dynasty, a regular script was formulated under the rule of Qin Shi Huangdi. This script is known as *Li Shu* (Official Script). The strokes of the characters were made more regular and compact. During the Han Dynasty, the invention of paper and the development of writing by brush led to a greater expressiveness in calligraphy. Two styles emerged. One of these was the *Kai Shu* (Regular Script), in which the characters were invested with an even greater regularity of form. There is a more geometric and angular shape to the characters; they are written as if placed in the centre of an imaginary square. During this period another script was developed, more cursive and free in form, which is called *Cao Shu* (Grass Script). Grass Script and the later script of *Xing Shu* (Running Script) both allow the writer a greater freedom of expression. Yet the strong and irregular strokes of the two scripts do have their conventions, which prevent the deforming of the characters. The brush may seem to dip and dash across the surface in a kind of shorthand Chinese, but the structural elements of the characters are still respected.

These five scripts of Chinese calligraphy—Seal, Official, Regular, Grass and Running—allow for great variety and experimentation of style within given, understood conventions. Chinese scholars who spend a lifetime perfecting their brushwork often try to master more than one style, using different scripts for different occasions. It is common to see the Grass and Running Scripts used for writing poetry at the side of paintings, while the more formal styles of Seal, Official and Regular Scripts are used for official inscriptions, letters and the scroll hangings, with their two-line quotations from a poem or homily, which used to hang in most peoples' houses.

Because of the value that Chinese people have traditionally placed on the words of their language, a character written out in good calligraphy was believed to have a good effect. Shops and restaurants in traditional China always paid large amounts of money to have their sign boards and advertisements written out in fine calligraphy, so as to attract business. And even a poor household, where nobody could read and write, would buy auspicious New Year couplets in good calligraphy, to hang on either side of their doors. The poorest peasant would often have the character *man,* meaning 'full', written out on his rice bucket as a good luck charm. Words were believed to possess the power of their meaning, and the writing of words was a revered art.

The appreciation of such an art form is difficult for those who cannot read Chinese, so it is doubly important to find out what you are looking at if you visit an exhibition of calligraphy. If you have a guide nearby, ask for a translation of the characters and an explanation of which style you are viewing. Then it is up to you to look at the balance of space and characters on the page, the ease or the tension, the regularity or irregularity of the script. Look for the way the brush has been used on the paper. Is the manner firm and tense, or fluid and rhythmic? Are the characters written out in bold isolated units or do they run together like a flowing stream? Answers to these questions will give you some idea of the calligrapher's intentions.

*(following pages) Women of Hui'an County in Fujian Province*

# Foreign Devil

I always objected to halt at a city, but arriving at that of Liang-shan Hsien late on the afternoon of the third day from Wan, it was necessary to change the chai-jen and get my passport copied. An imposing city it is, on a height, approached by a steep flight of stairs with a sharp turn under a deep picturesque gateway in a fine wall, about which are many picturesque and fantastic buildings. The gateway is almost a tunnel, and admits into a street fully a mile and a half long, and not more than ten feet wide, with shops, inns, brokers, temples with highly decorated fronts, and Government buildings "of sorts" along its whole length.

I had scarcely time to take it in when men began to pour into the roadway from every quarter, hooting, and some ran ahead—always a bad sign. I proposed to walk, but the chairmen said it was not safe. The open chair, however, was equally an abomination. The crowd became dense and noisy; there was much hooting and yelling. I recognised many cries of Yang kwei-tze! (foreign devil) and "Child-eater!" swelling into a roar; the narrow street became almost impassable; my chair was struck repeatedly with sticks; mud and unsavoury missiles were thrown with excellent aim; a well-dressed man, bolder or more cowardly than the rest, hit me a smart whack across my chest, which left a weal; others from behind hit me across the shoulders; the howling was infernal: it was an angry Chinese mob. There was nothing for it but to sit up stolidly, and not to appear hurt, frightened, or annoyed, though I was all three.

Unluckily the bearers were shoved to one side, and stumbling over some wicker oil casks (empty, however), knocked them over, when there was a scrimmage, in which they were nearly knocked down. One runner dived into an inn doorway, which the innkeeper closed in a fury, saying he would not admit a foreigner; but he shut the door on the chair, and I got out on the inside, the bearers and porters squeezing in after me, one chair-pole being broken in the crush. I was hurried to the top of a large inn yard and shoved into a room, or rather a dark shed. The innkeeper tried, I was told, to shut and bar the street-door, but it was burst open, and the whole of the planking torn down. The mob surged in 1500 or 2000 strong, led by some literati, as I could see through the chinks.

There was then a riot in earnest; the men had armed themselves with pieces of the doorway, and were hammering at the door and wooden front of my room, surging against the door to break it down, howling and yelling. Yang-kwei-tze! had been abandoned as too mild, and the yells, as I learned afterwards, were such as "Beat her!" "Kill her!" "Burn her!" The last they tried to carry into effect. My den had a second wooden wall to another street, and the mob on that side succeeded in breaking a splinter out, through which they inserted some lighted matches, which fell on some straw and lighted it. It was damp, and I easily trod it out, and dragged a board over the hole. The place was all but pitch-dark, and was full of casks, boards, and chunks of wood. The door was secured by strong wooden bars.

They brought joists up wherewith to break in the door, and at every rush—and the rushes were made with a fiendish yell—I expected it to give way. At last the upper bar yielded, and the upper part of the door caved in a little. They doubled their efforts, and the door in another minute would have fallen in, when the joists were thrown down, and in the midst of a sudden silence there was the rush, like a swirl of autumn leaves, of many feet, and in a few minutes the yard was clear, and soldiers, who remained for the night, took up positions there. One of my men, after the riot had lasted for an hour, had run to the yamen with the news that the people were "murdering a foreigner," and the mandarin sent soldiers with orders for the tumult to cease, which he might have sent two hours before, as it can hardly be supposed that he did not know of it.

The innkeeper, on seeing my special passport, was uneasy and apologetic, but his inn was crowded, he had no better room to give me, and I was too tired and shaken to seek another. The host's wife came in to see me, and speaking apologetically of the riot, she said, "If a foreign woman went to your country, you'd kill her, wouldn't you?"

Isabella Bird, The Yangtze Valley and Beyond, 1899

## WILDLIFE IN CHINA
—*Martin Williams*

Wildlife enthusiasts hoping to spot great numbers of unusual birds and mammals while on a sightseeing tour of China are likely to be disappointed. Damage to the environment, excessive trapping and hunting, along with pressure imposed on ecosystems by the huge population, have drastically reduced wildlife in much of the country. Visitors with only a casual interest in wildlife notice that few birds are to be seen, whether around tourist sites or on journeys through the countryside.

Yet there are areas which are rich in wildlife species that are unique to China or at least rare in other countries. The panda reserves in north Sichuan, whose forests also host rare pheasants; Poyang Lake, the winter home of over 90 per cent of the world's Siberian Cranes; the tropical forests in Xishuangbanna, which harbour over 400 species of birds and over half of China's mammal species—these are among the sites which even the most well-travelled naturalists would find rewarding. Giant Pandas, Manchurian Tigers, River Dolphins, Golden Monkeys and Crested Ibises are among the endangered species which have recently received protection due to the introduction of conservation measures by the Chinese government.

Reaching the prime wildlife areas may require some effort, and some are inaccessible to foreigners or restricted to visitors on organized tours. Hence—particularly for those with money but little time—joining a specialized tour may be the best means of seeing wildlife in China.

Some localities which may be visited by independent travellers are given below. The emphasis is on birds, since bird-watchers predominate among the naturalists who have explored China in recent years. Note that the environs of some tourist sites have proved convenient for bird-watching. The Great Wall at Badaling and the Summer Palace near Beijing are examples. Buddhist temples can also be good, since they are often surrounded by woodland in areas which are otherwise deforested.

*continues on page 252*

*A Giant Panda eating bamboo*

*Changbaishan,* Jilin Province (*see* picture on page 254). The slopes of this mountain have superb forests, and good numbers of birds breed here. Manchurian Tigers are occasionally reported.

*Zhalong Nature Reserve,* Heilongjiang (about 250 kilometres— 155 miles—south of Qiqihar) is a huge wetland. Red-crowned and White-naped Cranes breed here, and four other crane species breed nearby or pass in migration. Around 500 Siberian Cranes spend April and early May in the area.

*Beidaihe,* Hebei Province, is a seaside resort and one of Asia's best places for observing bird migration. Around 280 species of birds migrate each year. Over 700 cranes of four species pass in early spring (20 March to 4 April is usually the best period). Early April to late May is the main spring migration period for most other birds (late April to mid-May being the best). Early September is excellent for shorebirds and Pied Harries, and the autumn migration continues until the middle of November, with cranes, geese, Oriental White Storks and Great Bustards passing in numbers around the beginning of the month. By this time, most smaller birds have headed south.

*Yen Chinao Nature Reserve,* Jiangsu Province, is a coastal wetland where Sanders Gulls breed, and in winter over 200 Red-crowned Cranes and several thousand ducks and shorebirds are seen on the marshes. Though the reserve is large, one bird-watcher has reported seeing 50 Red-crowned Cranes during a half-day's walk from the village of Yancheng.

*Qinghai Lake,* Qinghai Province. It seems that the rather sparsely populated Qinghai-Tibetan plateau is relatively rich in birds, and visits to the environs of Koko Nor (beside Qinghai Lake) have yielded some very interesting species, including several which are unique to China.

*Jiuzhaigou,* in Sichuan Province, one of the areas where Giant Pandas live (wild pandas are very rarely seen). Visits to the area have produced sightings of some very rarely seen species, and pheasants may also be found.

*Emeishan,* in Sichuan Province, has forests which have proved very good for bird-watching. One species—the Emeishan Liocich-la—is unique to the mountain.

# Mountains

Mountain-climbing was a traditional pastime in ancient China. Emperors went to mountains to make sacrifices to heaven and the deities. Scholars went to draw inspiration for poetry and painting. Mystics went to become Buddhist monks or Taoist hermits. Ordinary people went to pray and worship. Thus mountain-climbing in China was more than a sport. It was a popular religious and cultural activity. This partly explains why Chinese mountains are so well laid out with walking trails, stone markers, hermitages, monasteries, guesthouses and tea pavilions.

The Chinese have divided their mountains between Taoist and Buddhist peaks. Taoists were philosophers with an interest in alchemy, herbal medicine and the general world of nature. They regarded the pursuit of immortality and oneness with the cosmos as a way of life. The common people, however, also established and worshipped a pantheon of Taoist deities. The Buddhists believed that the path to enlightenment lay in good works, a knowledge of the Buddhist scriptures, and in meditation far from the everyday world. Both Taoists and Buddhists therefore saw mountains as a natural refuge. In early times, the religious affiliation of a mountain was not so clearly defined—Buddhist and Taoist communities often shared the same mountain. Today, however, the divisions are clear. The four Buddhist mountains are Emeishan in Sichuan, Wutaishan in Shanxi, Putuoshan off the coast of Zhejiang, and Jiuhuashan in Anhui Province. The five Taoist mountains are Taishan in Shandong Province, Huashan in Shaanxi, Northern Hengshan in Shanxi, Southern Hengshan in Hunan and Songshan in Henan. Huangshan in Anhui Province belongs to neither category, and is not a holy mountain.

The Southern and Northern Heng mountains and Mount Song have not been included here, since they are not as yet easily accessible to foreign travellers. All of the mountains described here are open to foreign visitors; in fact, some of them have become so popular, especially with overseas Chinese and Hong Kong visitors, that they have been officially designated as 'Tourist Zones' (Jiuhuashan and Putuoshan, for example). Few travellers would plan to scale all the peaks of China's mountains, but a trip to at least one of them could be included as part of a regional tour. Some of the more enterprising international travel companies now include mountain trips as part of their itinerary.

## Taishan

Taishan (Mount Tai) rises above the folded landscape of the Shandong Peninsula in northeast China. As early as the time of Confucius (551–479 BC), it was famous as a centre for pilgrimage. As Confucius said, 'From the summit of Mount Tai the earth seems small'. Qin Shi Huangdi, the first emperor of China, climbed Mount Tai to

*(following pages) Tianchi, or Heaven Lake, straddles the Chinese–North Korean border at 2,194 metres. Several kilometres across, it formed in the crater of an extinct volcano, and is the main attraction in the forested Changbaishan Nature Reserve in Jilin Province*

make a sacrifice in the second century BC, but history records that he was buffeted by storms because he lacked the necessary righteousness!

Throughout the ages, emperors regularly visited Mount Tai, leaving behind records of their visits—a few characters written in their own calligraphy, for example, set in stone at favoured scenic points. The modern traveller can join the less grand pilgrims and sightseers who throng the mountain through the spring, summer and autumn months, and enjoy the climb of 7,000 steps and an overnight stay at the simple guest-house on the summit. (Even though the tourist influx has resulted in the installation of a cable car, walking is still the best means of experiencing the mountain.)

Mount Tai is just over 1,500 metres (5,000 feet) in height, and a fit person can usually climb to the summit in four to five hours. In order to arrive before sunset, the less fit should start the ascent early in the morning, since the steps on the last part of the climb are extremely steep and need to be negotiated in good light. The best time of year to climb the mountain is in spring, but people have climbed it in the dead of winter, when it was cloaked in snow, and have found the experience delightful—if a little chilly.

Most visitors hope for a clear morning on which to enjoy the sunrise over the sea of clouds that lies above the plain. This is best described by Mary Augusta Mullikin and Anna M. Hotchkis in their book, *The Nine Sacred Mountains of China*, written in the mid-1930s: 'On a clear day the view from the top is one continuous line of inter-lacing mountains lying to the north and east, whereas to the south the plain spreads out in a glory of light, as though the tawny soil had become a golden yellow carpet'.

Chinese city dwellers come to the mountain for sightseeing holidays, and they enjoy the **Dai Temple** at the foot of the mountain as well as the various shrines and temples en route. But many country folk, particularly the women, still visit the mountain as part of a pilgrimage. Taishan is dedicated to the Taoist deity, the Jade Emperor, but the most popular shrine and temple is dedicated to the Jade Emperor's daughter. It is called the **Princess of the Coloured Clouds Temple**. The peasant women of Shandong visit her temple to pray for sons and grandsons, a prayer of greater urgency in these days of one-child families, when all parents and grandparents wish for a male heir to carry on their name. They throw sweets, small coins and scarves as offerings to the princess.

## Huangshan

Huangshan (Yellow Mountain) in Anhui Province was never classified as a sacred mountain, but in recent years it has become one of the most popular destinations in eastern China, largely due to its proximity to Shanghai. That should serve as a warning. The mountain is a favourite with Chinese holidaymakers, and therefore the summer months should be avoided—unless, of course, you like crowds.

*A young Sani woman at the Stone Forest, Yunnan*

Unlike the smooth-topped Taishan, Huangshan rises in a series of craggy peaks which inspired a whole school of painting in the late Ming period. The peaks themselves have literary names which reflect the traditional reverence Chinese scholars feel for mountains— Lotus Flower Peak, Bright Summit and Heavenly Capital Peak, for example. Between Purple Cloud Peak and Peach Blossom Peak are hot spring pools which are a pleasure to bathe in after a stiff walk.

Huangshan, at just over 1,800 metres (6,000 feet), does not offer easy hiking, and a good pair of thick-soled shoes should be worn, since the granite trails are tough on the feet. Overnight guesthouses on the summits offer basic accommodation, but hikers should remember to bring warm and waterproof clothing (those swirling seas of clouds look wonderful from a distance, but walking through them can be damp and demoralizing without proper protective clothing), and some supplies of high-energy food such as chocolate and dried fruit.

## HUASHAN

Huashan, with its fearsome five peaks, rises over 2,400 metres (8,000 feet) above the plains of Shaanxi Province, to the east of Xi'an. The mountain used to be off-limits to foreigners, but it is now open to travellers, only the fittest and most well-prepared of whom should accept the invitation. The mountain paths are carved out of bare rock in many places, and some of the trails lead past dizzying precipices.

Like Taishan to the east, Huashan is a Taoist mountain and a site of imperial sacrifices. History records that the founders of the Shang and Zhou dynasties made sacrifices on this mountain, which dominated a strategic pass at a great bend of the Yellow River. Its peaks are dotted with small Taoist shrines and large temples, some of which are used as guesthouses. The most spectacular view can be had from the **West Peak Monastery**, which sits astride a narrow ridge of bald granite, topped with wind-sculpted pine trees.

## WUTAISHAN

To the northeast of the city of Taiyuan, in Shanxi Province, soars the five-peaked mass of Wutaishan. The mountain is sacred to Buddhists. It represents Manjusri, the Bodhisattva of Transcendent Wisdom, known in Chinese as Wenshu. Being close to the grasslands of Inner Mongolia, Wutaishan was a frequently visited place of pilgrimage for Mongolians who had adopted the Tibetan version of the faith.

Sadly, all but two of the numerous Buddhist monasteries, which once covered the slopes of Mount Wutai, have gone. Those surviving are **Nanshan Monastery** and **Foguang Monastery**, the latter being a rare example of original Tang temple architecture. The buildings from 850 still stand. In descriptions of Wutaishan in the

1930s, the mountain was a bustling centre of activity: Mongolian pilgrims arrived at the temples on their short ponies, and Tibetan lamas mixed with Chinese Buddhist monks in friendly confusion. The mountain is cold, even in midsummer, so hikers should bring adequate layers of clothing as well as basic supplies such as torches, high-energy foods, fold-away rainwear and comfortable shoes.

## EMEISHAN

Emeishan lies to the southwest of the city of Chengdu in Sichuan Province. It is a Buddhist mountain and represents Puxian, the Bodhisattva of Universal Kindness. As it is higher than most of China's other sacred mountains, rising to a lofty 3,000 metres (10,000 feet), Emeishan cannot be visited in less than three days—which include two overnight stops at monastic guesthouses scattered over the mountain slopes.

There is a wide choice of walking trails to be followed, but the ascent to the summit requires some steep climbing—so be prepared. Once you are up there, the view is breathtaking (assuming you are lucky enough to be there on a fine day). If all the circumstances are correct, you will not only see the sun from the summit but also strange light effect known as 'Buddha's Halo', which appears between the clouds.

The walks on Emeishan are truly beautiful. Unlike the trails on the northern mountains, which cut through rock and pines, those on Emeishan twist through cool bamboo thickets where countless butterflies dance in the summer sunlight. Farmers in the area have not yet discovered insecticides, which means that butterflies as well as many insects flourish amidst the mountain glades. Fast-flowing streams rush past small farmsteads, and a variety of shrubs grow along the mountain paths. At the overnight stop of the **Pavilion of the Clear Singing Waters**, two Streams—the Black and the White—meet each other in a frothing torrent (hence the name of the pavilion). Monks run the guesthouses, and their food is simple and vegetarian. Washing facilities are minimal, but on a warm afternoon you can have a bucket-bath out in the sun.

There are said to be pandas living on the western slopes of the mountain, where there are no walking trails. However, it is unlikely that you will catch a glimpse of these shy creatures. A hike to the summit will more probably bring you face-to-face with a horde of chattering monkeys. Beware of their friendship—they are unrepentant beggars, and dislike being refused anything.

Emeishan has become a popular tourist destination in the summer months, and holiday-makers, in addition to the pilgrims, have sometimes filled all the available accommodation. You are advised to inquire about advance booking of beds in the guesthouses on Emeishan; this can be done at the office in **Baoguo Monastery** at the foot of the mountain. Hikers who are pressed for time can take buses which make regular runs up a back road to a half-way point on the mountain. En route, the bus stops near a path that leads to **Wannian Temple**, which has a huge bronze statue of Puxian riding on an elephant. At the end of the road, you can ride a cable car to the

summit, thereby doing hardly any hiking at all. Otherwise, start walking from the bottom, armed with a map from the office at Baoguo Monastery, or from Wannian Temple. There are two main routes to the summit, the northern (shorter and more direct) and the southern (more winding, more rugged). Whichever route you follow, be sure to travel light—the walk is strenuous—and don't forget to pack snacks, waterproof clothing, a thick jersey and a complete change of clothing in case of bad weather.

## PUTUOSHAN

Putuoshan rises out of the sea off the coast of Zhejiang Province. This rocky island, seven kilometres (four miles) long by five kilometres (three miles) wide, is a remarkable sanctuary of peace and beauty, which has been a Buddhist site of pilgrimage since the Tang dynasty. In the early 13th century, it was dedicated to Guanyin, the Goddess of Mercy, by an imperial decree.

Now designated as a 'Tourist Zone', Putuoshan is reached by boat from Ningbo or via the larger island of Dinghai. Like other religious establishments, Putuoshan's monasteries were closed during the Cultural Revolution, and the thousands of monks and nuns who lived there were forced to return to their towns and villages. Some of the original Buddhist inhabitants have now returned, and in the last few years the island has again become an active centre of Buddhist worship.

The three great monasteries of Putuoshan are the **Puji Si**, **Huiji Si** and **Fayu Si**. The Pujisi buildings date from the Qing dynasty, but the tiles of the roof of the monastery's Great Hall come from the Ming palaces of Nanjing, destroyed by the Manchu troops when they conquered China in 1644. Located on Buddha's Peak, the Huiji Si is a Ming foundation which can be reached by bus or up a flight of 1,000 stone steps—a challenge for the very devout who ascend it by prostrating themselves at every third step. The Fayu Si, a later foundation than Puji Si, has an attractive setting, rising in terraces amidst tree-clad slopes.

## JIUHUASHAN

The Buddhist peaks of Jiuhuashan lie south of the Yangzi River in Anhui Province. Jiuhuashan is dedicated to the Bodhisattva, Di Zang. Its 90 peaks rise as high as 900 metres (3,000 feet) against the backdrop of a wooded plain. The trails make comfortable walking, except for those to the summit, and just under 100 monasteries have survived to this day. The most prominent of these, the **Dizangsi**, is dedicated to Di Zang. This Bodhisattva is believed to be able to open the gates of hell to release the suffering souls, so the monastery was by tradition a point of pilgrimage for bereaved relatives. Some of the mountain temples were founded as early as the fourth century, but most of the buildings that have survived to this day date from the Qing period.

*(preceding pages) The side of Hong Kong that few visitors see. Tai Long Wan, or Big Wave Bay, is situated in Sai Kung East Country Park, just one of 21 country parks covering some 40 per cent of the territory's total land area of 1,092 square kilometres*

# Hong Kong Special Administrative Region

By its bizarre, overnight change of ownership on June 30th–July 1st, 1997 (*see* picture overleaf)—one day the concern of British Cabinet ministers in London's Downing Street, the next that of the Chinese Communist Party's Politburo in Beijing's Zhongnanhai—Hong Kong's traditional attraction as a destination for travellers has been enhanced by its appointment with history decided upon in 1984 between the late Chinese leader Deng Xiaoping and the then British Prime Minister, Margaret Thatcher.

So long regarded as a gateway to China, Hong Kong is now part of the big country again, albeit a special one bearing the name of Special Administrative Region (SAR). According to the SAR's Basic Law, Hong Kong will be able to maintain its capitalist economy for 50 years, accomodated ideologically in Beijing by Deng Xiaoping's 'one country, two systems' concept.

As it has done since China opened its doors to tourism in the late 1970s, Hong Kong remains a good place to begin a China tour, being served by almost every major airline in the world at discount rates. Moreover, with purpose-built rail links, it is now possible to board a train in Kowloon and arrive on the same train in Beijing just 36 hours later. Hong Kong, a facinating blend of the Orient and Occident, scenic wonder, economic miracle and shopping paradise remains the perfect gateway to China.

The main centres of population in Hong Kong are Hong Kong Island itself and Kowloon. The Island and the tip of Kowloon peninsula were ceded to Britain 'in perpetuity' by the so-called 'Unequal Treaties' which concluded the two Opium Wars between Britain and China in the 19th century. Thereafter, Hong Kong flourished as the base for British opium trading. In 1898, Britain leased more of Kowloon and the New Territories from China for a period of 99 years. That lease expired in 1997, hence the historic agreement to return Hong Kong to Chinese sovereignty spelt out in the Sino-British Joint Declaration made in 1984.

The lease of 1898 gave Hong Kong a large number of offshore islands as well as the New Territories. It is these islands, and the remoter areas of the New Territories, which offer a glimpse into the older rural world of Hong Kong. The farmers of the New Territories and the outlying islands are mainly Hakka people; the women are easy to identify, since they wear a traditional headdress of a woven rattan hat with a black cloth fringe. In the New Territories, you can still see the traditional walled villages of the Hakka (fortified against their Cantonese neighbours, with whom they rarely inter-married in the past). One of these villages, Sam Tung Uk in Tsuen Wan, is now preserved as a museum in the middle of a highrise estate.

Hong Kong's rural life is slowly dying as farmers get older and their better-educated offspring take up work in the city. After all, Hong Kong is the fourth largest financial centre and one of the biggest ports in the world. Business dominates Hong Kong. If you walk down a busy street in Central, the financial district on Hong Kong Island, you will see people clustering around video displays in bank windows, getting an update on the stock market's movements. The value of trading on the Hong Kong Exchange may fall far short of Wall Street's, but it is still an important market for international dealers because of its regional position and its slot in the international time zones.

Business has made Hong Kong prosperous—and it shows. The biggest Paris and Italian fashion houses have several branches in Hong Kong, and the new buildings rising in Central are being designed by world-famous architects. The new Bank of China headquarters was designed by I. M. Pei, the Chinese-American architect who was also responsible for a controversial building at the Louvre in Paris. Norman Foster's Hong Kong Bank building has been written up in all the architectural magazines. Hong Kong's image in the world has changed radically since the 1960s, when it was known for its sweatshops and jeans factories. Although it is still a major exporter of garments, Hong Kong now manufactures for top designers. Gone are the days when the label 'Made in Hong Kong' meant something cheap and shoddy. 'Made in Hong Kong' now has prestige and style, as one can quickly see just by milling around Central—the business district—during the working week. Its citizens, ever fashion-conscious, not only dress elegantly but are also particularly susceptible to the acquisition of status symbols. Hong Kong has the greatest concentration of Rolls Royces per square kilometre in the world.

# City Sights

The visitor to Hong Kong has a dazzling variety of choice over ways to spend time profitably in the Special Administrative Region. Many people enjoy the shopping, of course, and the wonderful restaurants and nightlife. But there are are other ways to spend your days—which could mean anything from a ferry ride to one of the outlying islands, a day out at the marine centre of **Ocean Park** and its adjoining **Water World**, or a visit to one of the old temples or markets of Kowloon. Listed here is a small selection of possible sights and pleasures. The rest is up to the individual visitor.

**The Peak**, also known as Victoria Peak, is the mountain-top residential district of the rich and powerful. It is also a marvellous place to look out over the city, the harbour and the islands. If you are fit, and the weather is not too hot, you can walk to the top.

*(preceding pages) The British guard of honour carrying the Union flag departs the stage with the mainland guard of honour, after the raising of the Chinese and Hong Kong SAR flags seconds after the stroke of midnight on 1st July 1997, thus bringing to an end 156 years of colonial rule*

There are two shady, quiet paths—one starts from Magazine Gap Road, the other from Conduit Road. The most popular and comfortable way to the top is the eight-minute journey by the **Peak Tram**, which has its terminus just off Garden Road. Once at the top, you can walk up to the summit or take the circular trail which starts just to the right of the exit of the Peak Tram terminus. The **Peak Tower** (which looks like a cross between a lost spaceship and an antique Chinese vessel) has a coffee shop which offers good food with stunning window views. Over the road from the terminus, the **Peak Café** offers an airy setting for a meal or just a cup of tea.

Usually overlooked by foreign visitors but much loved by local residents, the **Botanical Gardens** can be found up the hill from Central, behind the former **Government House**. In the morning, old people gather to swap gossip and do their calisthenic exercises. The gardens are pleasant, but the small zoo is the main attraction with its leopards, orang-utans and wonderful landscaped aviaries full of rockpools, waterfalls and exotic foliage. The zoo is famous for its pioneer work in captive breeding of such endangered species as the Philippines Palawan Peacock and the Chinese Crane.

On the other side of Garden Road is **Hong Kong Park**, with a huge walk-in aviary, conseratory and Flagstaff House, a colonial relic from 1846, which was restored to house the **Museum of Tea Ware**.

For ordinary Hong Kong people, a ride on the **Star Ferry** is the cheapest way of crossing the harbour. For visitors, the Star Ferry is also the best way to enjoy a view of the whole harbour from the water. The fleet of ten green-and-white Star Ferries all have 'star' in their names—Celestial Star, Morning Star, Solar Star, for example.

Between Central district and Western district there are two parallel roads, Queen's Road and Des Voeux Road, bisected by a series of small lanes. It is fun to explore the lanes while they last—some of them have disappeared in recent years in the wake of urban development. However, much has been preserved in the cleverly-restored **Western Market**. Some of the Cloth (Wing On) Alley merchants have stalls here, along with arts and crafts stores and restaurants.

# Outings from Hong Kong

The largest 'outlying' island is **Lantau**, off the west coast of Hong Kong Island itself. It is still relatively undeveloped, but that will all change, since Hong Kong's new airport is being built on its southern shore. Nonetheless, for the moment Lantau is a haven of peace and quiet. The most well-known sights on Lantau are the **Po Lin Monastery** (gaudy and commercialized, but scenic) and a tea plantation, where rides on retired racehorses are offered. But the island is worth visiting for its grand landscapes of cloud-tipped mountains, pastoral valleys and cove beaches. The walking trails are well marked and take you through some lovely scenery.

To the south of Hong Kong Island, **Lamma Island** is smaller than Lantau and has no cars. Sadly, one side of it is disfigured by the three enormous chimney stacks of a coal-fired power station. It has a flourishing community of young people and is also visited on balmy evenings and at weekends by fleets of pleasure boats for its excellent waterfront seafood restaurants.

To the southwest of Hong Kong Island, **Cheung Chau** is famous for its Bun Festival, held every year in May. The festival features stilt-walkers, traditional costume parades and mountains of sticky buns (which, until the practice was discontinued as too dangerous, young men used to climb for a prize pinned to the top). Cheung Chau is now badly overbuilt and is a dormitory for Hong Kong commuters. Yet there are some pleasant pubs and bars, as well as a windsurfing school on the island.

Off the east coast of the New Territories lie the two lovely islands of **Ping Chau** and **Tap Mun**. Ping Chau, which lies close to China and is shaped like a grassy aircraft, can only be visited at weekends by public ferry. The absence of inhabited villages has made it a natural wildlife sanctuary, bright with butterflies, dragonflies and shy birds. The nearby island of Tap Mun is also small, but it has thriving villages, restaurants and a famous Tin Hau Temple popular with local seagoing fishermen (Tin Hau being a Taoist goddess worshipped in southern China and believed to protect fisherfolk). Tap Mun can be reached every day by ferry. Ferries to both islands depart from University, a stop on the Kowloon-Canton Railway.

In the eastern New Territories, the **Sai Kung** peninsula is the most beautiful and unspoilt area. This is because much of the land was designated as a Country Park in the 1970s (*see* picture on page 260). Visitors can explore the hills and seashore on walking trails, or pick up one of the small ferries which run between the villages. The beaches are clean and uncrowded, and the walks offer glorious views over **Mirs Bay** and the China coast. Further north, the town of **Fan Ling** is where the Royal Hong Kong Golf Club is sited.

## Shopping and Entertainment

Much of what is produced for export in China is on sale in Hong Kong. There are large **China Products** emporiums throughout the territory, which sell Chinese-made goods at reasonable prices. The advantage of shopping in these stores is that everything, from all the different regions of China, is under one roof. Also specializing in Chinese goods, but carrying a pricier and more up-market stock, are the **China Arts and Crafts** stores—one is near the Star Ferry terminus on Kowloon side, the other at the bottom of Wyndham Street in the Island's Central district.

*(preceding pages) Larger than San Francisco's Golden Gate Bridge, Tsing Ma Bridge was opened in May 1997. More than 200 metres high and with a main span of 1,377 metres, it is the world's longest suspension bridge carrying both road and rail traffic*

Central has all the most expensive brand-name shops. Prices may or may not be lower than New York or London, depending of course on currency fluctuations. Their best customers in recent years have been Asians, particularly Japanese and Taiwanese. Better value is offered at the factory outlet shops themselves, which sell goods made for export at knock-down prices. Lists of these factory outlets can be found in a shopping guide widely on sale in Hong Kong bookshops.

If you like shopping combined with some local colour, then try to visit some street markets by night. There are many throughout the Island and Kowloon, but the most popular with foreign visitors is **Temple Street Night Market** in Kowloon, near the Jordan Mass Transit or MTR (underground/subway) station. Here you can buy hand-painted T-shirts as well as taste a casserole of garlic snails. Another market is located around **Sai Yeung Choi Street**, near the Mongkok MTR station.

As far as eating is concerned, the choice is so diverse that it is best to consult the Hong Kong Tourist Association handbook for a comprehensive listing. If you have just come out of China and are longing for Western food, then Hong Kong has some of the best Western restaurants in the world. While the Continental restaurants in the top hotels, such as the Peninsula and the Mandarin, are always reliable, there is a host of independent French and Italian restaurants, not to mention fast-food outlets, in the gleaming shopping malls and areas such as Central, Tsim Sha Tsui and Causeway Bay.

Some of the most interesting local restaurants are the traditional teahouses, where the old-fashioned flavour of Chinese breakfast and lunch— *dim sum* (small steamed and fried snacks)—can be savoured. The best-known traditional teahouses are the Luk Yu in Stanley Street, on the Island, and the bird teahouse—where old men go with their pet caged birds—called Wan Loy, on Shanghai Street in Mongkok, Kowloon. It is almost impossible to find seats at these places, though, and one would do better to try a larger restaurant, possibly in an office-cum-shopping complex, which offers less 'atmosphere' but at least a reservation service.

Finally, Hong Kong is famous for its late, late nightlife. In Causeway Bay, the shops don't close until nearly 11 pm every night, and the discos can go on until 4 am. All the hotels have good bars and nightclubs, some with live music. Many karaoke bars are scattered in the bright lights districts of Tsim Sha Tsui and Wanchai. The local hostess bars range from the cheap and cheerful to the very, very expensive. These should be visited with some caution and a prior look at prices.

# Gazetteer of Secondary Destinations

Selected places of interest which are not included in the three main sections of this guidebook—Cultural Capitals, Cities Traditional and Modern and Cities in a Landscape—are presented here in alphabetical order. These 'secondary destinations' may be visited on side trips from places in the three aforementioned categories, particularly by travellers eager to get off the main tourist track.

## Changchun

Travellers may visit the capital city of Jilin Province en route to Harbin in Heilongjiang, to see the annual ice festival, or to one of the northeast's growing number of winter sports and hunting resorts, such as those within the Changbai Mountains bordering North Korea (*see* photograph on pages 254–255).

Changchun is located in the centre of one of the country's main resource bases. As such, the *Dongbei* region (the northeast) or Manchuria as it used to be known, was the natural first stepping stone for annexation by the Japanese in 1931 as they launched their grand militarist assault to occupy China. The annexation was completed on September 9th of that year when the Japanese launched an attack on Shenyang. However, some 200,000 Nationalist troops under General Zhang Xueliang's command were withdrawn from the city, without firing a shot, by Generalissimo Chiang Kai-Shek. He regarded the conflict with the Communists—'a disease of the heart'—to be more pressing than the Japanese invasion—'a disease of the skin'.

Designated Manchukuo, with Changchun being renamed Xinjing, New Capital, the city became the seat of Henry Puyi, the last emperor of the Qing dynasty who served as a Chinese figurehead to rule the new state, according to Japanese orders.

Puyi had arrived in Changchun after being allowed to remain in the northern part of Beijing's Imperial Place long after the fall of his dynasty in 1911. He had been permitted to retain his title Emperor Xuantong during those years. However, in 1924 he was forced out of the palace and taken to Tianjin where he was intercepted by Japanese agents and abducted first to Shenyang, then Changchun.

The Japanese 'offered' Puyi a role in 1932 as chief executive heading the annexed state. He accepted, and later, on March 1st, 1934, he was installed as Emperor Kangde in a purpose-built modern palace in Changchun. As such, the palace, open to visitors, can be regarded as the place where the man who lost a dynasty inherited power over a state that was never more than symbolic, hence the term 'puppet emperor,' with the

*Looking north across the harbour from Hong Kong Island, the neon lights of Nathan Road can be seen stretching towards the Kowloon hills. Central Plaza, for now Hong Kong's tallest building, dominates the foreground*

Japanese pulling all the strings. Puyi hoped his collaboration with the Japanese would eventually lead to the restoration of the Qing dynasty throughout China. For this reason he declined marriage with a Japanese woman to preserve the purity of the Manchu dynastic line.

Today the Changchun is home to the First Automobile Works, established in 1953, which produced China's state limousine, the Red Flag, which was used by Mao and state leaders until production was wound up in the latter part of the decade when imported vehicles started to win favour. A family-sized 'small Red Flag' is now produced.

# Changsha

Those interested in visiting sites connected with the life and times of Mao Zedong are advised to alight from their trains at **Changsha**, situated on the Xiang River and provincial capital of south China's Hunan Province. Trains which stop in this city include those running on the main Beijing–Guangzhou line and the recently opened Beijing–Kowloon line.

Mao Zedong arrived in Changsha as a 17 year old in 1910. The Double Tenth incident, on October 10th, 1911, was 'the spark that started a prairie fire' in Wuhan. The rebellion led to the downfall of the Qing dynasty and heralded the dawn of China's Republican period. Mao took this first opportunity to enlist in a rebel militia. Only when the fighting died down in the following year did he attend classes at the First Hunan Normal College. Although it was burned down by occupying Japanese troops, the wooden building has been renovated in tasteful period style to function once again as a place to train teachers. Visitors are welcome, and several paintings depict Mao as an activist, for example delivering a lecture on the 104th birthday of Karl Marx.

Before heading out of the city for Shaoshan, one can visit **Orange Island**, which lies in the middle of the Xiang River—ideally with a book of Mao's poems containing *Changsha*:

> *Alone I stand in the autumn cold*
> *on the tip of Orange Island,*
> *the Xiang flowing northward;*
> *I see a thousand hills crimsoned through*
> *By their serried woods deep-dyed,*
> *And a hundred barges vying*

*Over crystal blue waters.*
*Eagles cleave the air,*
*Fish glide in the limpid deep;*
*Under freezing skies a million creatures contend in freedom.*
*Brooding over this immensity,*
*I ask, on this boundless land,*
*Who rules over man's destiny?*

In travelling to **Shaoshan**, 104 kilometres west of Changsha, visitors are retracing the final leg of a pilgrimage made by millions of Red Guards as they embarked on so-called New Long Marches (sometimes in bare feet to temper their revolutionary spirits) during the height of the Cultural Revolution. Today, the bus ride through Hunan's red farm fields takes around four hours, while the village is also served by just one train per day. In fact rail is the most spectacular way to arrive in Shaoshan, for the town's station was built to handle tens of thousands of passengers per day. It now receives only a few hundred.

The station's empty, silent waiting room is interesting to see, as is the station forecourt, now devoid of the masses and watched over by a portrait of the Chairman and a statue of a young scholarly Mao in the park opposite. Meanwhile a huge billboard repeats the opening quotation from '*The Mass Line*' in Mao's Little Red Book: '*People, and people alone, are the motive force in the making of world history*'. Those arriving by bus shouldn't miss the remnant cult-status either. A white Mao statute takes pride of place in the waiting room of the bus station.

Mao was born on December 26th, 1893, into a family of middle-class peasants. The family actually occupied half of the building that tourists are shown, and their relative wealth can be determined by the fact their part of the building's roof is tiled as opposed to simply being thatched. Nearby is the Shaoshan Guesthouse, open to all, where Mao stayed when he returned to his hometown in 1959. That visit prompted what is regarded as one of his greatest poems, *Return to Shaoshan*:

*Like a dim dream recalled, I curse the long-fled past—*
*My native soil two and thirty years gone by.*
*The red flag roused the serf, halberd in hand,*
*While the despot's black talons held his whip aloft.*
*Bitter sacrifice strengthens bold resolve,*
*Which dares to make sun and moon shine in new skies.*
*Happy, I see wave upon wave of paddy and beans,*
*And all around, heroes homebound in the evening mist.*

Back in Changsha, the Hunan Provincial Museum tells the early Chinese revolutionary story. But the museum is now most famous for its exhibition of Han relics from the No.1 tomb at Mawangdui, just three kilometres from the city centre. Archaeologists excavating the site in 1972 unearthed a perfectly preserved corpse of a woman, thought to have been about 50 years old when she died in around 141BC. Organs from the mummy, and the contents of her stomach, including melon seeds, are displayed. The woman, the wife of a royal, was dressed in silk and linen garments for her funeral. Red and black lacquerware found in the tomb was also of high quality.

# Dalian

The Liaodong Peninsula juts out opposite the Shandong Peninsula to almost close off Bohai Gulf from the open sea. Situated at its southern tip, **Dalian** has for a long time been an important maritime settlement from which resource rich and strategic waters could be controlled. Travellers can reach the prosperous coastal city in 17 hours by train from Beijing, or by ferry from Xingang, the port of Tianjin, after a two-hour bus ride from Beijing.

At the start of this century the city was occupied by the Japanese, and then in 1945 under the Yalta Agreement it switched to Russian administration which ended in 1954. Electric trams still in use today are a reminder of eastern European influence, as are its numerous squares planted with flowers and grass. Locals call the grass *Xilai Cao*, after the given name of the current city mayor, Bo Xilai, a well-liked official credited with making Dalian one of the most beautiful, cleanest and smartest cities in China. All male government employees are required to wear shirts and ties, as are city taxi drivers. Mayor Bo is an outstanding yet rare example of a princeling (son of a leading comrade) who has actually earned his position on merit—he was elected mayor. His father is veteran revolutionary Bo Yibo.

Dalian is a favourite venue for meetings; often its hotels are booked up as whole management teams flock to the resort and enjoy the advantages of having swims and tasting the fruits of the sea between long speeches.

Travellers may visit Dalian en route to any other north-eastern destination, such as Harbin, Jilin, Changchun, Dandong on the North Korean border, or one of the mountain resorts in the Changbai Mountains. Just outside the city is the naval base of Lushun, once off limits, but now largely open. Nearby is Bullet Hill, site of a war memorial in the form of a massive obelisk-like bullet and erected in remembrance of Russian soldiers who fell in action assisting China at the end of the Second World War as they attacked the Japanese puppet state of Manchukuo. A war cemetery nearby contains thousands of graves bearing photographs of the Soviet war dead. After years of neglect and even desecration during the Cultural Revolution, the cemetery has been renovated and opened to visitors.

Chinese people say that Dalian is home to some of the most beautiful girls in the country, and that may be the reason why the city has developed into a leading fashion centre, staging an annual fashion fair featuring exhibitions, design and model contests.

# Datong

Less than 300 kilometres northeast of Beijing, or seven hours by overnight train, **Datong** seems centuries and much further removed from the breathtaking pace of development in the capital. It is dry, dusty and polluted—but few visitors come away disappointed from the city tucked just 30 kilometres south of the Great Wall.

The **Yungang Caves**, 15 kilometres west of the city proper boast the earliest, most extensive and spectacular collection of Buddhist stone carvings in the country. Most were produced during the Northern Wei period (460–494) when the capital of the small dynasty was located at Pingcheng, present-day Datong. There are 55 caves, of which 21 can be visited. A total of 51,000 bas reliefs and statues exist, ranging in size from a few centimetres to more than 16 metres. They exhibit Indian, Byzantine, Persian and Greek artistic influences. Cave five should not be missed. It contains the 16.8 metre seated Buddha in calm contemplation. The statue is one of the best preserved at the whole site as a result of its sheer size. Over the centuries traders have removed heads from thousands of Yungang's statuettes for sale to collectors.

While in Datong travellers are advised to visit the Great Wall at Shahukou to the west of Yungang, where the defence resembles a giant serpent of rammed earth or near Fengzhen to the north of the city.

# Hainan

In early Chinese history when the earth was believed to be flat, the rocky island of **Hainan** off the south China coast was thought to lie close to the edge of the world. It was left unexplored and unsettled by mainland Hans, but ethnic Li and Miao minorities dared to make the sea crossing from present-day Guangxi and Guangdong, eventually settling on the island's northern coast to dive for pearls. They named their home Zhuya, or Shore of Pearls. The first Hans to go to Hainan were sent there under duress as punishment for crimes, or as exiles, during the Tang dynasty. Communities developed, some making their livings by mining rose quartz, an activity which gave the island its early name: Qiongzhou, or Rose Jewel Kingdom. Today a map of Hainan is dotted with geographical reminders of its past. The straits between the mainland and island are called Qiongzhou Haixia, while villages bear names such as Qiongshan, Qionghai and Qiongzhong.

In recent history, Red Army soldiers took refuge on Hainan to escape Nationalist pursuit, where they were assisted by Li and Miao ethnics. Many women were recruited to the Communist cause and the story was dramatized into dance in one of the eight theatrical works permitted by Jiang Qing, Mao's third wife and most heinous member of the Gang of Four, during the Cultural Revolution. The bamboo hat—army cap ballet was called *The Red Detachment of Women*.

Hainan was part of Guangdong Province until 1988, when it was designated a province—China's smallest, and a special economic zone—the country's largest—at the same time. Favourable policies are being offered to foreign corporations setting up enterprises in any of the island's development zones. First and foremost though, Hainan remains a tropical paradise with sun, sea, palm trees, exotic fruits, water sports and an range of entertainments as its most lucrative natural resources. The topical joke that 'you don't realize how bad your health is until you've been to Hainan' is a not only a comment on the abundance of attractive women dressed in beach wear, but more on the large number of prostitutes which offer their services to mainly visiting Chinese businessmen. Authorities appear to turn a blind eye towards the vice. Chinese joke that Hainan is now occupied by a *yellow* detachment of women. The colour is a metaphor for things sexual and pornographic in the Chinese language.

**Sanya**, on the island's southern shore, is the top resort, reminiscent of a South Pacific paradise with curved, sandy beaches, swaying palms and blue ocean. Top hotel chains are starting to open up resort hotels overlooking the South China Sea, playing their role in converting Sanya into China's version of Hawaii. The resort can be reached from **Haikou**, the island's capital, where a large airport capable of accommodating jumbo jets has recently been opened. Direct flights are available from Beijing.

# Harbin

In geographical terms, **Harbin** is the most northerly provincial capital in all China, while Heilongjiang, literally Black Dragon River, is the most northerly and easterly province, sharing borders with the Russian Far East. For centuries, control of the region switched between the Chinese, Japanese and Russians. In 1917, half a million White Russians fled south to Harbin to dominate the city. Even as recently as 1930–54 the city was held in succession by the powers of the Black Bear and Rising Sun before being handed back to China in 1954. And in the late 1960s, Heilongjiang witnessed another invasion, this time by China's youth being sent to the countryside for re-education in the hands of poor peasants. The mass movement began in 1968, and over the next five years some half a million teenagers, mainly from Beijing and other big cities, were sent to *Beidahuang*, the Big Northern Waste. They carried out reclamation of barren land in the very northeastern corner of the province, supposedly to make more farmland suitable for wheat production. Only the most adventurous of travellers will ever see the results of these young peoples' labours.

Most visitors to Heilongjiang head there in winter, a few to ski or shoot, but most to see Harbin's ice sculpture festival, staged annually. Ice carvers from all over China, and other cold climes, converge on the city to make fantastic ice images, many embedded with coloured lights. Harbin is located on the Songhua River, which freezes solid and becomes a winter sleighing thoroughfare. The scene warms many a vistor's heart, despite a typical diurnal temperature ranging from minus 30 to minus ten degrees Celsius. All hotels have double glazing and fierce central heating.

The city outwardly hints of its previous occupant's architectural tastes. Many buildings have an aura of Russia, and city authorities have recently preserved and renovated a city centre street to protect such buildings. Sofia Cathedral, a Russian Orthodox church with onion domes reminiscent of the basilica on Moscow's Red Square and built in 1903 by Russian soldiers is currently being repaired.

Trains to Harbin start from Beijing Railway Station, and the journey time is now less than 20 hours.

# Hefei

The capital of Anhui Province, bisected by the mighty Yangzi River, has received an economic boost with recent plans to develop the Yangzi river basin as a main initiative to close the economic gap between booming coastal areas and poorly developed hinterland regions.

**Hefei** was only a town of 50,000 prior to the Communist victory in 1949; now it is a booming city surrounded by a bread basket region of the country. Any traveller approaching the city by rail will roll for hours across plains under wheat and rice paddies. Always dependent on agricultural production, Anhui has suffered from the climatic disasters over the centuries, often bearing the brunt of famines. Now, as farming has become more mechanized, the province is a major exporter of migrant labourers to all parts of China, particularly construction workers to prosperous cities, factory workers to economic development zones and domestic nannies to relatively well-off urban families in Beijing, Shanghai and booming coastal cities.

Visitors to Hefei should enjoy being where few foreign tourists bother to go, unless they have business motives. Hefei Museum contains 100,000 relics, while the Memorial Hall of Bao Gong, the most popular sight in the city, commemorates the public spiritedness of an upright and incorruptible Ming dynasty official. Today, the Communist Party finds itself having to deal with a rising wave of corruption described by one senior leader at a mid-1997 meeting as being 'worse than during the worst period of Nationalist rule'.

# Qingdao, Weifang and Yantai

Life on a peninsula is said to be more community-spirited than elsewhere, with the next town never seeming too far away. Although the Shandong Peninsula is larger than most, travellers will reap the most enjoyable experiences by touring a few of its cities and beach resorts.

The port of **Qingdao** was seized by German naval vessels on November 14, 1897 after the murder of two German missionaries in China. Under the terms of a treaty in March the following year, a territory of some 117 square miles given the name Kiao-chow, including Qingdao, was leased to Germany for 99 years.

Within a decade of occupation, the Germans had built Tsingtao, as they spelt it, into a European-looking city—those arriving by train will be struck by the architecture of the railway station. The Japanese took control of the port during World War I, and China regained the city in 1922. Today, apart from its beaches, Qingdao is most famous for its beer, said to be China's best; the culmination of German brewing know-how and nature. Overlooking the city is Lao Mountain, the source of mineral water used in the brewing process.

Next stop on a tour of Shandong is the inland city of **Weifang**, known as one of the kite flying centres of the world. The city stages an annual festival for enthusiasts and boasts an enormous kite museum with kites ancient and modern in every conceivable image, shape and size. Weifang makes a great stop for those on a seaside trip with children. It also plays a relatively little known part in Olympian history. Scottish sprinter Eric Liddell, immortalized in the movie *Chariots of Fire*, travelled to his birthplace, China, after winning the 400 metre gold medal at the 1924 Paris Olympics. He worked there, as his parents had done before him, as a missionary teacher. In the early 1940s when the Japanese seized control of Shandong, he was imprisoned in a camp at a Weifang school, where he continued to teach sports, despite the grave military situation. Just months before the end of the war he died of a brain hemorrhage and was buried in the school grounds. During the 1980s, the Eric Liddell Foundation was established in Hong Kong, and admirers of the athlete-missionary had a slab of Ross-of-Mull granite shipped from Scotland for a memorial. This can be seen in the grounds of the Weifang Number Two Middle School, together with a small museum in the hero's honour.

Continuing north from Weifang to the coast, the port of **Yantai** is reached. The city, once a treaty port under the name of Cheefoo, like Qingdao, has good beaches but is a graduation from the grain to the grape. The city's wineries and distilleries produce a range of alcoholic drinks which may be found on the shelves of stores nationwide. They include European-style grape wines; sherry-like sweet wines; cheap yet drinkable brandies; and champagnes, which are actually more like vintage ciders, but very refreshing all the same.

Those heading east out of the peninsula have a host of options. One could make stops at **Zibo**, a famous pottery and porcelain city; **Tai'an** in order to visit Taishan (*see* page 253); **Qufu**, the home of Confucius; and **Jinan**, the provincial capital for onward transport connections.

# Qinhuangdao, Shanhaiguan and Beidaihe

Incorporating the port city of Qinhuangdao itself, the seaside resort of Beidaihe and the ancient, fortified town of Shanhaiguan, **Qinhuangdao** is an ideal short trip from Beijing and can be reached in less than three hours by express train from the capital.

Hordes of Beijingers heading for **Beidaihe's** sandy beaches are following in the footsteps of the party's leadership. Chairman Mao took refuge from the capital's blazing heat at Beidaihe numerous times, and he wrote a poem by the same name. One of his most famous portraits, standing on the beach, was taken there, and later reproduced in pictorials and posters. Even today motorcades of black limousines sweep into the resort where leaders still hold summer meetings, especially before party congresses. Many Chinese 'units' too have rest houses in the town for the comfort of their high ranking cadres and model workers.

Thirty kilometres north of Beidaihe, passing through Qinhuangdao, a port of growing importance on the so-called Bohai Rim, one reaches the ancient town of **Shanhaiguan**. The name means mountain-sea-pass, and describes the strategic importance of the relatively narrow stretch of coastal plain between natural defences of mountain and ocean.

Shanhaiguan is widely regarded as marking the eastern terminus of the Ming dynasty Great Wall, which begins at Jiayuguan in Gansu Province. The Wall emerges from the Yan Mountains at Jiaoshan, seven kilometres west of Shanhaiguan, crosses the coastal plain, merges with the town wall then proceeds to the coast where it is known as Old Dragon's Head. The town is a must for Great Wall scholars.

The best site at which to view the Wall is at **Jiaoshan** itself. Active travellers would be advised to walk along or even on top of the Wall out of the town as it crosses fields of maize. Much of the Wall on the plain has been stripped of its bricks and stone blocks by locals in search of building materials. Nevertheless it is still a sturdy, prominent structure, about three metres in height. Its route across the plain is superbly appreciated from the peak of Jiaoshan (*see* pages 300 and 301), especially early in the morning. Depending on visibility, the whole route of the ramparts between mountain and sea can be traced.

A second must is the main gate in the town's wall bearing the name of **The First Pass under Heaven**. A pass is an extremely strategic and well-fortified section on the Great Wall. Atop the Wall, now reconstructed, figurines provide images of Ming dynasty scholars and soldiers, while gate towers hold exhibits of weaponry dating from the Ming, including a large iron cannon. The town's walls remain in magnificent dereliction, thickly overgrown and positively saturated with antiquity.

At the sea, six kilometres east of the town lies **Laolongtou**, Old Dragon's Head. The site has been heavily reconstructed with new stones and bricks. Nonetheless, experts working with ancient records have ensured that the building has accurately replicated the defences which existed during Ming times. In 1986 only stone blocks on the seashore gave any clue that this was once the terminus of the Great Wall.

By the early 17th century the Manchus from the northeast had displaced the Mongols as the major invading threat. In response, the Wanli Emperor (reigned 1572–1620) extended the Great Wall from Shanhaiguan, northeastwards through present-day Liaoning Province to the banks of the Yalu Jiang, the river which marks the boundary between China and North Korea. Called the Liaodong Sidewall, the structure was not of such a magnitude as the earlier, main line Ming Great Wall.

Just outside the town, the Temple of Meng Jiangnu encapsulates the suffering of the millions of ordinary people who built the Great Wall. Meng's husband was conscripted during Qin times (221–210BC) to labour on the Wall. During the winter his new wife set out for the border region to look for her husband in order to give him warm clothing. But she found he had perished. Legend tells she cried so frantically that her tears caused part of the Wall to collapse. When Emperor Qin Shihuang heard of this damage, he summoned her to his palace, to find that she was a stunning beauty and decided he wanted her as a concubine. Sickened by the thought of serving the tyrant, Meng Jiangnu escaped and threw herself into the ocean, supposedly off the coast near Shanhaiguan. The temple dates back to the Song dynasty (960–1217).

# Shenyang

Though the capital of Liaoning has a history dating back 2,000 years, **Shenyang** only rose to prominence prior to the establishment of China's final imperial dynasty, that of the Qing (1644–1911). The Manchus began their rise to power in the late 16th and early 17th centuries under Nurhachi (1559–1626). By this time the northeastern tribe had succeeded the Mongols as the main threat to native Han rule in China, and in response to menacing sorties by skilled Manchu horsemen and archers, the Wanli Emperor extended the Great Wall from Shanhaiguan to the Yalu River. In the end, the Manchus never actually breached the Great Wall, they were allowed to pass through the strategic coastal pass of Shanhaiguan by a renegade Ming general. They went on to Beijing, where Abukai, Nurhachi's 14th son, established the Qing dynasty and the new empire's capital.

Shenyang remained the Qing's secondary capital, largely because of the importance of the northeast region to the lucrative ginseng trade. Today, visitors to the industrial city can visit the Manchu Imperial Palace, a complex of some 70 buildings built between 1625 and 1636. The approach is marked by *xiamamen*, or dismount from horses tablets, steles in various scripts which pronounce the extent of the great Qing empire: they appear in Chinese, Uyghur, Mongolian, Tibetan and of course, Manchurian. The Qing rulers largely assimilated Han ways, and became great chroniclers and mappers of the empire.

Noteworthy sights, apart from the lacquered roof halls themselves, include the library which once housed more than 35,000 histories and chronicles, among them a comprehensive history of China, completed in 1782 during the Qianlong reign (1736–1795). Many of the great emperor's personal effects are also displayed.

Ironically, the last emperor, Xuantong (Henry Puyi) passed through Shenyang en route to Changchun in 1932, when he became puppet emperor of the Japanese controlled state of Manchukuo. He also underwent 're-education' in his ancestral northeast homeland after the Communists took power in 1949.

# Yan'an

Located 280 kilometres north of Xi'an, the small city of **Yan'an** and nearby towns of **Wuqi** and **Bao'an** give the traveller an insight into a vital period of Chinese revolutionary history between the end of the Long March in 1935 and the establishment of New China in 1949.

Almost a year to the day after some 80,000 Central Red Army soldiers departed from the Soviet Republic of China, the remnant Communist forces arrived in Wuqi, a village of north Shaanxi, in October 1935. There were only 4,000 survivors, among them Mao Zedong, Zhou Enlai and Deng Xiaoping. Safe in the incised river valleys of the loess tableland, Mao made nearby Yan'an his new base from 1936 until 1947. Before the move, he was interviewed by Edgar Snow, an American, whose eventual book *Red Star Over China* provided the outside world with its first and most detailed account of the Red Army's origin, evolution and motives, and more importantly what was effectively Mao's autobiography. The leader divulged his life story to the young mandarin-speaking journalist.

Once based in Yan'an, the Communists formulated specific policies for land reform which won broad support from the peasantry. Meanwhile, within the party and army the psychological victory of the 12,500-kilometre Long March was promoted. But ultimately, what came out of the Yan'an years was the Yan'an spirit of self sufficiency: it was in northern Shaanxi where the Reds became expert at growing food and making what they needed while defending themselves.

Yan'an can be reached in eight hours by bus from Xi'an, or in six hours via the new railway—one departure per day. The city sits clustered in the Yan River valley beneath the Yan'an Pagoda which became a national symbol, featured on stamps, coins and bank notes, after the Communists took power in 1949. Around the city, four of Chairman Mao's residences can be visited. He had several to avoid Japanese bombing raids. All are in the local *yaodong* cave-dwelling style.

Elsewhere, the Yan'an Museum recounts the full story of the revolution with an enormous display of artifacts, photographic and archive materials

# Zhengzhou

Located on the lower reaches of the Yellow River, the area around the present-day transport hub of **Zhengzhou** co-hosted the development of early Chinese civilization. Archaeologists have unearthed primitive villages of Neolithic age, evidencing that the Yellow River and its wide plains cradled human culture in the land that became unified as the Middle Kingdom.

But the Yellow River has often vented its wrath with seasons of flood and drought. And in 1937, as Japanese invaders closed in on Zhengzhou, the Nationalists bombed the river's dykes to flood the city's surrounds, sacrificing tens of thousands of lives—but saving Zhengzhou.

Today, this the capital of Henan Province, can serve as a centre from which to visit **Anyang**, capital of the Shang dynasty (c.1600–1027BC); Kaifeng, capital of the Northern Song dynasty (960–1127AD) (*see* page 89); and Luoyang, capital during the

Sui dynasty (581–618AD) (*see* page 86). However, Zhengzhou itself is usually visited during a pilgrimage to **Shaolin Monastery** on Song Shan, a sacred mountain which exhibits the coexistence of Buddhism, Daoism and Confucianism side by side.

Shaolin, or Little Forest Monastery was founded by Bodhidharma, the monk who introduced Zen Buddhism to China. When he arrived at the beautiful mountain, around 510AD, he is said to have meditated in a cave continuously for nine years. Shaolin's worldwide fame stems not from this peaceful act, but from the martial arts practiced for generations by its monks. A number of training camps for *wushu* students have developed around the monastery, while Shaolin's monks still live spartan lives which they say are conducive to their high level development of *wushu* skill.

# Nanchang

On the eve of August 1st, 1997, a major meeting attended by all of China's leaders and many of its surviving veteran revolutionaries was convened in Beijing's Great Hall of the People. The celebration marked the 70th anniversary of the foundation of China's armed forces after an event which took place in **Nanchang**, capital of the southeastern province of Jiangxi. A peasant army led by Zhou Enlai and Zhu De successfully staged an uprising in the city, seizing control of the Nationalist stronghold for several days. The action on August 1st, 1927, regarded as the first of its kind under the direct organization of the Chinese Communist Party, was later chosen as the founding day of China's armed services. The date, abbreviated to 8-1, appears in Chinese characters on army, navy and air force insignia.

The visitor to Jiangxi will seldom encounter other foreign travellers, yet the province offers sites by the dozen which provide insights into various aspects of Chinese history and culture. Nanchang, and numerous other places of interest can be reached by passengers on the Yangzi River by alighting at **Jiujiang**, a river port west of Poyang Lake. The city was once one of the three greatest tea trading ports on the river. Tea clippers would load up here with freshly picked leaves and then race downstream, across seas and oceans to London. The fastest could reach England in just over 30 days. These handsome full-sailed ships graced the Yangzi River following the opening its port cities to foreign trade after the 1858 treaty of Tianjin, until the introduction of the steamship in the middle of the 19th century.

Long before the tea trade, Jiujiang hosted two of China's greatest poets: Li Bai (701–762) was imprisoned here for a short time, while Bai Juyi (772–846) was exiled in the town.

A train links the bustling port with Nanchang, 150 kilometres to the south, but most other places have to be reached by bus. En route between Jiujiang and Nanchang the mountain resort of **Lushan**, more than 1,400 metres above sea level, can provide refuge from the torrid heat which afflicts life in the lower reaches of the Yangzi basin. While Jiujiang swelters at perhaps 38 degrees Celsius in July, Lushan is a comfortable 24 degrees.

The town's history goes back to the days of foreign merchants and missionaries who sought a resort in which their families could escape the summer heat. More than 100 villas were constructed. Later, both Nationalist and Communist leaders followed in their footsteps. Chiang Kai-shek had a villa here, as did Mao and Jiang Qing. And it was in the small village that the Communist Party convened the notorious Lushan conference at which one of China's ten commanders, Peng Dehuai, was dismissed. The eighth plenary session was held in the wake of the disastrous Great Leap Forward, and while most leading officials were too afraid to tell Mao the truth about the farcical falsifying of economic production figures, Peng was not; and the Chairman dismissed the People's Liberation Army's Commander-in-Chief.

In Nanchang, the headquarters of the Nanchang Uprising on Zhongshan Road can be visited. Next, travellers could go by bus to the eastern side of Poyang Lake to **Jingdezhen**, site of China's most famous porcelain town. Those with a passion for following the story of the Chinese revolution should go southwest by bus to Jinggan-shan, then further south to the towns of Yudu and Ruijin in southern Jiangxi.

**Jingganshan** is the mountain top stronghold from where the roots of the Red Army stem. After the split in the Nationalist-Communist United Front of 1923–27, Mao staged the unsuccessful Autumn Harvest Uprising in his home province of Hunan. He led his defeated rebels to Jingganshan, a range straddling the Hunan-Jiangxi border. The following year, in 1928, forces led by Zhu De joined those of Mao to establish the first mountain-top Soviet. Memorials around the small town immortalize the heroes and heroines who congregated in Jingganshan.

In 1929, the Mao-Zhu army migrated south to Ruijin, a town adjacent to the Fujian Revolutionary Base Area to establish the first Soviet Republic of China, which was soon encircled by Nationalist forces. Today, **Ruijin** is abundant in revolutionary shrines, including the Soviet Government Headquarters, meeting halls, residences of leaders and museums. It is most famous for being the starting point of the Long March, which commenced in mid-October, 1934 with thousands of Red Army soldiers crossing a pontoon bridge across the town's river during the night to escape detection and break out of the encirclement. More than two weeks later, the *New York Times* reported that 40,000 bandits were looting their way across Hunan. In fact there were 80,000 well disciplined soldiers on the march, looking for a new revolutionary base area. It was eventually found one year and 11,500 kilometres away in northern Shaanxi Province after what must be regarded as the most incredible mass exodus in human history.

# Guiyang

Guizhou Province is one of the least visited of all China's provinces, regions and municipal areas, yet it presents a face of China rarely seen elsewhere by foreign travellers. It hardly ever features in tour itineraries, and, until recently, few independent travellers bothered to spend time in the province. Now some informed visitors with time to linger are savouring Guizhou's vibrant ethnic culture.

**Guiyang**, the provincial capital, lies at the centre of the province, and can conveniently be reached by rail from either Kunming in the west or Chongqing, the Yangzi river port, in the north, both of which are popular destinations. The city has also opened a new airport and offers flights to and from almost every large city in China including Hong Kong. But perhaps the best way to reach Guiyang is by train: railway lines pass pinnacled limestone mountain ranges which rise up like thin cones from cool, misty plateaus.

The capital, lying at more than 1,000 metres above sea level and being hemmed in by hills, is compact by comparison to many of the country's sprawling provincial metropolises. The city and surrounds are rich in Long March history, as the Central Red Army crossed the province by a tortuous route to escape from the clutches of pursuing Nationalist and allied warlord factions. Chiang Kai-shek arrived in Guiyang in March 1935, but Mao's forces were well away from the city by then. During the next decade, Guiyang can almost claim to have served as temporary capital during the Anti-Japanese War (1937–45). The Nationalist-led United Front set up government offices in the city before relocating to Chongqing.

Within the city there are only a few sites as such to see: the charm of Guiyang is its community feel and ethnic mix. Here the visitor meets brightly-dressed minority nationalities who visit the city from outlying areas. However, the Provincial Museum, Botanical Gardens and Scholar's Pavilion are worth a day's sightseeing, while the city's bustling evening snack markets offer the best night-life, frequented by locals for their tasty snacks. An interesting one is the roast potato, dipped in pepper and chilli powder according to taste. Another day may well be needed for shopping. The Miao and Bouwei nationalities are the main producers of the wax-dyed material known as batik, while their jewellery and other embroidered and appliquéd adornments make tasteful souvenirs. The province also produce some of China's finest social materials: liquor, cigarettes and tea. The Maotai distillery (*see* below) produces a fragrant liquor from sorghum and wheat which sells nationwide for more than 350 yuan (approximately US$45) per bottle. Fake Maotai is a problem: even the liquor's distinctive white glass flask can be sold to 'recyclers' for 10 yuan (US$1.3).

For trips out of Guiyang, there are options in all directions depending upon one's field of interest. Nature lovers in this vast, over-populated and highly-urbanized land might head for the **Huangguoshu** waterfall, near Anshun, west of Guiyang. The fall is the largest in Asia at 68 metres in height and 84 metres wide. Huangguoshu could be a stopping off point for those travelling on to Kunming in neighbouring Yunnan Province.

A trip east by bus or train to the city of **Kaili**, specifically to see the Sunday market, seldom disappoints, unless there is a deluge to dampen the economic enthusiasm and social spirits of tens of thousands of its merchants and minglers. Miao women, dressed in black pleated skirts, embroidered tops and decked in jewellery converge on the market in droves. Products available include vegetables, fruit, meat, poultry, birds, ethnic textiles and adornments, snack foods, herbal medicines—and virtually everything else if one has time to look for it. Kaili could be a stopping off point for travellers making their way towards Huaihua, a rail hub in eastern Hunan, or that province's capital, Changsha.

North is the direction to experience a sizeable chunk of Long March history. The city of **Zunyi** was the site in January, 1935, where Mao Zedong took control of both the Red Army and the Chinese Communist Party. The Politburo meeting, convened in a former landlord's mansion built in 1920, judged leadership under Bo Gu and Wang Ming, Moscow-trained communists influenced by the German Comintern agent Otto Braun, as being detrimental to the party's and army's good. Since the commencement of the Long March three months before, the army's migration across Hunan, Guangxi and Guizhou had been a funeral march with 30,000 Reds losing their lives. The site of the watershed Zunyi Meeting includes the meeting room and private rooms of its participants. It should be followed by a visit to the Red Army Political Department Site—once a church—now housing an exhibition detailing Long March history. Also in the city is a striking monument to Red Army Martyrs, erected in 1985 by the Sichuan Art Academy.

Further north, more Long March sites can be visited. **Loushan Pass**, a strategic route through the Dalou Mountains, was seized by the Red Army from Nationalists in February 1935. The victory lifted the spirits of weary, young soldiers who had been literally marching round in circles for two weeks with little rest, crossing and re-crossing the Chishui River, before sweeping south to take Loushan. Mao wrote a song to commemorate the magnificent victory. A suitable circular route to encompass Loushan Pass, the Chishui river and Maotai distillery would be by bus from Zunyi to Tongzhi, then Tucheng and Maotai, before returning to Zunyi. The Maotai distillery however, does not accept visitors.

*One of the most impressive and spectacular sections of the Great Wall, at Jinshanling,*
*120 kilometres north-east of Beijing (see page 302)*

# THE GREAT WALL
### - William Lindesay

The only historical feature marked on maps of the world is represented by a castellated symbol which zig zags across the cartographer's ochre-brown hues of central-east Asia. It is the Great Wall of China

Daunted by neither landscape nor distance on its tortuous journey from desert to sea, this superlative-defying defence system, the longest, oldest, most time-consuming, labour-intensive and material-demanding construction project in mankind's history, is far more than a landmark: it is part of the geography of North China, the world, and beyond.

Snaking along mountain ridges, the Great Wall dominates the landscape from miles around, then vanishes over the ridges. From the air, where horizons are wider, the Wall still astrides the horizons, reaching from where the sun rises to where it sets. And from the heavens, courtesy of satellite photography, we know the Great Wall is as prominent a geographical feature as the hand of nature at its most powerful in carving out the mighty valleys of the Yangzi and Yellow rivers.

## Origins

In history there have been three sub-continental scale Great Walls, built during Qin (221–206BC), Han (206BC–AD220) and Ming (1368–1644) times. Intervening dynasties, including the Northern Wei (386–534), Northern Qi (550–577) and the conquest dynasties of the Liao (916–1125) and Jin (1115–1234), also built Walls and dug trenches for defensive purposes, but not on such grand scales. However, by definition, having been constructed at the northern edges of the empires on imperial orders, they too were Great Walls of China.

No major threats to the security of Chinese empires ever came from the south, but in the north a variety of peoples—Xiongnu, Quitans, Jurchens, Mongols and Manchus—ethnically different to Han Chinese, inhabited the steppes and desert fringes. The Hans settled in the fertile central plains, cultivated crops and built settlements, often walled, while the northerners were nomads and hunters who habitually invaded Han territory on horseback.

# Evolution

High walls, running for long distances across open country and manned by guards, had been used as a means of preventing mass invasions since the Warring States period (475–221 BC). They were made from rammed earth. Wall-building continued to play an important role in national defence strategies, with increasing sophistication. Rocks, bricks and mortar were used; construction scales grew ever greater; routing through the mountains was more ambitious to accentuate defensive capacity; and patroling garrisons were provided with arsenals of ingenious weaponry for close and remote combat.

Wall-building innovation reached its acme during the Ming dynasty. Ironically, Manchu horsemen were allowed to pass through one of the Wall's most-fortified passes, at **Shanhaiguan** on the Yellow Sea coast, by a renegade general (*see* pictures on pages 300 and 301). The invaders established the Qing dynasty (1644–1911) and Wall-building was abandoned: future enemies would come not from the north, but from across the globe by sea to China's coast.

The Ming's brilliant construction therefore, designed to be insurmountable to the most-determined and well-armed invader, was never truly tested.

# The Ming Dynasty Defence

Remains of the Ming Great Wall stretch from Jiayuguan, along the Hexi corridor of Gansu Province, across the Ningxia Hui Autonomous Region and Shaanxi, along the Shanxi-Inner Mongolia provincial boundary, north of Beijing and through Hebei to Shanhaiguan on the coast. In the early 17th century, in response to the growing threat to Manchu invasion, this main-line structure was extended by the addition of the so-called Liaodong sidewall, stretching from Shanhaiguan, northeast to the Yalu Jiang, a river which today marks the border between China and North Korea.

The Beijing region boasts the most-magnificent remaining sections since the Hongwu emperor (reigned 1368–1398) ordered the routing of the Great Wall through the Yanshan mountains. According to recent satellite surveys, the Beijing Municipality has 673 kilometres of Great Wall within its boundaries. Most of it was reinforced during the Yongle (reigned 1403–1423) and Wanli (reigned 1573–1620) periods.

*(opposite page) An invader's view of the formidable defenses of the Great Wall
(above) This section at the western end of the Great Wall at Jiayuguan shows
the ledge on top of the wall along which guards would have walked between watchtowers.
The well-known landmark of the Jiayuguan fortress can be seen in the distance*

Having suffered under barbarian rule for more than three centuries, the Hongwu emperor, who re-established native Han rule, decided that the building of a Great Wall was the basic means of border defence necessary to ensure that the Chinese empire would never again be conquered by the northerners. At the time, the Ming had their capital in Nanjing, which was in the centre of the fertile Yangzi region and well-supplied with grain, but distant from the volatile northern border where, as history had proved time and time again, dynastic stability was most at stake.

To guarantee good military control and loyalty in the north, the Hongwu emperor adopted a policy of *pan wang*, or princes guarding the border, by assigning some of his 27 sons to northern fiefdoms.

When the Yongle emperor took power in 1403, he decided to move the capital from Nanjing to Beijing. He had spent his youth in the Beijing region after his father's establishment of the dynasty in 1368, and was later given the title Prince of Yan and military control of a fiefdom. Very much a professional soldier with strong allegiance in the north, he was a veteran at thwarting Mongol threats and realized that keeping the hordes at bay would secure him a long reign, and the empire's stability.

To do that, he had the Great Wall reinforced on a massive scale and built lines of beacon towers to facilitate the conveyance of signals to the new capital. Meanwhile, Beijing was built into a bastion just south of this stupendous defence. The Imperial City had a moat and high defensive walls, and within it was constructed the Imperial Palace, also behind a moat and palace walls. All building materials were shipped along the Yuan-built Grand Canal, whose renovation and improvement allowed the new capital to be kept well-supplied with grain from the south.

Most of the Wall north of Beijing follows mountain ridges and scales peaks: here the ramparts are virtually impossible for an invader to breach, let alone access on horseback. There were however, a few valleys through the mountains which had been used as passes since ancient times. These became strategic passes (most heavily-fortified sections) on the Great Wall: thicker, high ramparts were built at these points, and watchtowers were closer together. Double Walls created loops in which invaders could be trapped and annihilated. Larger garrisons of men were stationed at passes.

To the invader, the system of ramparts must have appeared impregnable, master-minded by militarily-brilliant strategists and architects. The Ming Wall should be regarded as being as technically advanced and militarily advantageous in its day as systems of spy satellites, radar and the nuclear deterrent are today.

In terms of its communicative role, the Great Wall can be likened to an optic fibre in medieval times. Guards in beacon towers would initiate information concerning

Mongol threats by smoke signal, cannon fire or drum beats, depending on weather conditions. The message could be carried along the Wall, then south to the emperor in the Imperial Palace.

Within a matter of hours the emperor and his ministers could be made aware of threats and swiftly decide on counter-attacking measures. Had the capital remained in Nanjing, information might have taken several days to reach its destination.

The Great Wall's system of defence and communication was also supplemented by military expeditions into the heart of Mongolian territory to destroy encampments and burn grasslands. The Yongle emperor personally led many of them: Beijing served as the ideal platform from which to launch campaigns. Thus the Great Wall in many ways was the last line of defence and by no means the border of the empire.

Built to withstand attack from Mongol hordes but never seriously breached, Beijing's Ming Great Wall stands as a permanent monument to glorify the ingenuity of architects ad military strategists, a memorial to mourn the countless millions who were conscripted and died during its construction.

## Visiting the Wall

Badaling, Juyongguan, Mutianyu, Jinshanling and Simatai have, to greater and lesser degrees, been reconstructed and 'opened' to tourism. It is necessary to purchase tickets (costing between 18 and 40 *yuan* for foreigners) to access the Wall at these places. Three sites have cable cars to spare less-able visitors heart- and leg-strain on the steep climbs. Those who enjoy walking however, and who have time, can venture onto the derelict sections beyond reconstructed sections at all locations.

Moreover, there is simply too much Great Wall around Beijing to reconstruct, and that means several hundred kilometres of it exists in a wild, authentic state—remote, overgrown and crumbling—starkly exhibiting the timeless flight of centuries.

**Badaling** was the first section of Wall renovated for tourism. Just 65 kilometres north of Beijing, and accessible via the newly-built Badaling Expressway toll road, it is about one and a half hours' drive from the city. This most-crowded section is beginning to show signs of tourism overuse as more than 10,000 people a day converge on the site during the high season and on holiday weekends. The strategic pass is quite magnificent, with the lower sections of the ramparts being composed of huge, pink granite blocks which are topped with kiln-baked bricks bound with mortar. Beacon towers are located within an arrow's flight of each other, and looking east and west

*(following pages) Dawn panorama over the jagged Jiankou section, west of Mutianyu, that spectacularly illustrates the enormous feat of engineering achieved by its Ming dynasty builders*

the ramparts thrust and dip in and out of sight. From April to October the Wall is floodlit in the evenings.

The **China Great Wall Museum**, with nine exhibition rooms, is located at Badaling. Many weapons and Wall-related relics discovered in the vicinity are exhibited: a battle scene is recreated with models; and Wall-building techniques and battles are explained and chronicled with charts and drawings. Photographs of famous visitors, including 276 foreign heads of state from 143 countries, are also on show. Open 8am–4pm daily. Admission 10 *yuan*. Telephone 6921-1890 or 6921-1228. Another attraction adjacent to the museum, especially recommended for younger visitors, is the Great Wall Circular Vision Theater where a dramatized 15-minute film about the Wall's history and legends is projected onto an Omnimax circular screen. Admission is 30 *yuan*.

Badaling is accessible by five tourist line public buses (*see* Beijing map on page 100). Frequent departures are made from the Qianmen quadrangle bus station; Qianmenxi, 200 metres west of KFC outside the Tai Feng Lou Restaurant; Qianmendong, one kilometre east of Qianmen outside the Ren Ren Restaurant; Beijing Railway Station west forecourt; and from opposite Beijing Zoo. From 6am–10am daily, April to November; 7am–9am, December to March. Buses travel directly from the city to the Ming Tombs (9 *yuan*), then Badaling (11 *yuan*). Travel time is more than 90 minutes. Return services start from 1:30pm and end at 5:30pm in summer, earlier in winter. Most hotels offer minibus tours to the Wall and prices may range from 60–200 *yuan*. Taxis can be hired for between 300 *yuan* and 500 *yuan* depending on how long the driver is required to wait, and vehicle type. The local train from Xizhimen Railway Station is another option, especially good in winter if the roads are snow bound. Train numbers 579 and 575 depart at 8.10am and 8.30am respectively. Return tickets can be bought, and travel time is more than two hours.

**Juyongguan** can be seen by all en route to Badaling. Entering the valley heading north from Nankou, the sharp-eyed will detect linearities which describe a massive loop on the distant mountainside. Juyongguan was a second, 'insurance' line of defence, and reconstruction since 1990 has replicated the bastion's elaborate defence system of ramparts, gates and towers. A total of 150 million *yuan* (US$18 million), a record sum for relics reconstruction in China, has been invested in this site.Very little of the building material is original: most was removed by locals in search of readily-available building materials during the Qing and Republican periods. However, the view from the Wall's highest point on the western ridge is magnificent, affording one clear appreciation of the strategic nature of this pass  which links the northern steppes with the plain of the south.

The main reason to stop at Juyongguan lies at the foot of the Wall, between the old and new roads. Yuntai, the **Cloud Terrace**, once formed the base for three successively-built Yuan dynasty (1254–1368) pagodas. The remaining hexagonal 'language' archway has Buddhist reliefs of the Four Heavenly Kings in white marble on its northern and southern faces, while the interior of the structure has scripts in six languages which reflect both the extent of the Mongol empire and the many nationalities of Buddhism's adherents. The scripts are Nepalese Sanskrit, Tibetan, Phags-pa Mongolian, Uyghur, Xi Xia and Han Chinese.

**Mutianyu**, 80 kilometres (50 miles) north of Beijing in Huairou County is the second most-visited section. Less crowded, visitors can climb up 1,000 steps or take the cable car (50 *yuan* one-way, 90 *yuan* return) to reach the Wall.

Magnificent panoramas lie in wait, especially in fall. The thickly wooded slopes around Mutianyu provide a palate of autumnal tints to contrast with the whitish blocks of the Wall. For the energetic, a walk to the west is recommended. After one kilometre derelict ramparts are reached. A further 30–40 minutes' walk will take hikers to a prominent loop called the Oxhorn. The highest beacon tower for miles around still stands a few hundred metres further west. It rewards the adventurous with a bird's eye view westward across the precipitous Jiankou section which is extremely difficult to negotiate due to its crumbling condition, bushy overgrowth and near-vertical inclines (see picture on pages 296–297).

Mutianyu is accessible by public bus tourist line number 6, departing from outside the Southern Cathedral (north-east corner of the Xuanwumen intersection, accessible from the subway station of the same name—*see* Beijing map on page 100). There are frequent departures daily between 6am and 10pm from April to November, and only on Saturdays and Sundays, 7am to 9am, in other months. Buses also visit Hongluo (Red Conch) Temple and Yanqi Lake after leaving Mutianyu.

Travel time is about two hours and the return fare is 24 *yuan*. Return buses leave Mutianyu between 1.00pm and 5.00pm. Minibus tours also depart from various hotels, while taxis can be hired for 300–600 *yuan*. Public buses leave Dongzhimen Bus Station, close to the subway of the same name, for Huairou, starting from 6.00am and every 15 minutes thereafter. From Huairoiu there are onward buses for the short trip to Mutianyu. If necessary, accommodation can be found in Huairou, and a Ming-dynasty style barracks has been constructed as lodgings on the Mutianyu Wall itself, about one kilometre west of the cable-car station.

*(following pages)The Great Wall at Shanhaiguan snakes down the mountains and across the coastal plain to the sea. These two pictures show the stark contrast in the landscape between winter and summer, and some reconstruction. Despite having built the strongest Great Wall in history, the Ming dynasty's defences were breached here on this coastal plain by Manchu horsemen in 1644, who went on to establish the Qing dynasty*

Jinshanling and Simatai, adjacent sections of the Great Wall to the east of Gubeikou, are located 120 kilometres (75 miles) north-east of the capital on the boundary between Beijing Municipality and Hebei Province. These sections are regarded by most as Wall par excellence for their heights, solitude and plethora of watchtowers which dot the ramparts like fins on a might dragon. Formal access points for both sections are about 5 kilometres (3 miles) apart as the crow flies, or 25 kilometres (15 miles) by road.

At Jinshanling (see picture on page 289), the Wall zig zags up inclines and straddles between peaks like a suspension bridge of stone. Every turn in the defence and peak is marked with a tower. A particularly striking feature here are barrier walls, best described as mini battlements on the Wall pavement itself. They were built as a precaution against invaders mounting the Wall. Defenders could combat invaders while seeking protection from missiles behind the mini-battlements. In clear weather Miyun Lake, Beijing's main reservoir, can be seen.

A few kilometres further east (about three hours' walk) at Simatai, awaits one of the most hair-raising challenges on the Great Wall around Beijing. Soon the reconstructed section is left behind as one climbs eastward and upward towards the perilous Simatai ridge.

The highest watchtower, dubbed the 'Tower for Viewing Beijing' for the vista available to its conquerors, can be reached only by negotiating an extremely narrow section of Wall. Sharp drops loom on both sides of this one-metre-wide path. Beyond is the Stairway to Heaven of barrier walls: this is a challenge even for those who do not suffer from vertigo. Those who lose their nerve halfway across are best advised to crawl on all fours.

Public bus tourist line number 12 from Xuanwumen, outside the Southern Cathedral, provides a service to Simatai. Departures, approximately every 30 minutes, are limited to weekends and state holidays. Travel time is three hours plus, and buses stop briefly at Bailongtan Pool on the way back. The return fare is 50 *yuan*.

Jinshanling and Simatai are east of Gubeikou which is on the Beijing-Chengde railway line. There are three departures daily from Beijing Railway Station: train numbers 11, 551 and 553 at 7.12am, 10.02am and 16.26pm respectively. Hard seats cost 18 *yuan*, soft seats 36 *yuan*. Transit time to Gubeikou is three hours for the dawn departure, and four and a half hours for the other two. An alternative is the minibus (30 *yuan*), from the east forecourt of Beijing Station. Frequent departures leave throughout the day from about 5.00am. Public bus (13 *yuan*) from Dongzhimen is a slow alternative at 7.30am and 8.30am; or minibuses run the same route for 30 *yuan*.

All these modes of transport to Gubeikou would necessitate short onward travelling to Jinshanling and Simatai. Motorcabs are available.

However, an alternative is to take the bus from Dongzhimen to Miyun, where minibuses are then available direct to Simatai.

A thoroughly enjoyable full-day trip to Simatai is organized by Wall-aficionado Jarrah Pour, a Persian expatriate, long-term Beijing resident and fluent English speaker (Tel: mobile phone 9089-3026 or 13810-04866). Affectionately know as Ati and based at the Jingtai Hotel, he runs a 20-seater minibus to Simatai twice weekly, usually on Tuesdays and Fridays. But can set up a reasonably-priced trip to the Wall anywhere, anytime for anyone. He always climbs up the Wall himself and imparts his experience (of more than 160 ascents) to his guests. Tickets are 80 *yuan* round trip. Buses depart from the Jingtai Hotel at 8.30am (with pick-ups at the Friendship Store and Hard Rock Cafe, or by arrangement); arrive at Simatai around noon; three to four hours are then spent climbing the Wall, and buses arrive back in Beijing around 7.00pm.

Purists who want to visit a non-tourist section would be advised to head for **Huanghuacheng**, 60 kilometres north of Beijing. Heavily reinforced during the reign of Wanli, these derelict, mighty ramparts cross a small valley in which a reservoir has been built. A special feature of the Wall and towers here are rocks of various provenance: pink granite, white dolerite and grey gabbro. This is a fine location to start a high-level hike, either east or west from the road. To the West, the first tower still contains a memorial plaque, dating from 1580, recording the good deeds of the garrison stationed there for the defence of the capital. To the East, the Wall climbs steeply towards the peak of the highest mountain around.

This section can only be reached by public bus from Dongzhimen, changing at Huairou for Huanghuacheng. Taxis cost between 300 and 500 *yuan*, but although the route is actually very easy to follow, it is hard to find a Beijing taxi driver who knows the way. Take the road north from the Asian Games Village towards Lishui Qiao, then keep going north through Xiazhuang, following signposts for Sihai.

(William Lindesay travelled alone and on foot for a distance of 2,470 kilometres along the whole length of the Ming Great Wall between Jiayuguan and Shanhaiguan in 1987. He recounted his adventure in '*Alone on the Great Wall*' (Hodder, UK 1989; Fulcrum USA 1991; Lubbe, Germany 1997). He has since made return trips to the Wall in Gansu, Shanxi and Hebei, and spent a further 45 weekends exploring Beijing's Great Wall.

# Practical Information

## Hotels

The following is a select list of the hotels most frequently used by foreign visitors to China. The list is by no means comprehensive, but it covers the major cities described in this guide. In the less visited or remote destinations, of course, travellers will find little or no choice at all in the way of accommodation. At the time of writing, rates range from US$180 for a standard double room in a five-star, centrally located hotel in Beijing, to around Rmb50 for a double room in Ürümqi. Of course, travel agents are able to obtain more competitive rates for group tours. For the latest details, you are advised to check with your local travel agent or branch of CITS .

### BEIJING

■ SUPERIOR

**Beijing Hotel**
33 Dong Chang'an Dajie. Tel. (010) 6513-7766; tlx. 222755; fax. (010) 6513-7703
北京饭店　东长安大街33号
Beijing's oldest (1900) and best known hotel. Centrally located near Tiananmen Square. Equipped with all the facilities expected of an international-standard hotel.

**Beijing Hilton**
1 Dongfang Road, Dongsanhuan Beilu. Tel. (010) 6466-2288; fax. (010) 6465-3052
北京希尔顿酒店　东三环北路东方路1号
Well located on the third ring road, this hotel has all the class and qualities expected from a Hilton hotel.

**China World Hotel**
1 Jianguomenwai Dajie. Tel. (010) 6505-2266; tlx. 210578; fax. (010) 6505-3167/8/9
中国大饭店　建国门外大街1号
Part of a huge new complex which includes the Traders Hotel and the China World Trade Center, packed full of all sorts of facilities (20 restaurants and bars, for example). Managed by Shangri-La Hotels.

*Beyond the length of restored wall at Badaling, the most popular destination with around 10,000 visitors per day, lies this derelict section of original Ming dynasty wall*

### Beijing International Club Hotel

21 Jiangoumenwai Dajie. Tel. (010) 6460-6688; fax. (010) 6460-3299
北京国际俱乐部饭店　建国门外大街21号
One of the Sheraton's 49 'Luxury Collection' hotels, this complex comprises a 287-room hotel with office tower and athletic club.

### Grand Hotel Beijing

35 Dong Chang'an Dajie. Tel. (010) 6513-7788; tlx. 210617; fax. (010) 6513-0048/50
北京贵宾楼饭店　东长安大街35号
Westernmost wing of the Beijing Hotel, but independently managed. Recognized by 'The Leading Hotels of the World'. With health club and business centre.

### The Great Wall Sheraton Hotel

Dongsanhuan Beilu, Chaoyang. Tel. (010) 6500-5566; tlx. 222002;
fax. (010) 6500-1919
长城饭店　朝阳区东三环北路
Joint-venture hotel situated near Sanlitun, the area with the largest concentration of embassies and foreign residents. Shuttle to city centre. 1,007 rooms. Splendid garden.

### Holiday Inn Crowne Plaza

48 Wangfujing Dajie, Deng Shi Xi Kou Tel. (010) 6513-3388; tlx. 210676;
fax. (010) 6513-2513
北京国际艺苑皇冠假日饭店　北京灯市西口王府井大街48号
Centrally located, ten minutes from the Forbidden City. Comprehensive facilities include art exhibition gallery and art salon featuring cultural activities. 385 rooms.

### Holiday Inn Lido Beijing

Jiangtai Lu, Chaoyang. Tel. (010) 6437-6688; tlx. 22618; fax. (010) 6437-6237
北京丽都假日饭店　朝阳区将台路
Located on the way to Beijing's airport. Wide range of facilities including ten restaurants, health club, indoor swimming pool, supermarket and delicatessen and a 20-lane bowling alley. Shuttle bus service to city centre. Part of the hotel complex consists of residential apartments housing some of Beijing's expatriates.

### Jianguo Hotel

5 Jianguomenwai Dajie. Tel. (010) 6500-2233; tlx. 22437; fax. (010) 6500-2871
建国饭店　建国门外大街5号

A favourite with foreign business people due to proximity to what has become Beijing's business district. Indoor swimming pool and delicatessen, among the usual facilities.

### Jing Guang New World Hotel

Hu Jia Lou, Chaoyang District. Tel. (010) 6501-8888; tlx. 210489; fax. (010) 6501-3333

京广新世界饭店　朝阳区呼家楼

In a commercial and residential skyscraper, east of the city centre. Managed by New World Hotels International.

### Jinglun Beijing-Toronto

3 Jianguomenwai Dajie. Tel. (010) 6500-2266; tlx. 210012; fax. (010) 6500-2022

京伦饭店　建国门外大街3号

Within walking distance of major business centres; very efficient service. Joint-venture hotel with business centre and ballroom. 659 rooms.

### Kempinski Hotel, Beijing Lufthansa Centre

50 Liangmaqiao Rd. Tel. (010) 6465-3388; tlx. 210601; fax. (010) 6465-3366

北京燕莎中心凯宾斯基饭店　朝阳区亮马桥路50号

540 rooms, 13 restaurants, bar, business and health centres, pool, tennis, squash, six function rooms and a small Bavarian brewery. Located on the new outer ring road.

### The Palace Hotel Beijing

8 Goldfish Lane, Wangfujing. Tel. (010) 6512-8899; tlx. 222696; fax. (010) 6512-9050

王府饭店　王府井金鱼胡同8号

Managed by the Peninsula Group of Hong Kong in efficient Hong Kong style. Lots of facilities including indoor swimming pool.

### Shangri-La Hotel Beijing

29 Zizhuyuan Lu. Tel. (010) 6841-2211; tlx. 222322; fax. (010) 6841-8002

香格里拉饭店　紫竹院路29号

Location a bit remote (ten to 15 minutes by car to Tiananmen Square). Shuttle bus service available. The rooms are among the best in Beijing. Has health club and indoor swimming pool plus office suites which can be rented.

### Swissôtel, Hong Kong Macau Centre

Gongren Tiyuchang Bei Lu, Chaoyang District. Tel. (010) 6501-2288;
tlx. 222527; fax. (010) 6501-2501

北京港澳中心　朝阳门北大街工人体育场北路

First hotel in Asia with full facilities for the handicapped. Located in large
commercial and hotel complex. With health club, swimming pool, tennis courts.

■ FIRST CLASS

### Beijing Airport Mövenpick Hotel

Xiaotianzhu Village, Shunyi County. Tel. (010) 6456-5588; tlx. 222986;
fax (010) 6456-1234

北京国都大饭店　首都机场南小天竺路

Five minutes from the airport, 40 minutes from town. Business centre, tennis courts.

### Beijing International Hotel

9 Jianguomennei Dajie. Tel. (010) 6512-6688; tlx. 211121; fax. (010) 6512-9972

北京国际饭店　建国门内大街9号

Massive complex with tennis courts, health club, indoor-outdoor swimming pools,
bowling alley, billiards and shopping arcade. Five-minute taxi ride to Tiananmen
Square. Built by the China International Travel Service.

### Changfugong New Otani Hotel

Jianguomenwai Dajie. Tel. (010) 6512-5555; tlx. 222936; fax. (010) 6513-9810

长富宫饭店　建国门外大街

Japanese-managed and, as expected, a favourite with Japanese tour groups. Good
location in the commercial district. Tennis courts, indoor pool, Japanese restaurant.
Located near the Friendship Store in the embassy district.

### Exhibition Centre Hotel

135 Xizhimenwai Dajie. Tel. (010) 6831-6633; fax. (010) 6832-7450

北京展览馆宾馆　西直门外大街135号

Friendly, well-managed joint venture, near the Beijing Zoo in the grounds of the
Russian-built Exhibition Centre.

### Holiday Inn Downtown

98 Beilishi Lu. Tel. (010) 6833-8822, tlx. 221045; fax. (010) 6834-0696

北京金都假日饭店　西城区北礼士路98号

Economical, unpretentious hotel in non-tourist neighbourhood. Swimming pool, health club, Indian restaurant.

### Kunlun Hotel
21 Liangmaqiao, Chaoyang District. Tel. (010) 6500-3388; tlx. 210327; fax. (010) 6500-3228
昆仑饭店　朝阳亮马桥21号
Range of facilities including tennis courts and indoor swimming pool.

### Landmark Hotel
8 Beisanhuan Lu. Tel. (010) 6501-6688; tlx 210301; fax. (010) 6501-3513
亮马饭店（亮马公寓）　北三环路8号
Close to Great Wall Sheraton and Hard Rock Cafe. Medical clinic, health club and baby-sitting.

### Olympic Hotel
52 Baishiqiao Lu. Tel. (010) 6217-6688; tlx. 222749; fax. (010) 6217-4259
奥林匹克饭店　海淀区白石桥路52号
Friendly, attractive joint-venture hotel in pleasant surroundings near Purple Bamboo Park and Capital Gymnasium.

### SAS Radisson Hotel
6A East Beisanhuan Rd. Tel. (010) 6466-3388; tlx. 211241; fax. (010) 6465-3186
北京皇家大饭店　北三环东路6号A
Next to China International Exhibition Centre, best known among those on conference and exhibition business. Has all the facilities you would expect of a luxury hotel.

### Traders Hotel
1 Jianguomenwai Dajie. Tel. (010) 6505-2277; tlx. 222981; fax. (010) 6501-0818
国贸饭店（国贸中心）　建国门外大街1号
Business hotel with access to China World Hotel facilities (listed on page 305).

### Xin Dadu Hotel
21 Chegongzhuang Lu. Tel. (010) 6831-9988; tlx. 221042; fax. (010) 6833-8507
新大都饭店　西城区车公庄路21号
Well-renovated hotel run by Beijing Municipality. Located in residential area near Beijing Zoo. Business centre, bowling alley.

## Xiyuan Hotel

Erligou. Tel. (010) 6831-3388; tlx. 2222835; fax. (010) 6831-4577

西苑饭店　二里沟

In two sections, with the newer wing offering health club, indoor swimming pool, business centre. Most of the rooms in the older section, which has been renovated, are occupied by long-term foreign residents. Located near Beijing Zoo.

## Zhaolong Hotel

2 Gongren Tiyuchang Bei Lu. Tel. (010) 6500-2299; tlx. 210079; fax. (010) 6500-3319

兆龙饭店　朝阳工人体育场北路2号

Health club, indoor/outdoor swimming pools, theatre and banqueting centre.

## Capital Hotel

3 Qianmen Dong Dajie. Tel. (010) 6512-9988; tlx. 222650; fax. (010) 6512-0323

首都宾馆　前门东大街3号

## Friendship Hotel

3 Baishiqiao Lu. Tel. (010) 6849-8888; fax. (010) 6849-8866

友谊宾馆　白石桥路3号

## Fragrant Hills

Xiangshan. Tel. (010) 6259-1166; fax. (010) 6259-1762

香山饭店　香山

■ STANDARD

## Jinlang Hotel

75 Chongnei Dajie. Tel. (010) 6513-2288; fax. (010) 6512-5839

北京金朗大酒店　东城区崇内大街75号

Convenient downtown location near Beijing Railway Station and historical neighbourhoods. French brasserie, health club and business centre.

## Minzu

51 Fuxingmennei Dajie. Tel. (010) 6601-4466; tlx. 200912; fax. (010) 6601-4849

民族饭店　复兴门内大街51号

**Qianmen**

1 Yongan Lu. Tel. (010) 6301-6688; tlx. 222382; fax. (010) 6301-3883

前门饭店　永安路1号


**Taiwan Hotel**

5 Goldfish Lane. Tel (010) 6513-6688; tlx. 210543; fax. (010) 6513-6596

台湾饭店　王府井北金鱼胡同5号


**Zhuyuan Guesthouse**

24 Xiaoshiqiao Hutong, Jiugulou Dajie. Tel. (010) 6403-2299; cable 3428;
fax. (010) 6401-2633

竹园宾馆　旧鼓楼大街小石桥胡同24号


■ BUDGET

**Hadamen Hotel**

2A Chongwenmenwai Dajie. Tel. (010) 6711-2244, tlx. 210337;
fax. (010) 6711-6865

哈德门饭店　崇文门外大街2号A


**Huguosi Hotel**

Huguosi Jie, Western District. Tel. (010) 6618-1113; tlx. 222958;
fax. (010) 6618-0140

护国寺饭店　西城区护国寺街


**Qiaoyuan**

Dongbinhe Lu, You'anmenwai. Tel. (010) 6303-8861; fax. (010) 6318-4709

侨园饭店　右安门外东宾河路


**Tiantan Tiyu Guesthouse (Sportsmen's Inn)**

10 Tiyuguan Lu. Tel. (010) 6711-3388; tlx. 22738; fax. (010) 6711-5388

天坛体育宾馆　体育馆路10号


# CHENGDU

**Jiaotong (Transport) Hotel**

Xinnanmen Bus Station. Tel. (028) 555-4962; fax. (028) 558-2777

交通饭店　新南门汽车站内

Popular budget hotel.

### Jinjiang Hotel

36 Renmin Nan Lu (second section). Tel. (028) 558-2222; fax. (028) 558-1849
锦江饭店　人民南路二段36号
Built in the 1960s and since renovated, a bustling hotel with offices of many travel agents. Slightly shabby now but it is still the best known and most patronized hotel in Chengdu among foreign visitors.

### Holiday Inn Anrong Chengdu

Heng Street, Chadianzi District. Tel. (028) 752-6688; fax. (028) 751-0689
成都市茶店子区横街　成都安榕假日酒店

### Holiday Inn Crowne Plaza Chengdu

31 Zhongfu Jie. Tel. (028) 678-6666; fax. (028) 678-9791
成都总府皇冠假日酒店　总府街31号
It is conveniently located in the heart of the city centre, being one of the tallest buildings in town and only 20 minutes away from Chengdu's Shuangliu International Airport.

### Minshan Hotel

17 Renmin Nan Lu (second section). Tel. (028) 558-3333; fax. (028) 558-2154
岷山饭店　人民南路二段17号
Newer and smarter than the Jinjiang, located across the road. Pleasant and comfortable rooms.

### Sichuan Hotel (Sichuan Binguan)

31 Zongfu Jie. Tel. (028) 675-5555; fax. (028) 674-5263
四川宾馆　总府街31号
Convenient location; used to be the Dongfeng Hotel, now renovated.

## CHONGQING

### Chongqing Hotel

Xinhua Lu. Tel. (023) 6384-9301; fax. (023) 6384-3085
重庆饭店　新华路

### Chongqing Renmin Hotel

Renmin Lu. Tel. (023) 6385-1421; fax. (023) 6385-2070
重庆人民宾馆　人民路

**Holiday Inn Yangtze Chongqing**
15 Nan Ping Bei Lu. Tel (023) 6280-3380; tlx. 62220; fax. (023) 6280-0884
重庆扬子江假日饭店　南坪北路15号
Located on the south bank of the river, about ten minutes' drive to the city centre.

## DALIAN

**Holiday Inn Dalian**
18 Sheng Li Square, Zhong Shan District. Tel. (0411) 280-8888;
fax. (0411) 280-9704
大连九州假日饭店　中山区胜利广场18号
15 minutes from Dalian Port (second largest in China). Features Asian and Western restaurants and business centre.

## FUZHOU

**Lakeside Hotel**
Hubin Lu. Tel. (0591) 783-9888; tlx. 92255; fax. (0591) 783-9752
西湖大酒店　湖滨路1号
Situated by Fuzhou's West Lake, 20 minutes' drive from the airport. Four-star standard.

**Hot Springs Hotel**
Wusi Lu (middle section). Tel. (0591) 785-1818; fax. (0591) 783-5150
温泉大饭店　五四路中段
Located in downtown centre, four-star standard. Mineral-rich hot spring water is piped to the rooms.

**Overseas Chinese Mission**
Wusi Lu. Tel. (0591) 755-7603; tlx 92275; fax. (0591) 755-0648
华侨大厦　五四路
Renovated in the late 1980s. China Travel Service office located in the hotel.

## GUANGZHOU
■ SUPERIOR

**China Hotel**
111–118 Liu Hua Lu. Tel. (020) 8666-6888; fax. (020) 8667-7288, 8667-7014
中国大酒店　流花路111-8号
1017 rooms, plus a 15-storey office tower, shopping arcade, 17 restaurants and

lounges and 190 apartments. Located opposite the Trade Fair Exhibition Hall. Business centre, and convention facilities for up to 1,200 people. Outdoor pool, tennis court, gym, sauna and bowling alley.

## Garden Hotel
368 Huanshi Dong Lu. Tel. (020) 8333-8989; tlx. 44788; fax. (020) 8335-0467
花园酒店　环市东路368号
Large conference hall makes this a popular hotel for holding international events and exhibitions. Range of facilities including sports club and swimming pools.

## Guangdong International Hotel
339 Huanshi Dong Lu. Tel. (020) 8331-1888; tlx. 44788; fax. (020) 8331-1666
广东国际大酒店　环市东路339号
This is the tallest hotel in China and part of a large complex of offices, apartments, shops and a huge McDonalds. It has a good and varied range of restaurants and entertainment facilities.

## White Swan Hotel
Shamian Island. Tel. (020) 8888-6968; tlx. 44688; fax. (020) 8886-1188
白天鹅宾馆　沙面南街1号
The first of Guangzhou's joint-venture hotels, opened in 1983, expanded in 1988. Many offices of foreign corporations in Guangzhou are located here. Full array of facilities including health club, jogging track and golf driving range. Furnished apartments available for rent to long-term guests.

■ FIRST CLASS

## Dongfang Hotel
120 Liuhua Lu. Tel. (020) 8666-9900; tlx. 44439; fax. (020) 8668-1618
东方宾馆　流花路120号
The oldest of the up-market hotels in Guangzhou which accommodated almost all the foreign visitors to the annual trade fairs before a wider choice was opened up with the construction of joint-venture hotels. Originally built in the 1950s, then expanded in the 1980s. Full range of facilities.

## Holiday Inn City Centre Guangzhou
Huanshi Dong, 28 Guangming Lu. Tel (020) 8776-6999; tlx 441045;
fax (020) 8775-3126
广州文化假日酒店　环市东路华侨新村光明路28号

Good location in commercial district, 20 minutes from the airport, ten minutes from the main railway station. Excellent facilities include Western and Chinese restaurants, discotheque, swimming pool and a 500-seat cinema.

### Hotel Landmark Canton

Giao Guang Rd. Tel. (020) 8335-5988; tlx. 441288; fax. (020) 8333-6197

华厦大酒店　侨光路

On the river front in the heart of town this hotel will, when its second phase is completed, be one of the best equipped and serviced in town.

### Ramada Pearl

9 Ming Yue Lu. Tel. (020) 8737-2988; fax. (020) 8737-7481

广州凯旋华美达大酒店　东山区明月一路9号

Riverside location in Dongshan area with excellent sporting facilities including two swimming pools, tennis and squash courts and a golf driving range. Business centre, office space, and meeting and banquet services.

## GUILIN

### Guishan Hotel

Chuanshan Lu. Tel. (0773) 581-3388; tlx. 48443; fax. (0773) 581-4851

桂山大酒店　穿山路

On the east bank of the Li River with good recreational facilities.

### Holiday Inn Guilin

14 Ronghu Nan Lu. Tel. (0773) 282-3950; tlx. 48456; fax. (0773) 282-2101

假日桂林宾馆　榕湖南路14号

Situated near the Ronghu (Banyan) Lake, this comfortable hotel is in a quiet part of town. All the usual facilities and services expected of a Holiday Inn.

### Lijiang Hotel

1 Shanhu Bei Lu. Tel. (0773) 282-2881; tlx. 48470; fax. (0773) 282-2891

漓江饭店　杉湖北路1号

Downtown location, and convenient for the main shopping area.

### Osmanthus Hotel

451 Zhongshan Nan Lu. Tel. (0773) 383-4300; tlx 48455; fax. (0773) 383-5316

丹桂大酒店　中山南路451号

Managed by a Hong Kong-based company.

**Royal Garden Hotel**

Yanjiang Lu. Tel. (0773) 581-2411; tlx. 48445; fax. (0773) 581-5051/2

帝苑酒店　沿江路

Situated across the Li River from Fubo Hill.


**Sheraton Guilin Hotel**

Binjiang Nan Lu. Tel. (0773) 282-5588; tlx. 48439; fax. (0773) 282-5598

喜来登桂林文华大饭店　滨江南路

Located on the Li River, with usual facilities including swimming pool and health club.

# HANGZHOU

**Dragon (Huanglong) Hotel**

Shuguang Lu. Tel. (0571) 799-8833; tlx. 351048; fax. (0571) 799-8090

黄龙饭店　曙光路

Swimming pool, tennis court, fitness centre, conference rooms and disco. Managed by New World Hotels International of Hong Kong.


**Hangzhou Shangri-La Hotel**

78 Beishan Lu. Tel. (0571) 707-7951; tlx. 35005; fax. (0571) 707-3545

杭州香格里拉　北山路78号

Overlooks the West Lake and offers a number of lake-view rooms. Previously the Hangzhou Hotel, and has two restaurants serving Chinese and European cuisine, and a coffee shop and bar.


**Wanghu Hotel**

2 Huangcheng Xi Lu. Tel. (0571) 707-1942; tlx. 35003; fax. (0571) 707-1350

望湖饭店　环城西路2号

On the north side of the West Lake, with the usual services and amenities.

There is a small selection of lower-priced hotels such as the **Huagang Hotel**, Huanhu Xi Lu, tel. (0571) 799-8899, tlx. 35007, fax. (0571) 799-2481; **Huajiashan Hotel**, 2 Xishan Lu, tel. (0571) 707-1224, tlx. 35063, fax. (0571) 707-3980; and **Zhejiang Guesthouse**, 68 Santai Shan Lu, tel. (0571) 808-2924, fax. (0571) 806-4966.

# HARBIN

**Holiday Inn City Centre Harbin**

90 Jingwei Lu, Daoli District. Tel. (0451) 422-6666; fax. (0451) 422-1661

哈尔滨万达假日酒店　哈尔滨市道里区经纬街90号

30 minute drive from Harbin airport and ten minutes from railway station.

# HEFEI

**Holiday Inn Hefei**

1104 Changjiang Dong Lu. Tel. (0551) 262-0099; fax. (0551) 262-0066

合肥古井假日酒店　合肥市长江东路1104号

# HOHHOT

**Inner Mongolia Hotel**

1 Wulanchabu Lu. Tel. (0471) 696-4233; fax. (0471) 696-1479

内蒙古饭店　乌兰察布西路1号

Hotel with modern facilities; CITS has its office here.

**Xincheng Guesthouse**

Hulun Nan Lu. Tel. (0471) 6292288; fax. (0471) 6931141

新城宾馆　呼仑南路

Older than the Inner Mongolia Hotel, and more run-down. Double rooms with bath as well as dormitories available.

**Zhaojun Hotel**

53 Xinhua Dajie. Tel. (0471) 696-2211; tlx. 85053; fax. (0471) 696-8825

昭君大酒店　新华大街53号

Facilities include three restaurants, beauty parlour and disco.

# KAIFENG

**Dongjing Hotel**

14 Yingbin Lu. Tel. (0378) 398-9388

东京大饭店　迎宾路14号

**Kaifeng Guesthouse**

102 Ziyou Lu. Tel. (0378) 595-5589

开封宾馆　自由路102号

# KUNMING

**Golden Dragon Hotel**

575 Beijing Lu. Tel. (0871) 313-1402; fax. (0871) 313-1082

金龙饭店　北京路575号

Newest international-style hotel in Kunming, with a hot-spring swimming pool, tennis courts, business centre, karaoke and several restaurants offering Chinese and Western cuisine. Located in the commerical centre of the city. Office of Hong Kong airline, Dragonair, in the lobby.

### Green Lake Hotel

6 Cuihu Nan Lu. Tel. (0871) 515-8888; fax. (0871) 515-7867
翠湖宾馆　翠湖南路6号
Recently renovated and very comfortable. Helpful staff complement good services including an excellent arts and crafts shop, ticket booking and sightseeing tours.

### Holiday Inn Kunming

25 Dong Feng East Rd. Tel. (0871) 316-5888; fax. (0871) 313-5189
樱花假日大酒店　东风东路25号
252 rooms, seven restaurants, banqueting hall, swimming pool, health club and sauna.

### King World Hotel

28 Beijing Rd. Tel. (0871) 313-8888; telx. 64143; fax. (0871) 313-1910
锦华大酒店　北京路南段28号

### Kunming Hotel

145 Dongfeng Dong Lu. Tel. (0871) 316-2063; fax. (0871) 313-8220
昆明饭店　东风东路145号
Old hotel completely remodelled recently. Tours and bicycle rental can be arranged. China Youth Travel Service office in the lobby.

## LANZHOU

### Lanzhou Huayi Hotel

14 Xijin Xi Lu. Tel. (0931) 233-3051; tlx. 72143; fax. (0931) 233-0304
兰州华谊大酒店　西津西路14号
Soviet-style hotel, adequate rooms.

### Jincheng Hotel

Tianshui Lu. Tel. (0931) 841-6638; fax. (0931) 841-8438
金城宾馆　天水路
The city's newest and most up-market hotel offering business centre, beauty parlour and seven restaurants. Conveniently next door to CITS.

### Lanzhou Hotel

204 Donggang Xi Lu. Tel. (0931) 841-6321; fax. (0931) 841-8608
兰州饭店　东岗西路204号
Another Soviet-style hotel with fairly stark facilities, close to markets and railway station. Dormitory beds available.

**Shengli Hotel**

127 Zhongshan Lu. Tel. (0931) 846-5221; fax. (0931) 846-1531

胜利饭店　中山路127号

Displaced by the Jincheng as Lanzhou's newest hotel. Located near the bus terminus. Silk Road Travel Service on the second floor organizes tours of the relevant sites, cars for hire, and books tickets.

# LHASA

**Lhasa Hotel**

1 Minzu Lu. Tel. (0891) 633-2221; tlx. 68010; fax. (0891) 633-4632

拉萨假日饭店　民族路1号

Top hotel in Lhasa, once a Holiday Inn. Equipped with international communications facilities and oxygen tanks for any guest stricken with altitude sickness. Restaurants serving Chinese and Western fare.

**Tibet Guesthouse**

221 Beijing Xi Lu. Tel. (0891) 633-4966; tlx. 68013; fax. (0891) 633-6787

西藏宾馆　北京西路221号

Close to the Lhasa Hotel, this small hotel (96 guest rooms) was built in a Tibetan style.

# LUOYANG

**Friendship Guesthouse**

6 Xiyuan Lu. Tel. (0379) 491-2708; fax. (0379) 491-3808

洛阳友谊宾馆　西苑路6号

**Luoyang Peony Hotel**

15 Zhongzhou Xi Lu. Tel. (0379) 491-3699; tlx. 473047; fax. (0379) 491-3668

洛阳牡丹大酒店　中州西路15号

New hotel with 200 rooms, coffee shop, bar, health centre, disco and the inevitable karaoke.

# NANJING

**Jinling Hotel**

2 Hanzhong Lu, Xinjiekou. Tel. (025) 445-5888; tlx. 34110; fax. (025) 470-3396

金陵饭店　新街口汉中路2号

Centrally located high-grade hotel, the first choice of most foreign businessmen and tourists. The revolving lounge on the 36th floor has a dance floor. An annexe to the hotel houses a variety of arts and crafts shops.

### Holiday Inn Yihua Nanjing

259 Zhongshan Bei Lu. Tel. (025) 343-8716; tlx. 34102; fax. (025) 342-6676
南京怡华假日酒店   南京市中山北路259号

### Dingshan Hotel

90 Chaha'er Lu. Tel. (025) 880-1868; tlx. 34103; fax. (025) 882-1729
丁山宾馆   察哈尔路90号
In the northeast of the city centre—not a terrific location but reasonably priced and
comfortable hotel.

### The Central Hotel (Zhongxin Da Jiudian)

75 Zhongshan Lu, tel. (025) 440-0888; tlx. 34083; fax. (025) 441-4194
中心大酒店   中山路75号
Good location and comprehensive facilities.

## QUANZHOU

### Golden Fountain (Jinquan) Hotel

Baiyuanqing Chi. Tel. (0595) 228-5078; fax. (0595) 228-4388
金泉饭店   白源清池旁

### Overseas Chinese Mansion (Huaqiao Dasha)

Baiyuanqing Chi. Tel. (0595) 228-5601; fax. (0595) 228-4612
华侨大厦   白源清池旁

## SHANGHAI

■ SUPERIOR

### Holiday Inn Crowne Plaza Shanghai

388 Pan Yu Rd. (corner of Pan Yu and Xin Huan roads). Tel. (021) 628-8808;
tlx. 30310; fax. (021) 628-2788
上海银星皇冠假日酒店   番禺路388号
About half an hour from the airport, the Bund, and the Jade Buddha Temple.

### Holiday Inn Pudong (opening December 1997)

899 Dong Fang Jie, Pudong District. Tel. (021) 6875-2895; fax. (021) 6875-1605
上海浦东假日酒店   上海市东方路899号

### Huating

1200 Caoxi Bei Lu. Tel. (021) 6439-1000; tlx. 33589; fax. (021) 6255-0830
华亭喜来登宾馆   漕溪北路1200号

Huge S-shaped building with two exterior glass elevators. Modern facilities plus ten-pin bowling alley. The location is southwest of city centre; there is a shuttle bus service.

## Jinjiang Hotel

59 Maoming Lu. Tel. (021) 6253-4242; tlx. 33380; fax. (021) 6472-5588
锦江饭店　茂名南路59号
In the heart of the old French concession, the Jinjiang was originally a private hotel for French residents of Shanghai. The hotel's oldest building, the north block, with its grand curving steps leading up to the columned entrance, dates from 1931. Several restaurants, a large shopping arcade, disco, fitness centre.

## Portman Shanghai

1376 Nanjing Xi Lu. Tel. (021) 6279-8888; tlx. 33272; fax. (021) 6279-8999
波特曼香格里拉酒店　南京西路1376号
Striking new hotel, part of the Shanghai Centre and flanked by office and residential apartment blocks which house the bulk of Shanghai's foreign businesses and expatriates. Comprehensive services, including theatre and lawn bowls. Management is by Shangri-La Hotels International.

## Shanghai Garden

58 Maoming Lu. Tel. (021) 6415-1111; tlx. 30159; fax. (021) 6415-8866
上海花园酒店　茂名南路58号
Built on the site of the former Cercle Sportif Français (later the Jinjiang Club), this new high-rise hotel incorporates a part of the pre-1949 building in its ground and first floors. The magnificent oval ballroom, carefully restored to its former art deco grandeur, is worth a visit. Opened in 1990, run by Japanese group Okura Hotels. All the usual sports and business facilities.

## Shanghai Hilton International

250 Huashan Lu. Tel. (021) 6248-0000; tlx. 33612; fax. (021) 6248-3848
上海静安希尔顿酒店　华山路250号
Conveniently located between the city's established commerical districts and the Hongqiao development zone. Full array of amenities—health centre, tennis and squash courts, swimming pool, business centre etc.

## Shanghai JC Mandarin

1225 Nanjing Xi Lu. Tel. (021) 6279-1888; tlx. 33939; fax. (021) 6279-1822
上海锦沧文华酒店　南京西路1225号

Opened in mid-1991, well located hotel which stands opposite the Shanghai Centre. Efficient management by Singaporean group. Boasts all-weather swimming pool, fitness centre and other top-class services.

### Westin Tai Ping Yang Hotel

5 Zunyi Nan Lu. Tel. (021) 6275-7576; tlx. 33345; fax. (021) 6275-5420
上海威斯汀太平洋大饭店　遵义南路5号
Considered the top hotel in the Hongqiao development zone. Opened in 1990 under Westin management. All modern amenities. It is 15 minutes by car from the hotel to the western end of Nanjing Xi Lu.

■ FIRST CLASS

### Hotel Equatorial

65 Yanan Rd West. Tel. (021) 6248-1688; tlx. 33345; fax. (021) 6248-1773
上海国际贵都大饭店　延安西路65号
A large hotel next door to the Hilton.

### Jinjiang Tower

161 Changle Lu. Tel. (021) 6433-4488; tlx. 33265; fax. (021) 6433-3265
新锦江大酒店　长乐路161号
Striking cylindrical tower, the flagship of Shanghai's Jinjiang Group, a business and property conglomerate. Set in the same complex as the older Jinjiang hotel buildings, the Tower has all the facilities of a top-class international hotel.

### Peace Hotel

20 Nanjing Dong Lu. Tel. (021) 6321-1244; tlx 33914; fax. (021) 6329-0300
和平饭店　南京东路20号
Built in the late 1920s and formerly known as The Cathay, this landmark with its distinctive green-roofed tower is probably the most famous hotel in Shanghai. The Peace was renovated in 1990, but much of the art deco interior has been retained and continues to echo the hotel's glamorous past.

### Yangtze New World

2099 Yan'an Xi Lu. Tel. (021) 6275-0000; tlx. 33675; fax. (021) 6275-0750
上海杨子江大酒店　延安西路2099号
Run by Hong Kong's New World Hotels International, this is a pleasant four-star hotel favoured by business visitors. Located on the airport road, next to the Westin. Amenities include gym, sauna, karaoke lounge and business centre.

■ STANDARD

### Overseas Chinese Hotel (Huaqiao Fandian)

104 Nanjing Xi Lu. Tel. (021) 6327-6226; tlx. 33909; fax. (021) 6372-3634

华侨饭店　南京西路104号

Built more than 60 years ago, this hotel with its Italian-style portico enjoys one of the best locations in Shanghai. Its rooms remain popular with overseas Chinese visitors.

### Park Hotel

170 Nanjing Xi Lu. Tel. (021) 6327-5225; fax. (021) 6327-6958

国际饭店　南京西路170号

This 1930s hotel is conveniently situated by Renmin Park, close to the Overseas Chinese Hotel and similarly popular for its excellent location.

### Shanghai Mansions

20 Bei Suzhou Lu. Tel. (021) 6324-6260; tlx. 33007; fax. (021) 6306-5147

上海大厦　北苏州路20号

Another relic from the 1930s. Located on the north bank of Suzhou Creek and overlooks the waterfront. This used to be Broadway Mansions, a smart residential hotel.

■ BUDGET

### Pujiang Hotel

15 Huangpu Lu. Tel. (021) 6324-6388; fax. (021) 6324-3179

浦江饭店　黄浦路15号

Located across the street from Shanghai Mansions; overlooks the Huangpu River. Renovated in 1990, it now houses the Shanghai Stock Exchange on the first floor.

### Seagull Hotel

60 Huangpu Lu. Tel. (021) 6325-1500; tlx. 33003; fax. (021) 6324-1263

海鸥饭店　黄浦路60号

Built as an appendage to the International Seamen's Club in 1985, this hotel is open to the general public.

## SUZHOU

### Aster Hotel

156 Sanxiang Lu. Tel. (0512) 829-1888; tlx. 363023; fax. (0512) 829-1838

雅都有酒店　三香路156号

Managed by Hong-Kong based New World Hotels International, this 29-storey hotel has top-class guest-rooms and as well as a swimming pool, business centre, and bowling alley. 'Food Street' on first floor serves a wide choice of Western, Asian and Chinese specialities which are prepared in open kitchens. Located in the west of the city.

## Bamboo Grove Hotel

Zhuhui Lu. Tel. (0512) 520-5601; fax. (0512) 520-8778

竹辉饭店　竹辉路

Consisting of a low-rise complex, this new hotel is run by the Lee Gardens International Group of Hong Kong. Amenities include a health club and business centre. The hotel is situated within 10-15 minutes' walk of the Garden of the Master of Fishing Nets.

## Gusu Hotel

115 Shiquan Jie. Tel. (0512) 520-0393; tlx. 34401

姑苏饭店　十全街115号

This was built as an extension to the Suzhou Hotel and shares some of its facilities.

## Nanlin Hotel

22 Gunxiu Fang, Shiquan Jie. Tel. (0512) 522-4641; tlx. 363063;
fax. (0512) 523-1028

南林饭店　锦绣坊2号

Well located on Suzhou's main shopping street, this medium-range hotel is comfortable and pleasant.

## Suzhou Hotel

115 Shiquan Jie. Tel. (0512) 520-5733; tlx. 36302; (0512) 520-4015

苏州饭店　十全街115号

Older hotel offering several grades of rooms in its two buildings.

# TIANJIN

## Hyatt Tianjin

Jiefang Bei Lu. Tel. (022) 2331-4222; fax. (022) 2331-0021

天津凯悦　解放北路

Favoured by business visitors on account of its location in the heart of the commercial district, this hotel also provides leisure facilities such as health spa and jogging track.

## Holiday Inn Tianjin

290 Zhongshan Rd. Tel. (022) 2628-8888; fax. (022) 2628-6666

天津假日酒店　天津市中山路290号

Opened in June 1997.

**Sheraton Tianjin**

Zijinshan Lu, Hexi District. Tel. (022) 2334- 3388; fax. (022) 2335-8740

天津喜来登酒店　河西区紫金山路

Convenient location; usual sports and business facilities. One of its restaurants offers Italian cuisine.

## URUMQI

**Holiday Inn**

53 Xinhua Bei Lu. Tel. (0991) 281-8788; fax. (0991) 281-7422

新疆假日大饭店　新华北路53号

Only international-style hotel in Urümqi; features swimming pool, health club, business centre, and three restaurants (Western, Chinese, Muslim). China International Travel Service is next door.

**Kunlun Hotel**

Youhao Lu. Tel. (0991) 484-0411; fax. (0991) 484-0213

昆仑宾馆　友好路

Large hotel with friendly staff north of the city. Facilities include four restaurants (two Chinese and two Muslim) and ticket purchase service. Dormitory beds available in the old section of the hotel.

**Xinjiang Hotel**

107 Changjiang Lu. Tel. (0991) 585-2511; fax. (0991) 581-1354

新疆饭店　长江路107号

Located near the railway station. Double room with bath available; also rooms for three or four guests sharing.

## WUHAN

**Holiday Inn Tian An Wuhan**

868 Jie Fang Da Dao, Wuhan. Tel (027) 586-7888; fax. (027) 584-5353

武汉天安假日酒店　解放大道868号

Facilities in this 400-room hotel include three Chinese restaurants, a coffee shop, disco and bar, business centre and fitness centre.

## WUXI

**Hubin Hotel**

Liyuan Lu. Tel. (0510) 510-1888; tlx. 36202; fax. (0510) 510-2637

湖滨饭店　蠡圆路

Found opposite the Li Garden and has quiet setting.

### Shuixiu Hotel

Liyuan Lu. Tel. (0510) 510-1888; tlx. 36202; fax. (0510) 510-2637
水秀饭店　蠡圆路
Adjacent to the Hubin, a two-storeyed hotel in a pleasant setting.

### Holiday Inn Milido Wuxi

2 Liangxi Rd. Tel. (0510) 676-5665; fax. (0510) 670-1668
无锡美丽都假日酒店　梁溪咯2号
Situated on the banks of the Grand Canal in the heart of the city's business and financial district and 10 minutes drive from the railway station and 20 minutes from Wuxi airport. Lake Taihu is only a short trip away.

## XIAMEN

### Holiday Inn Crowne Plaza Harbour View Xiamen

8–12 Zhen hai Road. Tel. (0592) 202-3333; tlx. 93138; fax. (0592) 203-6666
厦门假日皇冠海景大酒店　镇海路8-12号
This is the only world-class chain hotel in Xiamen. Centrally located, it is five minutes' drive to the ferry pier for Gulangyu. It is well equipped with a business centre, karaoke/disco, swimming pool and delicatessen, among other amenities.

### Mandarin (Yuehua) Hotel

Foreign Trade Residential Area, Huli. Tel. (0592) 602-3333; fax. (0592) 602-1431
厦门悦华酒店　湖里外商住宅区
Four-star villa-style hotel out of the town centre. Features sports facilities such as tennis courts and swimming pool, and business services.

### Jinbao Hotel

124-126 Dongdu Lu. Tel. (0592) 601-3888; tlx. 93034; fax. (0592) 601-3122
金宝酒店　东渡新港路
Small medium-priced hotel, much used to accommodate tour groups.

### Lujiang Hotel

54 Lujiang Dao. Tel. (0592) 202-2922; tlx. 93024; fax. (0592) 202-4664
鹭江大厦　鹭江道54号
Well located on the seafront opposite the ferry pier for Gulangyu Island.

### Xiamen Guesthouse

16 Huyuan Lu. Tel. (0592) 202-2265; tlx. 93065; fax. (0592) 202-1765
厦门宾馆　虎园路16号

## Xiamen Plaza
908 Xia He Lu. Tel. (0592) 505-8888; fax. (0592) 505-8877
厦门东南亚大酒店  厦禾路908号
Next to the railway station, this hotel caters for Asian business visitors and groups.

# Xi'an

## Bell Tower Hotel
Bell Tower. Tel. (029) 727-9200; fax. (029) 721-8767
钟楼饭店  钟楼西南角
Under Holiday Inn management, this hotel has been recently refurbished. Good central location overlooking Bell Tower Square.

## Dynasty Hotel
55 Huancheng Xi Lu (northern section). Tel.(029) 862-6262; fax. (029) 862-7728
秦都酒店  环城西路55号
Four-star joint-venture hotel, opened in 1990. Restaurants serve Western, Cantonese and Korean cuisines. Managed by Chains International Hotels.

## Grand New World Hotel
48 Lian Hu Lu. Tel. (029) 721-6868; fax. (029) 721-9754
古都新世界大酒店  莲湖路48号
Managed by New World International, this hotel, in the old walled city, is famous for its restaurants and the massive bas relief of Emperor Qin.

## Grand Castle Hotel
12 Xi Duan Huan Cheng Nan Lu. Tel. (029) 723-1800; fax. (029) 723-1500
长安城堡大酒店  环城南路西段12号
This modern recreation of a Tang dynasty castle, managed by ANA Hotels, has space, elegance and excellent service.

## Hotel Royal Xi'an
334 Dong Da Jie. Tel. (029) 721-0305; fax. (029) 723-5887
西安皇城宾馆  东大街334号
On the main street in the old walled town, this Nikko-managed hotel has fine decor and some excellent dining.

## Hyatt Xi'an
158 Dongda Jie. Tel. (029) 723-1234; fax. (029) 721-6799
西安凯悦（阿房宫）饭店  东大街158号
New luxury hotel with over 400 rooms, with all the usual facilities associated with an

international chain—fitness centre, business centre, function rooms. Convenient central location.

### Shangri-La Golden Flower Hotel
8 Changle Xilu. Tel. (029) 323-1221; fax. (029)
西安香格里拉金花大酒店　长东西路8号

### People's Mansion (Renmin Dasha)
319 Dongxin Jie. Tel. (029) 721-5111; fax. (029) 721-8152
人民大厦　东新街319号
Medium-priced hotel; excellent location. Western and Chinese restaurants and bicycle rental.

### Sheraton
12 Fenggao Lu. Tel. (029) 426-1888; fax. (029) 426-2983
西安喜来登大酒店　丰镐路12号
Luxury hotel established outside the west gate of the city wall. Large, with several restaurants and comprehensive recreational amenities.

### Xi'an Garden (Tanghua Binguan)
4 Yanyin Lu. Tel. (029) 526-1111; tlx. 70027; fax. (029) 526-1998
西安唐华饭店　雁引东路4号
Top-class hotel, a joint venture with a Japanese corporation, located east of the Big Goose Pagoda in the south of the city. Built in Tang-dynasty style.

### Xi'an Guesthouse
26 Chang'an Lu. Tel. (029) 526-1351; fax. (029) 526-1796
西安宾馆　长安路26号
Located just south of the city wall, this comfortable medium-priced hotel is close to CITS and features standard facilities as well as an outdoor café in the summer.

## ZHENGZHOU
### Holiday Inn Crowne Plaza Zhengzhou
115 Jinshui Lu. Tel. (0371) 595-0055 fax. (0371) 599-0770
河南中州皇冠假日宾馆　郑州市金水路115号
Three kilometres from Zhengzhou airport and four kilometres from the railway.

# Useful Addresses

## CHINA INTERNATIONAL TRAVEL SERVICE

■ BRANCHES IN CHINA

### Beijing

**Beijing Tourism Building**

28 Jianguomenwai Dajie

北京市建国门外大街28号

北京旅游大厦

Tel. (010) 6515-8562; fax 6515-8603

**FIT Service/Ticketing**

Multi-Service Department

China International Travel Service

2 Chongwenmen Xi Dajie

北京市崇文门西大街2号

中旅社票务部

Tel. *FIT*: (010) 6512-2211 ext. 371 (Sales)

352 (American/Canadian)

351 (European)

375 (Japanese)

252 (Australia/ Hong Kong Region)

*Ticketing*: (010) 6512-6688 ext. 1752 (air)

1750 (international rail)

Tlx. 22004; fax. 6512-2006

### Chengdu

65 Renmin Nan Lu (section two)

成都市人民南路二段65号

Tel. (028) 667-3689; fax. 666-3794

### Chongqing

Renmin Lu. 人民路

Tel. (0811) 6385-1248

### Fuzhou

44 Dongda Lu

福州市东大路44号

Tel. (0591) 753-7869; fax 7537447

### Guangzhou

179 Huanshi Lu

广州市环市路179号

Tel. (020) 8667-1450; fax 8667-8048

### Guilin

14 Ronghu Bei Lu

桂林市榕湖北路14号

Tel. (0773) 282-3518; fax. 282-2936

### Hangzhou

1 Shihan Lu

杭州市石函路1号

Tel. (0571) 515-2888; fax 515-6576

### Hohhot

95 Yishuting, Xincheng District

呼和浩特市新城区艺术厅南95号

Tel. (0471) 692-4494; fax 696-1182

### Kaifeng

64 Ziyou Lu

开封市自由路64号

Tel. (0378) 595-5130; fax 595-5131

### Kunming

8 Heping Xincun

Huancheng Nan Lu

昆明市环城南路和平新村8号

Tel. (0871) 313-2895; tlx. 64027

### Lanzhou

361 Tianshui Lu

兰州市天水路361号

Tel. (0931) 841-6164; fax 841-8556

### Lhasa

Beijing Dong Lu

拉萨市北京东路

Tel. (0891) 633-0353

**Luoyang**
Xiyuan Lu
洛阳市西园路
Tel. (0379) 491-3701

**Nanjing**
202-1 Zhongshan Bei Lu
南京市中山北路202-1号
Tel. (025) 334-6444; fax 330-8954

**Shanghai**
33 Zhongshan Dong Lu
上海市中山东路33号
Tel. (021) 6321-7200; fax 6329-1788

**Suzhou**
115 Shiquan Jie
苏州市十全街115号
Tel. (0512) 522-3783; tlx. 36302

**Tianjin**
20 Youyi Lu, Hexi District
天津市友谊路20号
Tel. (022) 2835-0102; fax 2835-2619

**Urümqi**
51 Xinhua Bei Lu
乌鲁木齐市新华北路51号
Tel. (0991) 282-1444; fax 281-0689

**Wuxi**
7 Xinsheng Lu
无锡市新生路7号
Tel. (0510) 270-6702; fax 270-1489

**Xiamen**
15th Floor, Zhenxing Building
Hubin Bei Lu
厦门市湖滨北路振兴大厦十五楼
Tel. (0592) 505-1825; fax 505-1819

**Xi'an**
Chang'an Lu
长安路
Tel. (029) 526-2066; fax 526-1453

■ OFFICES ABROAD
OF CHINA NATIONAL TOURISM
ADMINISTRATION

**Australia**
China National Tourist Office
Level 19, 44 Market Street, Sydney,
NSW 2000
Tel. (61) 02–299–4057; tlx. AA177886
CNTOS; fax (61) 02–290–1958

**France**
Office du Tourisme de Chine
116, Avenue des Champs-Elysées
75008 Paris
Tel. (33) 1–44–21–82–82; tlx. 612866;
fax. (33) 1–44–21–81–00

**Germany**
China National Tourist Office
Fremdenverkehrsamt der VR China,
Ilkenhans str. 6,
D–60433 Frankfurt AM Main-1
Tel. (49) 69–597–3412; tlx. 4170360
FACD; fax. (49) 69–597–3412

**Hong Kong**
China International Travel Service (HK)
Ltd, 6th Floor, Tower 2,
South Seas Centre, 75 Mody Road,
Tsim Sha Tsui East, Kowloon
Tel. (852) 2732–5888; tlx. 38449 CITC
HX; fax. (852) 2721–7154

**Japan**
China National Tourist Office
6th Floor, Hanchidai Hamamatsu Cho
Bl., 1-27-13 Hamatsu-Cho,
Minato-ku, Tokyo
Tel. (81) 3–4331461; fax (81)
3–4338653

**United Kingdom**
China National Tourist Office
4 Glentworth Street, London NW1
Tel. (44) 71–935–9427; tlx. 291221
CTCLONG; fax (44) 71–487–5842

**USA**
China National Tourist Office
Suite 6413, Empire State Building,

350 Fifth Avenue, New York NY 10118
Tel. (1) 212–760–9700/8218
CITSNYC; fax (1) 212–760–8809

China National Tourist Office
Suite 201, 333 West Broadway, Glendale,
CA 91204
Tel. (818) 5457505; tlx. 9102508906
CNTOLA; fax (818) 5457506

## CHINA AIRLINES
(Booking Offices)

**Air China**
Aviation Building, 15 West Chang'an
Avenue, Beijing
Tel. (10)601–3336 (domestic);
(10) 601–6667 (international)

**China Northwest Airlines**
Beijing Airport Office: Tel: (10)456–2367
Beijing City Office: Tel: (10)601–7589,
601–7574
Xi'an Booking Office, 269 Xishaomen:
Tel: (029) 426–4111; fax (029) 426–3763

**China Eastern Airlines**
Beijing Airport Office: Tel. (10) 456–2135
Beijing City Office: Tel. (10) 602–4070,
602–4071
Shanghai Booking Office, 789 Yan'an
Zhong Lu. Tel. 021–247–1960/2255 (int.)
Tel. 021–247–5953/1805 (domestic)

**China Southern Airlines**
Beijing Airport Office: Tel. (10) 456–4089
Beijing City Office: Tel. (10) 601–6899,
601–6799
Guangzhou Booking Office, 181 Huanshi
Xilu. Tel. (020) 669–3950

**China Southwest Airlines**
Beijing Airport Office: Tel (10) 456–2870
Beijing City Office: Tel. (10) 601–7579,
501–6828
Chengdu Booking Office, 15 Renmin
Nanlu. Tel. (028) 666–5711

**China North Airlines**
Beijing Airport Office: Tel (10) 456–2170
Beijing City Office: Tel. (10) 602–4078,
601–7594
Shenyang Booking Office, 117 Zhonghua
Lu, Heping District. Tel. (024) 386–3705

**China Xinjiang Airlines**
Beijing Airport Office: Tel (10) 456–2803
Beijing City Office: Tel. (10) 602–4803
Urumqi Booking Office, 62 Youhao
Nanlu. Tel. (0991) 484–2391

# Recommended Reading

For more detailed cultural and practical guidance to the cities, provinces and themat-
ic journeys of China, check out Odyssey/Passport's regularly-updated titles which
now include: *Beijing; Beijing Walks; Shanghai; Xi'an; Sichuan; Guizhou; Tibet; Yunnan;
the Silk Road, and the Yangzi River.*

    *China: A Short Cultural History* by C. P. Fitzgerald (Cresset Press, London 1961)
is an excellent chronological introduction to Chinese civilization. An anthology,
edited by R. Dawson, entitled *The Legacy of China* (Oxford University Press 1964)
covers, section by section, the philosophy, literature, arts, science and politics of
China. Jonathan Spence's *Gate of Heavenly Peace* (Viking Press 1981) is a well-written
survey of recent Chinese history. His *Search for Modern China* (Hutchinson 1990) is
an epic narrative from around 1600 to the present.

    *The Story of the Stone* by Cao Xueqin, translated by David Hawkes and John Min-
ford in five volumes (Penguin 1973-88), is that great 18th-century novel of manners
better known as *The Dream of the Red Chamber*. There are other excellent translations
of Chinese literature. *The Romance of the Three Kingdoms* is available in various translations. The poems of the two Tang masters, Li Bai (Li Po) and Du Fu (Tu Fu), have
been translated by Arthur Cooper in the collection *Li Po and Tu Fu* (Penguin 1973).

    Chinese archaeology has attracted world attention in recent years. *China: Ancient
Culture, Modern Land* (University of Oklahoma Press 1994) is a highly informative
and well-illustrated tome. *Style in the Arts of China* by William Watson (Penguin
1974) is an interesting handbook, analyzing the forms of Chinese art in terms of
style. Mary Tregear's *Chinese Art* (Thames and Hudson 1980) is a good short introduction to a vast subject. *Chinese Monumental Art* by P. C. Swann (Thames & Hudson 1963) covers a number of topics, including the four principal Buddhist cave sites
and the Great Wall. *The Nine Sacred Mountains of China* by M. A. Mullikin and A. M.
Hotchkis (Hong Kong 1973) describes the five Taoist peaks and the four Buddhist
mountains, as does *Travels through Sacred China* by Martin Palmer (Thorsons 1994).

    Sven Hedin, the great Swedish explorer of the early 20th century, produced some
very exciting material on Xinjiang and Tibet. He wrote *The Silk Road* (Routledge &
Sons, London 1938) and *Trans-Himalaya: Discoveries and Adventures in Tibet* (Mac-
millan 1909). A more recent publication about early travellers in Central Asia is
*Foreign Devils on the Silk Road* by P. Hopkirk (Oxford University Press 1986). For
those interested in both exploration and botany, *Plant Hunting in China* by E.H.M.
Cox (Oxford University Press 1986) is recommended.

    There are many books attempting to interpret the Chinese revolution. *Red Star
Over China* by E. Snow (Gollancz 1938) is the classic report on the communists at
the beginning of the anti-Japanese war, illuminated by the author-journalist's long

conversations with Mao Zedong. *Fanshen: A Documentary of Revolution in a Chinese Village* by W. Hinton (Vintage Books 1966) describes in detail the dynamics of revolution in a peasant society, while *Life and Death in Shanghai* (Grafton Books, London 1986) is an autobiographical work by Nien Cheng about her seven-year imprisonment during the Cultural Revolution. For a taste of contemporary travel off the beaten track, *Alone on the Great Wall* by William Lindesay (Hodder 1989/Fulcrum 1991) is a thrilling account of an Englishman's journey on foot along the Great Wall. Other epic journeys can be relived by reading William Lindesay's *Marching with Mao: A Biographical Journey* (Hodder 1993) retracing the route of the Long March and Kevin Bishop's *China's Imperial Way* (Odyssey 1997) following the ancient trade route between Beijing and Hong Kong.

# A Guide to Pronouncing Chinese Names

The official system of romanization used in China, which the visitor will find on maps, road signs and city shopfronts, is known as *Pinyin*. It is now almost universally adopted by the western media.

Some visitors may initially encounter some difficulty in pronouncing romanized Chinese words. In fact many of the sounds correspond to the usual pronunciation of the letters in English. The exceptions are:

### Initials

c    is like the *ts* in '*its*'

q    is like the *ch* in '*cheese*'

x    has no English equivalent, and can best be described as a hissing conso nant that lies somewhere between *sh* and *s*. The sound was rendered as *hs* under an earlier transcription system.

z    is like the *ds* in 'fa*ds*'

zh   is unaspirated, and sounds like the *j* in 'jug'

a    sounds like 'ah'

e    is pronounced as the *o* in 'mother'

i    is pronounced as in 'ski'(written as *yi* when not preceded by an initial consonant). However, in *ci, chi, ri, shi, zi* and *zhi*, the sound represented by the *i* final is quite different and is similar to the *ir* in 'sir', but without much stressing of the *r* sound.

o    sounds like the *aw* in 'law'

u    sounds like the *oo* in 'ooze'

ü    is pronounced as the German *ü* (written an *yu* when not preceded by an initial consonant). The last two finals are usually written simply as *e* and *u*.

### Finals in Combination

When two or more finals are combined, such as in *hao, jiao* and *liu*, each letter retains its sound value as indicated in the list above, but note the following:

ai    is like the *ie* in 'tie'

ei    is like the *ay* in 'bay'

# Index of Places

Practical information, such as telephone
numbers and opening hours, is notoriously subject to change. We welcome
corrections and suggestions from guidebook users; please write to:
The Guidebook Company,
G/F 2 Lower Kai Yuen Lane,
North Point, Hong Kong.
E-mail: odyssey@asiaonline.net